ALVARADO'S PIN-UP NUDES

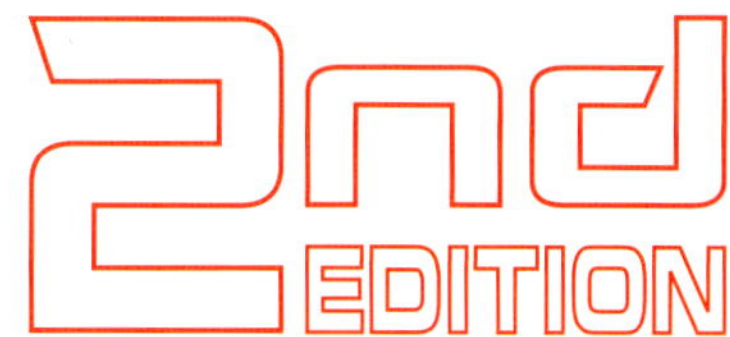

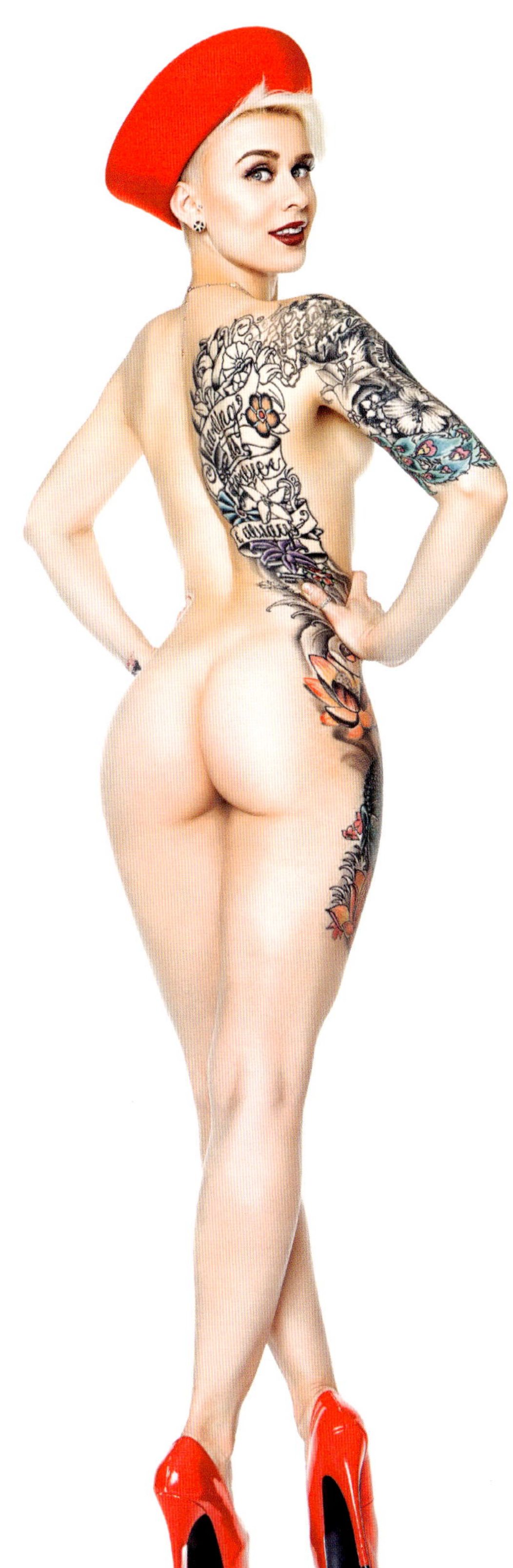

ROBERT ALVARADO

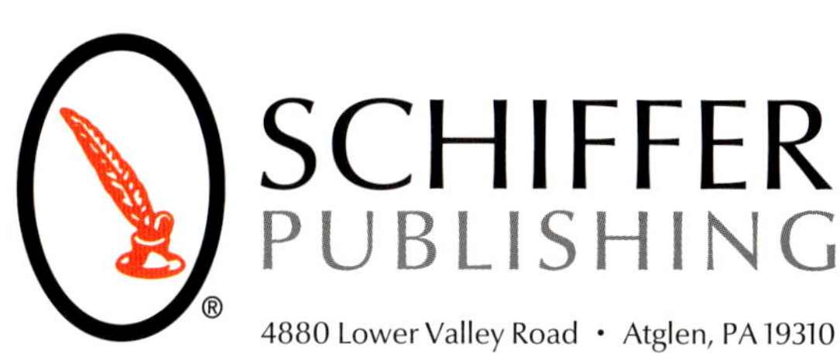

Other Schiffer Books by the Author:

Alvarado's Classic Modern Pin-ups, 978-0-7643-3892-2, $34.99
Alvarado's All-American Girls, 978-0-7643-5141-9, $34.99
Alvarado's Cosplay Pin-ups, 978-0-7643-5141-9, $29.99

Library of Congress Control Number: 2019934820

Cover and book designed by: Jack Chappell

ISBN: 978-0-7643-5807-4
Printed in Hong Kong

Published by Schiffer Publishing, Ltd.
4880 Lower Valley Road
Atglen, PA 19310
Phone: (610) 593-1777; Fax: (610) 593-2002
E-mail: Info@schifferbooks.com
Web: www.schifferbooks.com

For our complete selection of fine books on this and related subjects, please visit our website at www.schifferbooks.com. You may also write for a free catalog.

Schiffer Publishing's titles are available at special discounts for bulk purchases for sales promotions or premiums. Special editions, including personalized covers, corporate imprints, and excerpts, can be created in large quantities for special needs. For more information, contact the publisher.

We are always looking for people to write books on new and related subjects. If you have an idea for a book, please contact us at proposals@schifferbooks.com.

Hard to believe it's been five to six years since this edition first came out, and the passion has not left me one iota. I still look forward to working with every model and I'm always excited to see what we can create.

Working with different models and people is such a huge joy in my life; I really have such a drive to create and make things happen to an image.

My mission (didn't realize I had a mission!) is to bring the pin-up style of pictures into the twenty-first century. My inspiration is Norman Rockwell, and he is why I try and make the images look illustrated or painted.

Once a model leaves the real fun begins—let's see what I can do with these images. The editing process for me is half the fun; I cannot wait to edit the images after a shoot. I will usually text the model at least one image before she gets home from the shoot! Ha! Yes, it's just the big kid in me.

Depending on the model, I usually shoot around 300–500 images, and from that I only edit 6–8 images. Usually two from each set we do. The most I shot one model in one session was just more than 900 images—took us all day! She was a trooper. As far as time, It takes me about 45 minutes to edit an image on average. Understand, I've been doing it for a long time and I have actions built in to help speed up the process. On the other hand, I've spent 4–6 hours on one image—it just depends. The longest image took me a day and half . . . ugh . . . but it came out really cool.

It's been a heck of a ride! I am grateful to everyone that appreciates my work, and thank you so much!

Robert Alvarado

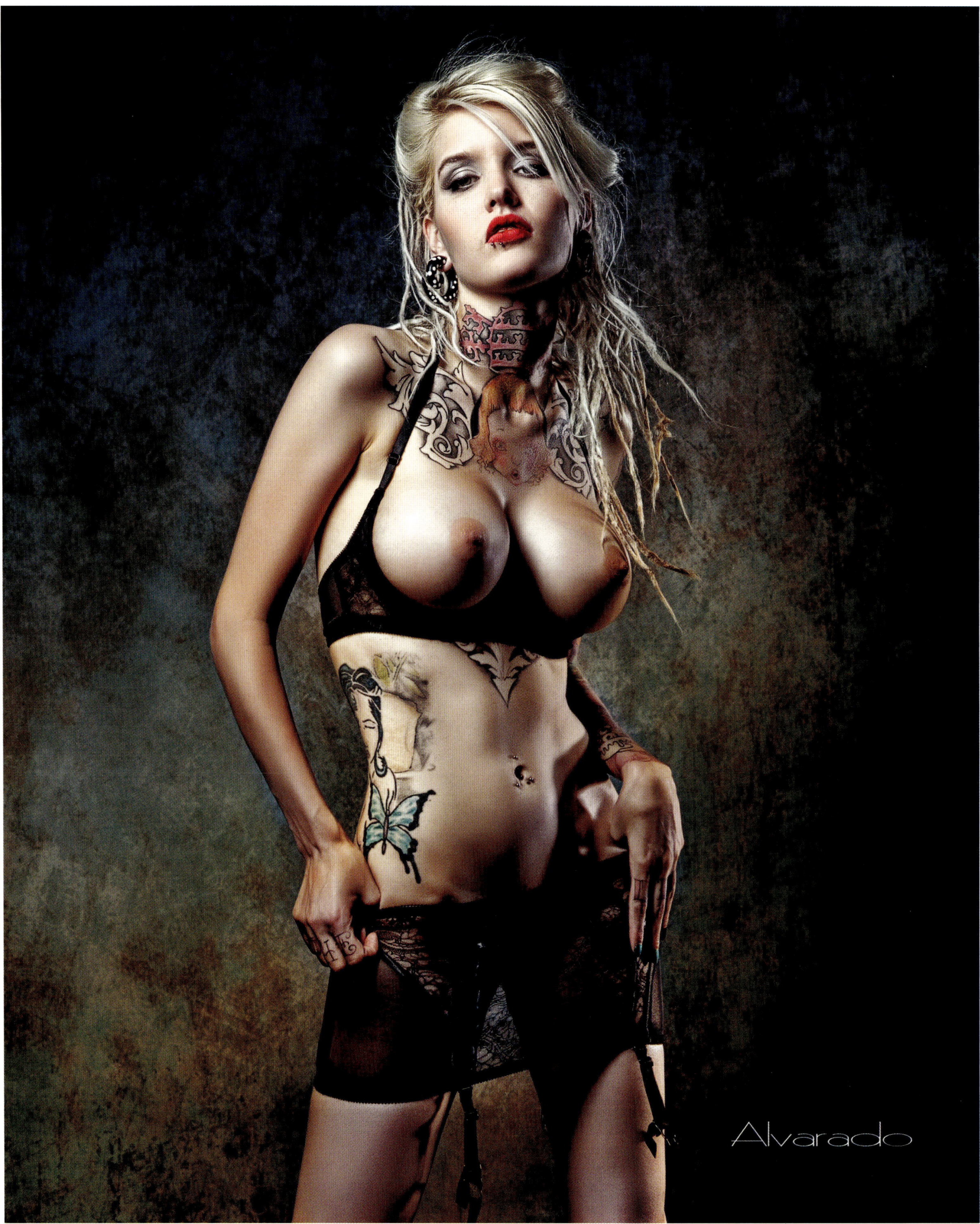
Alvarado

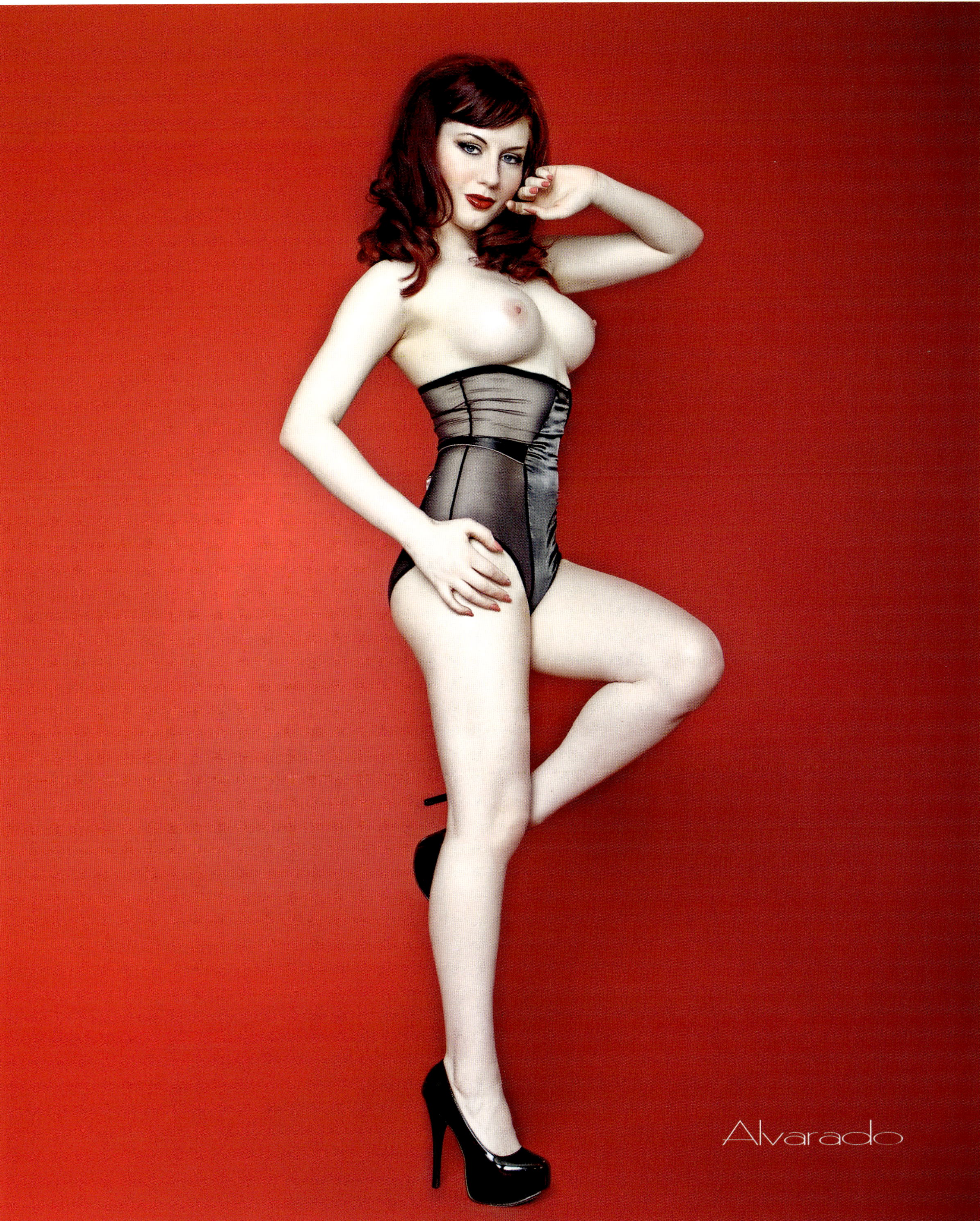
Alvarado

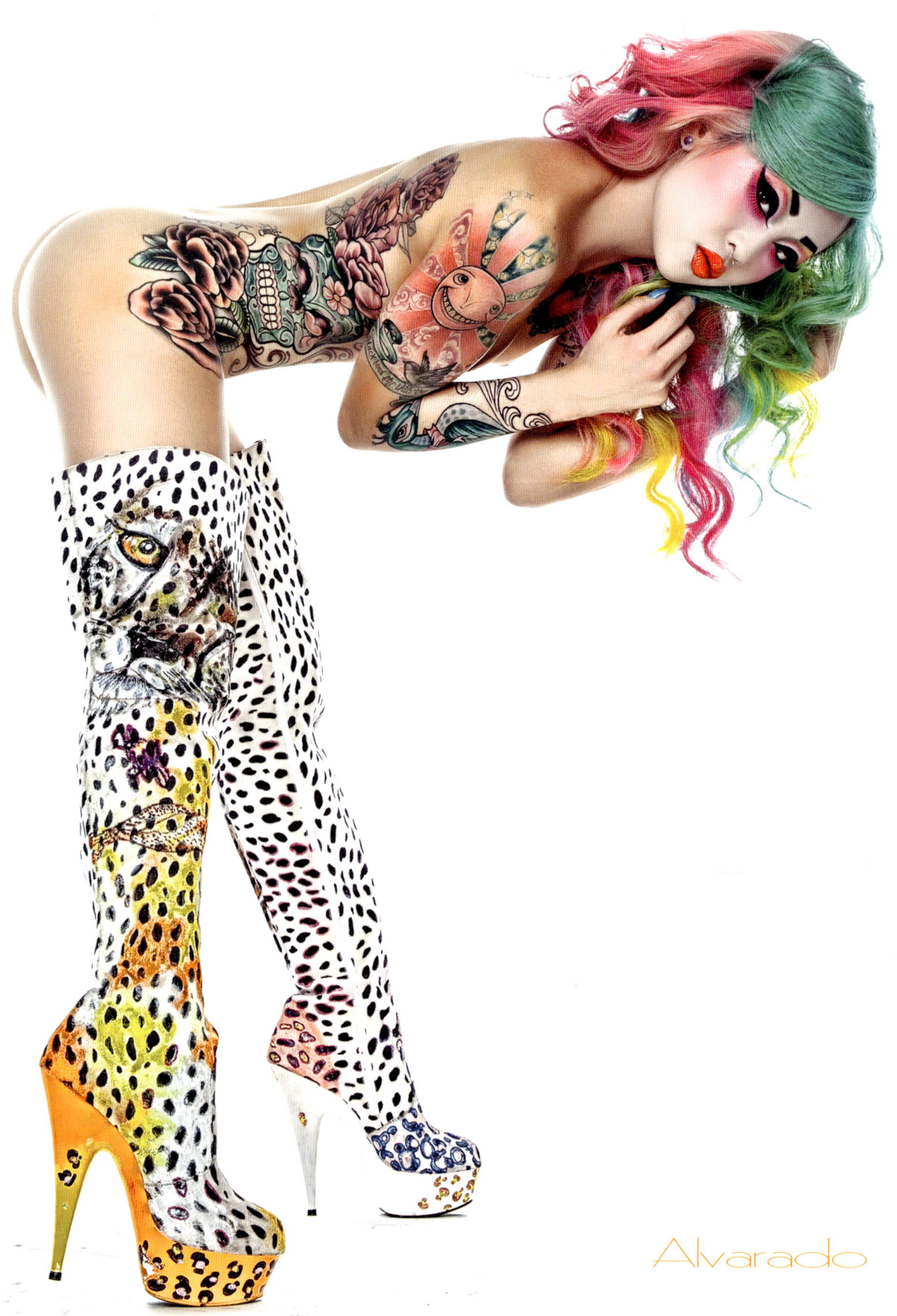

Alvarado

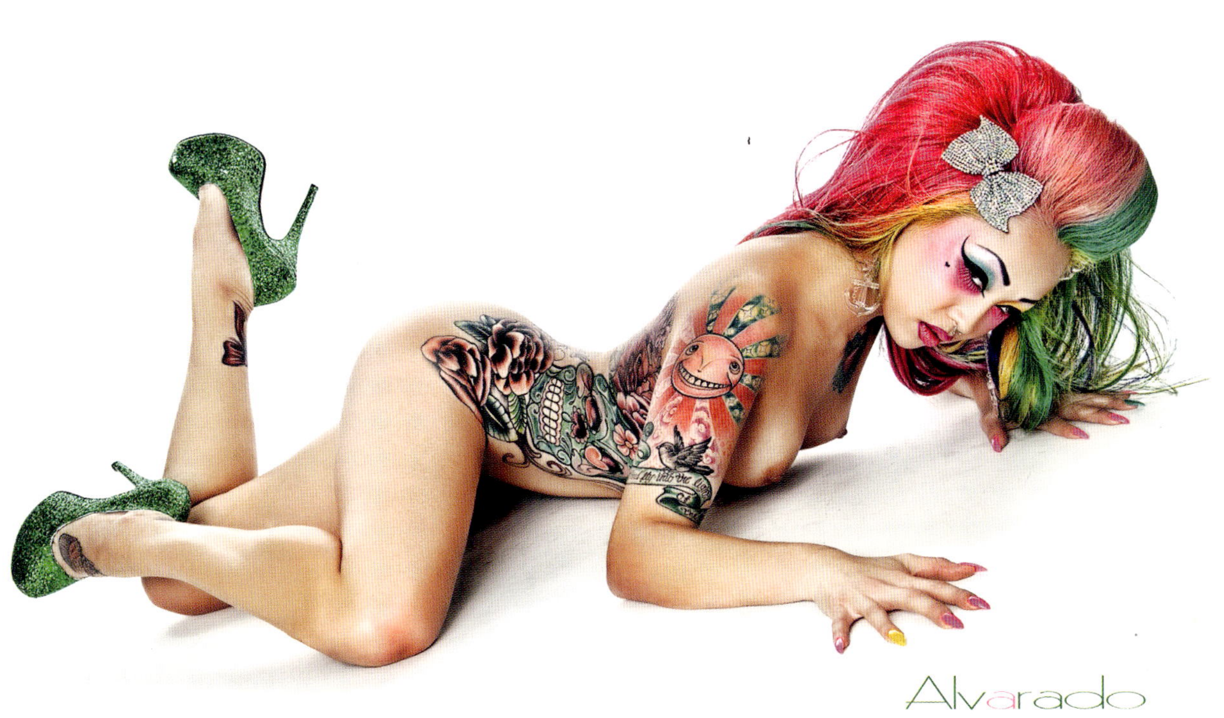
Alvarado

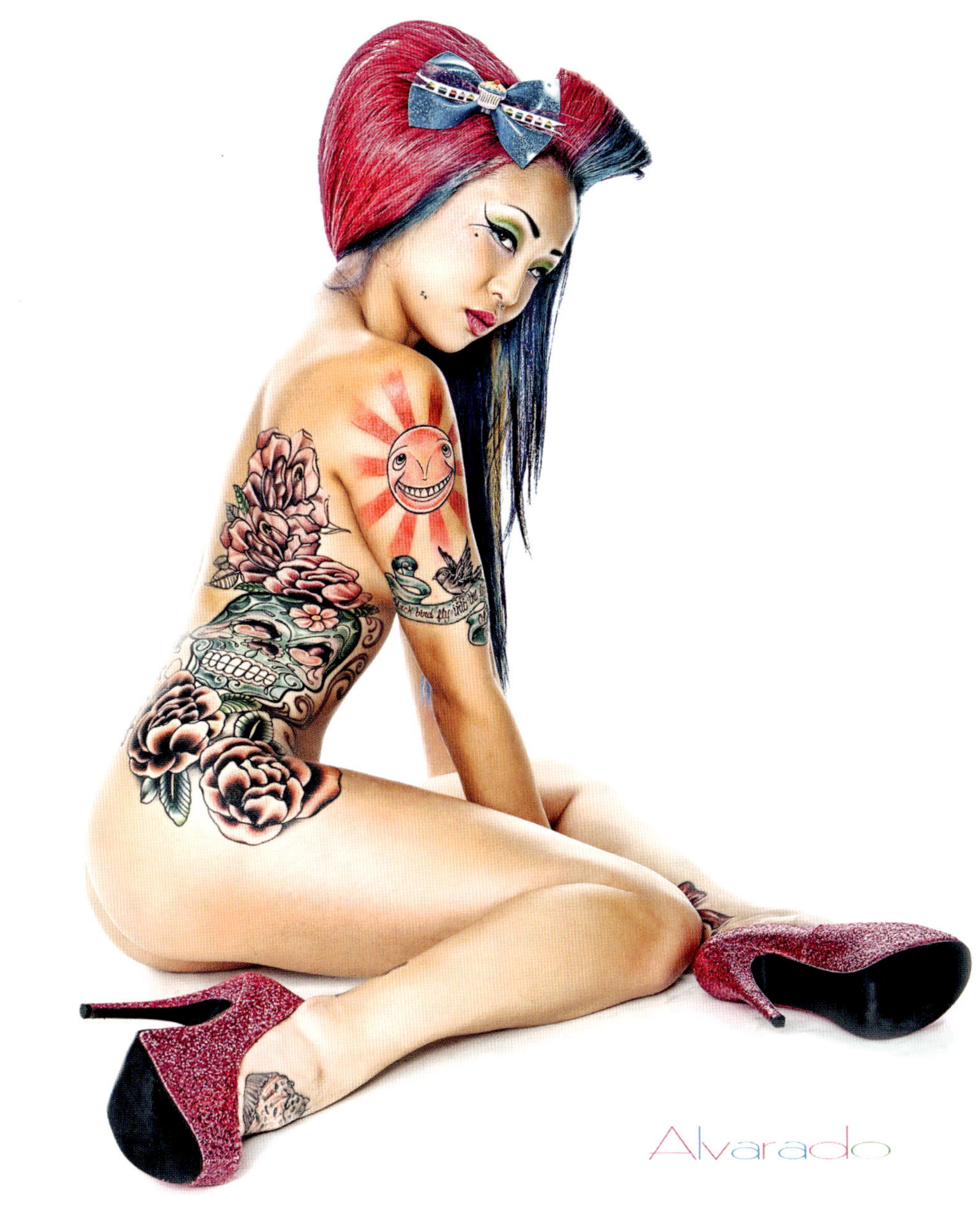
Alvarado

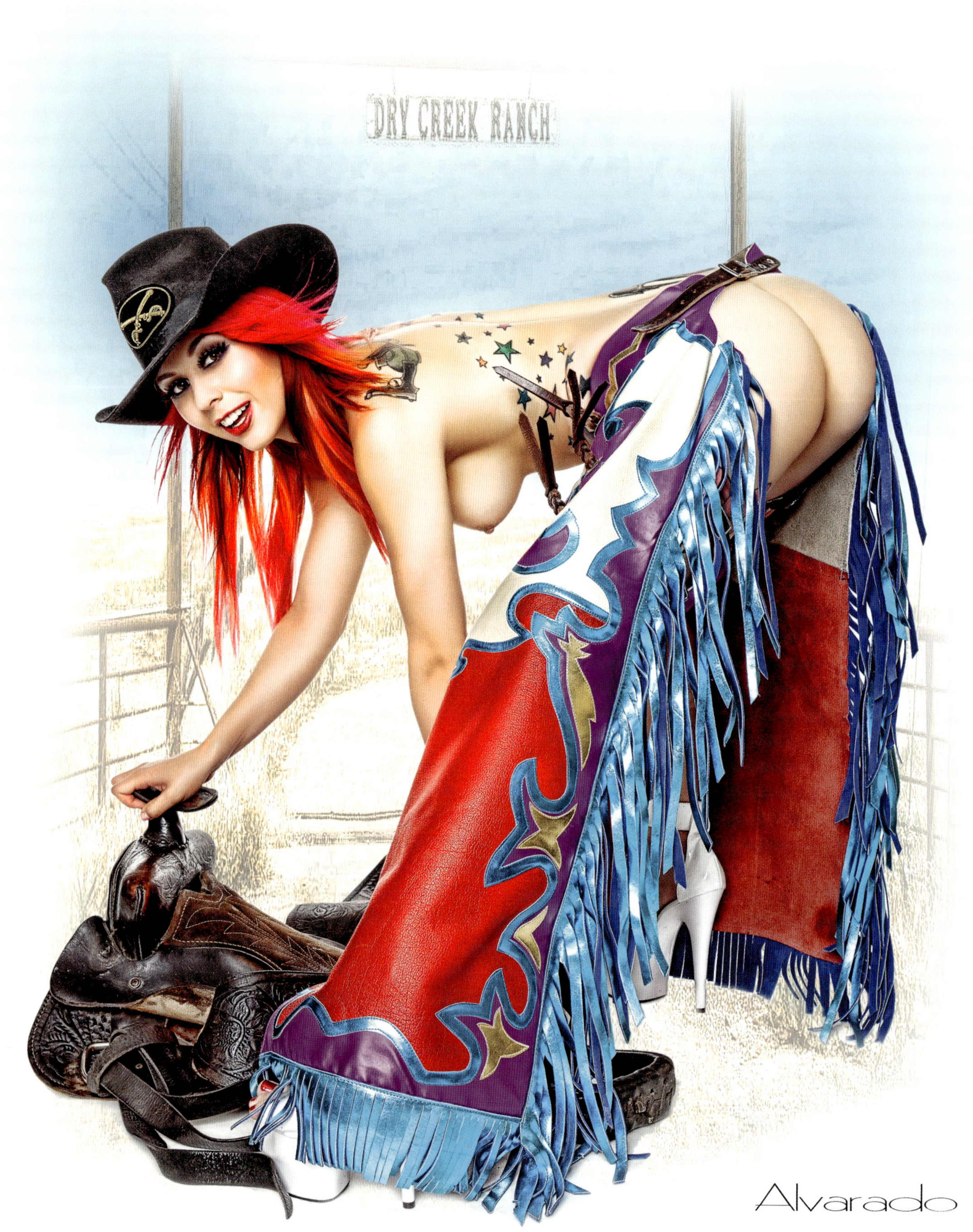
DRY CREEK RANCH
Alvarado

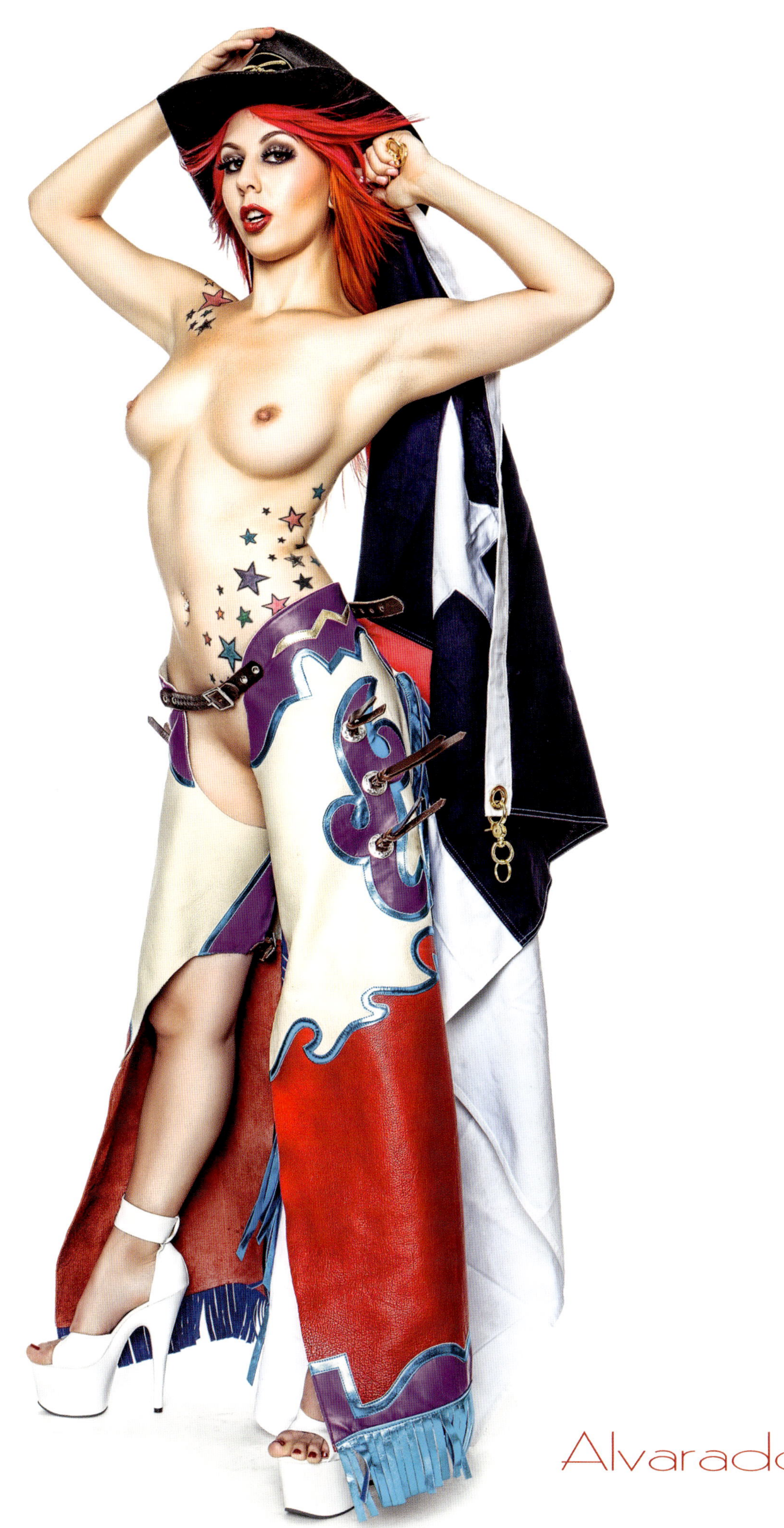

Alvarado

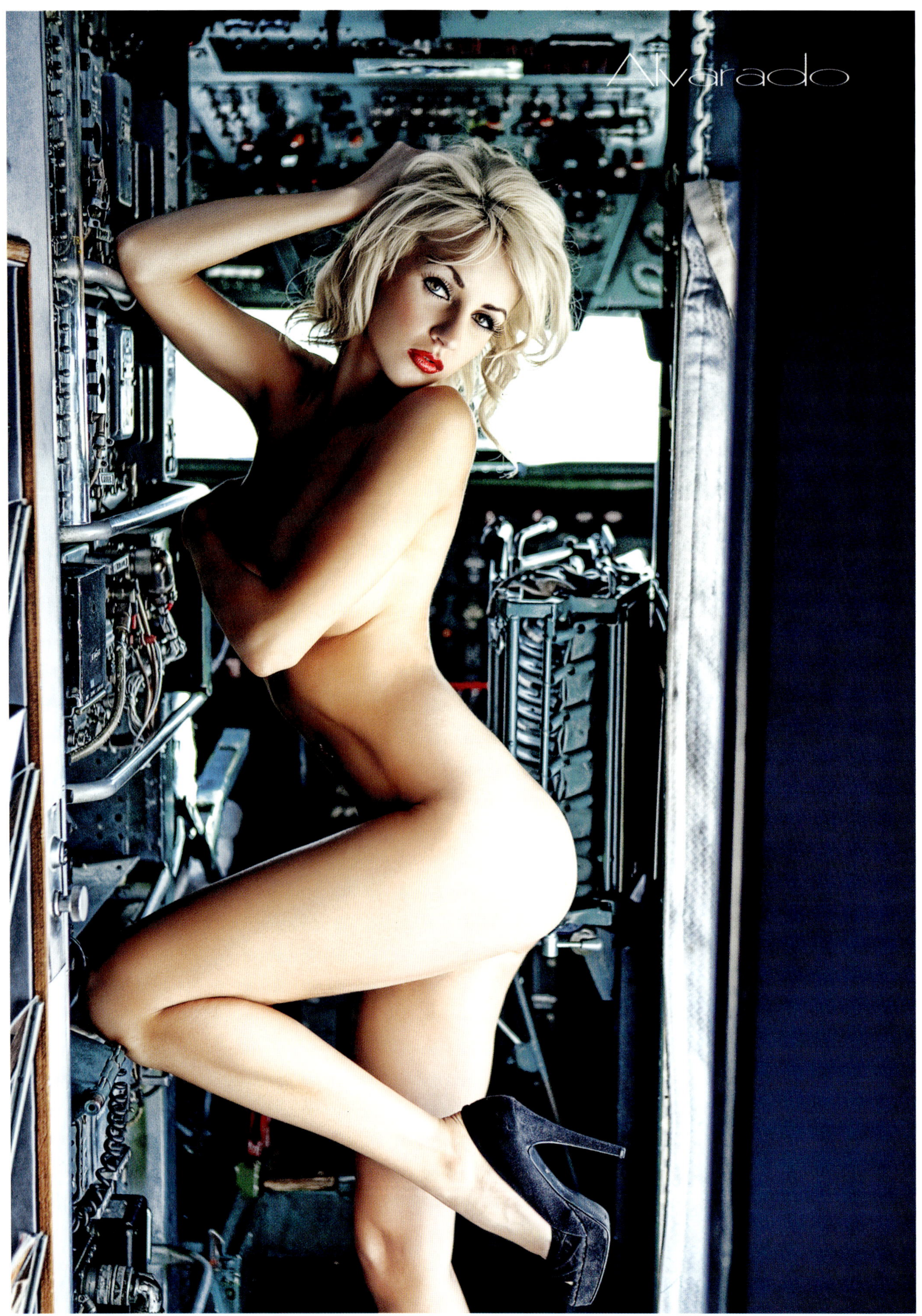
Alvarado

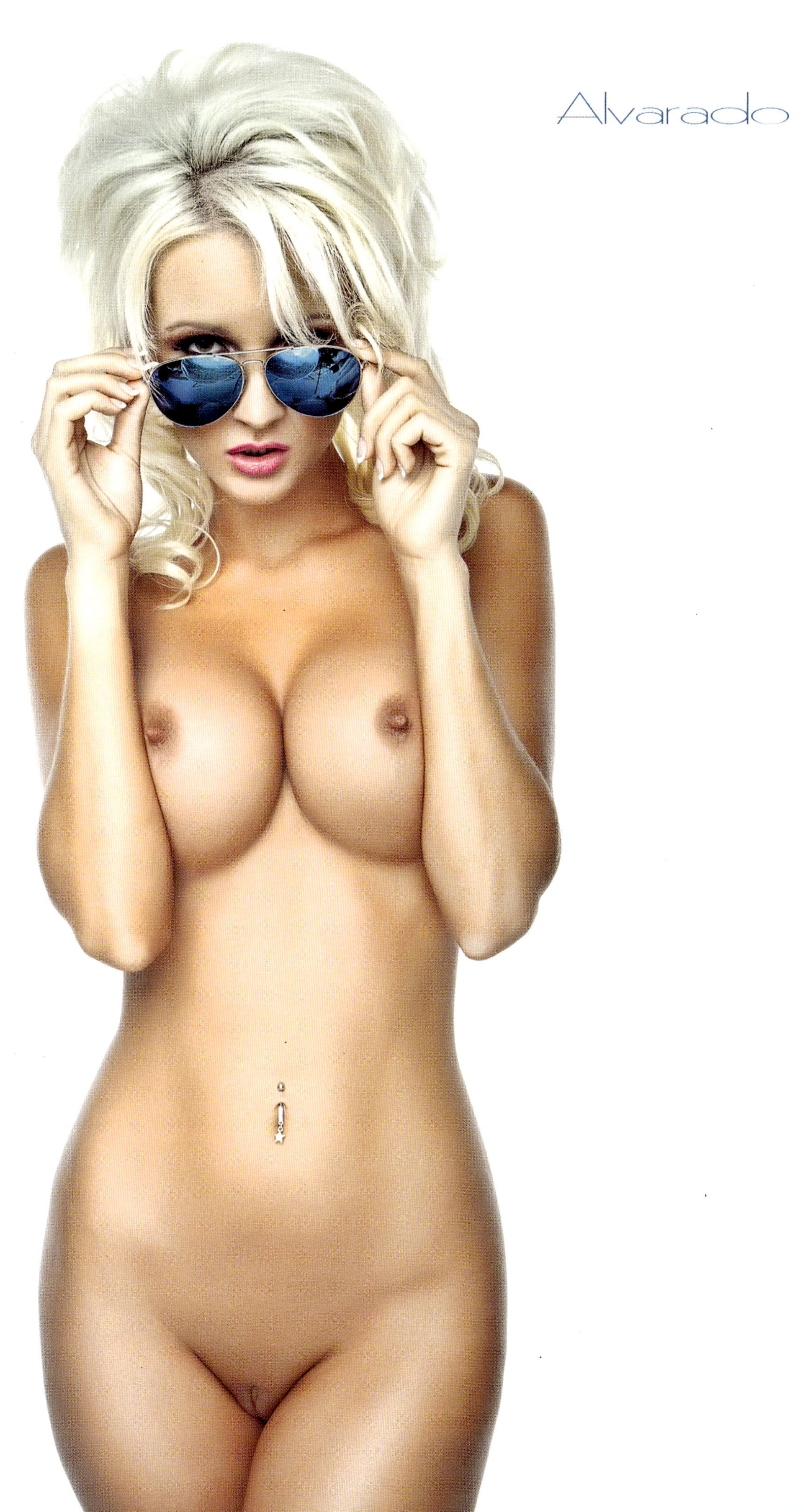

Alvarado

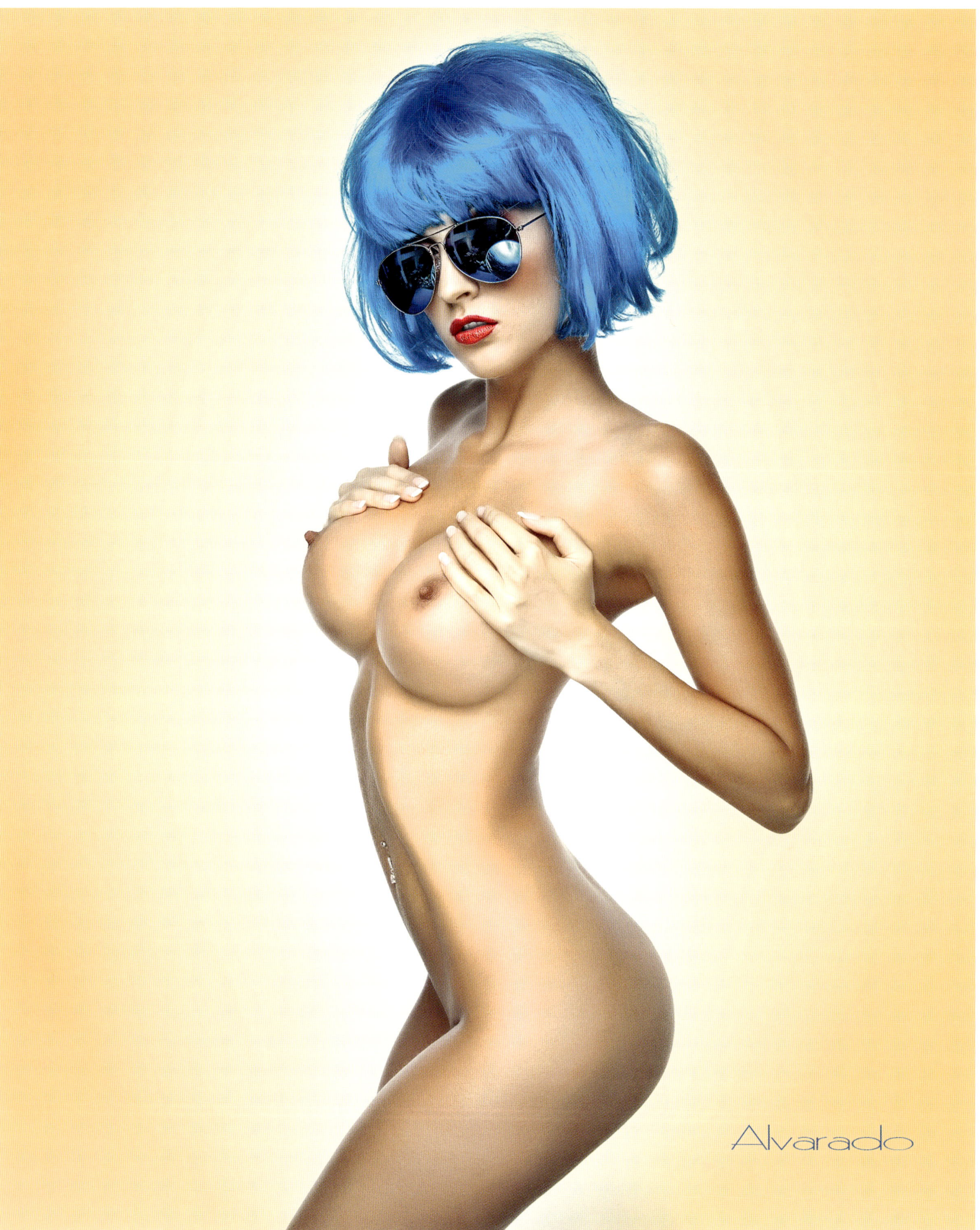
Alvarado

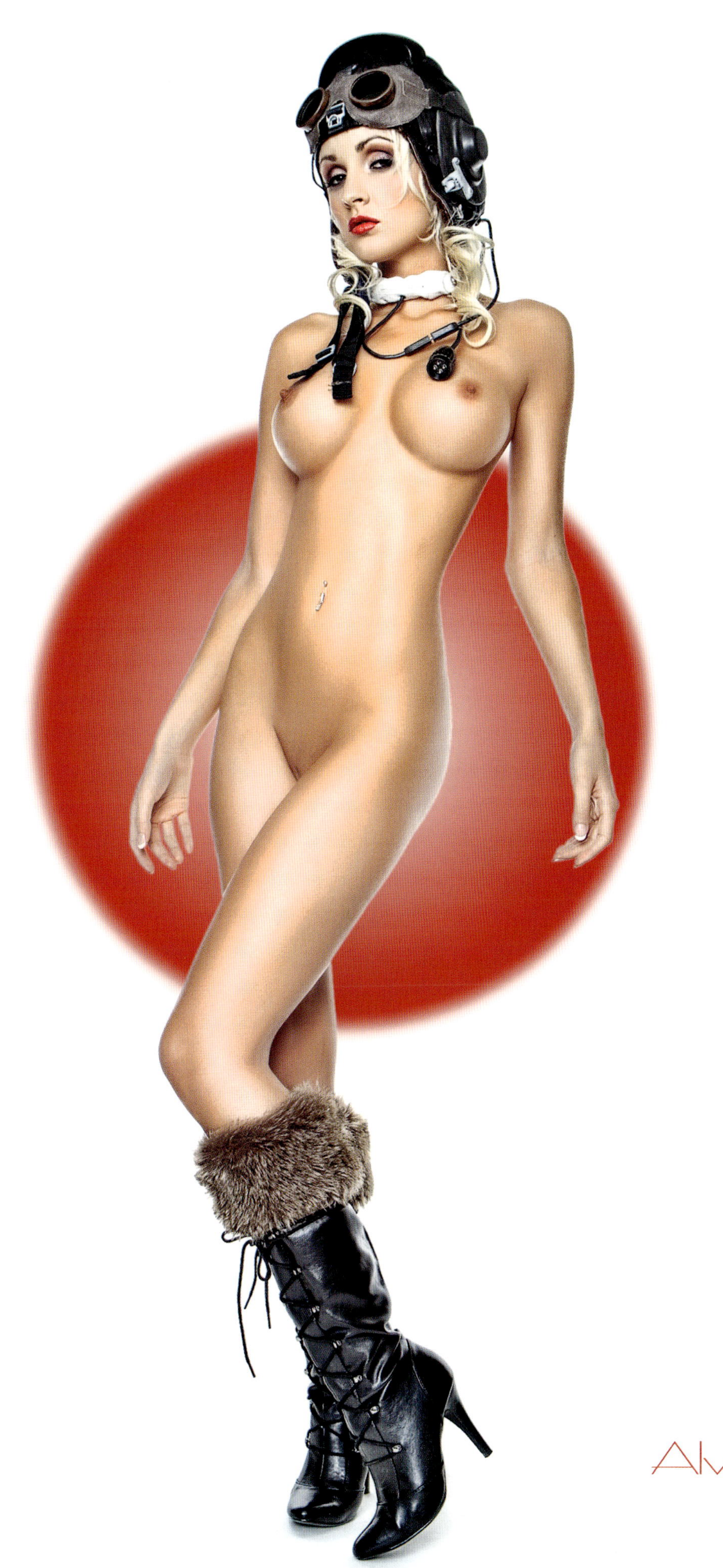

Alvarado

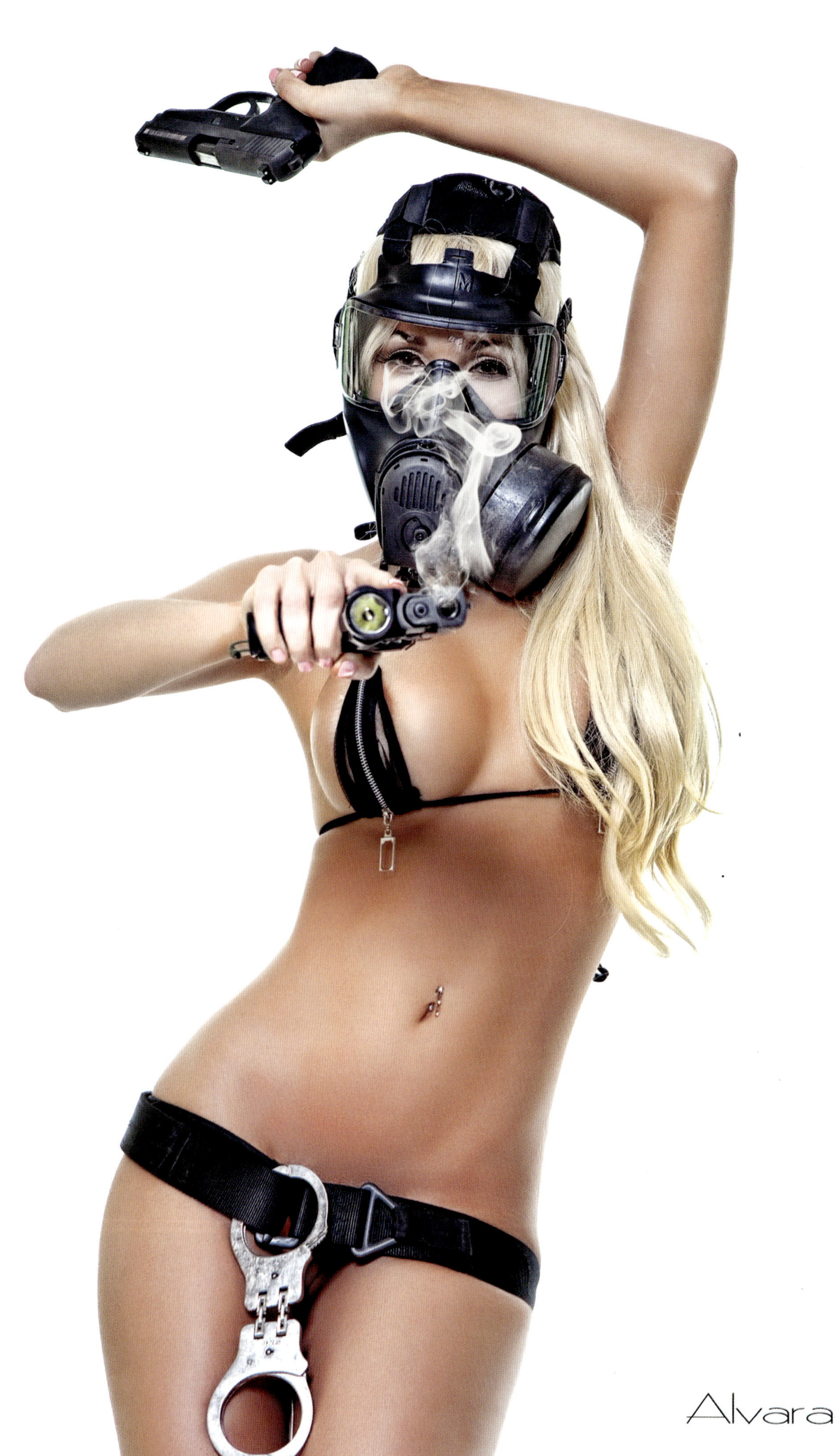

Alvarado

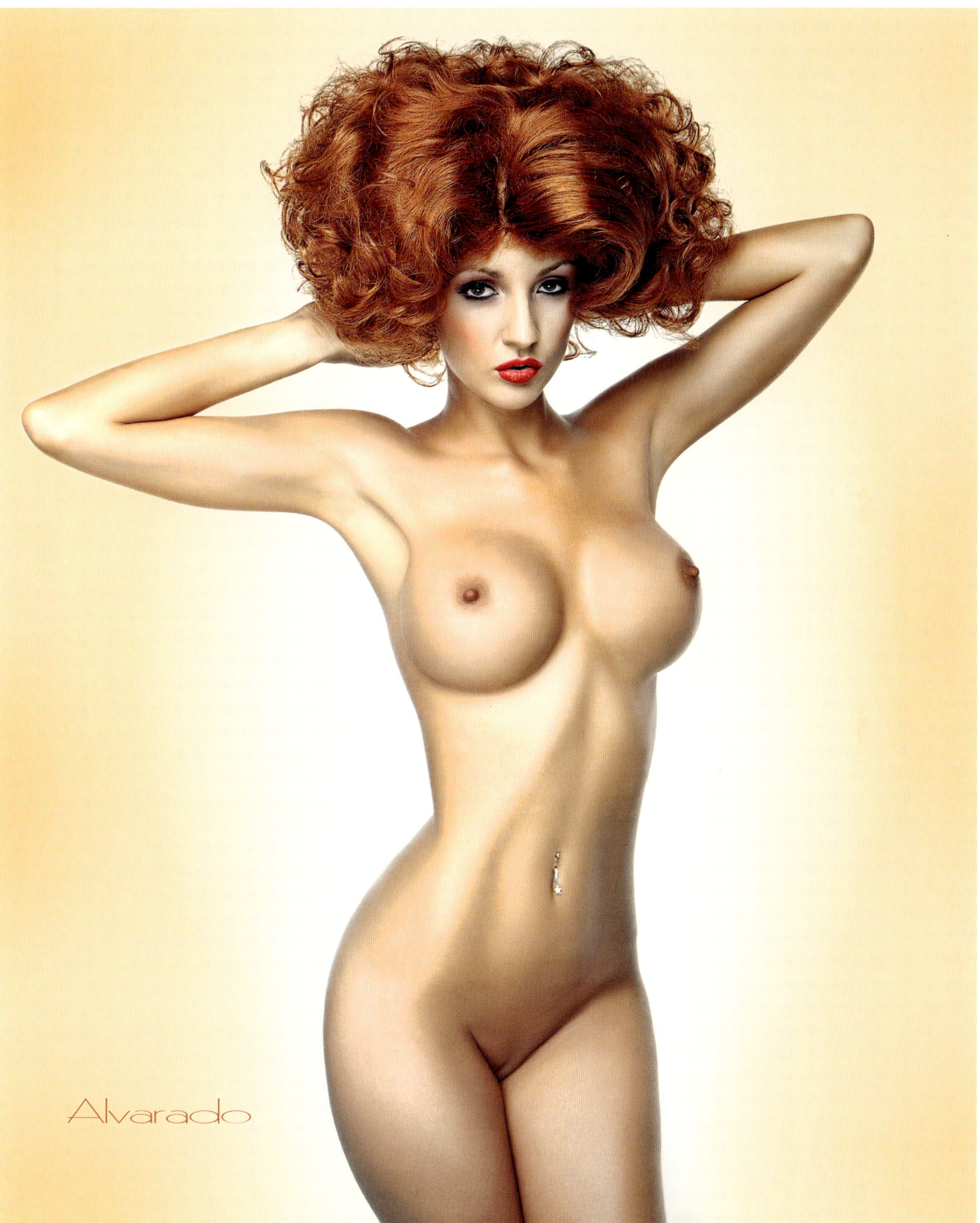
Alvarado

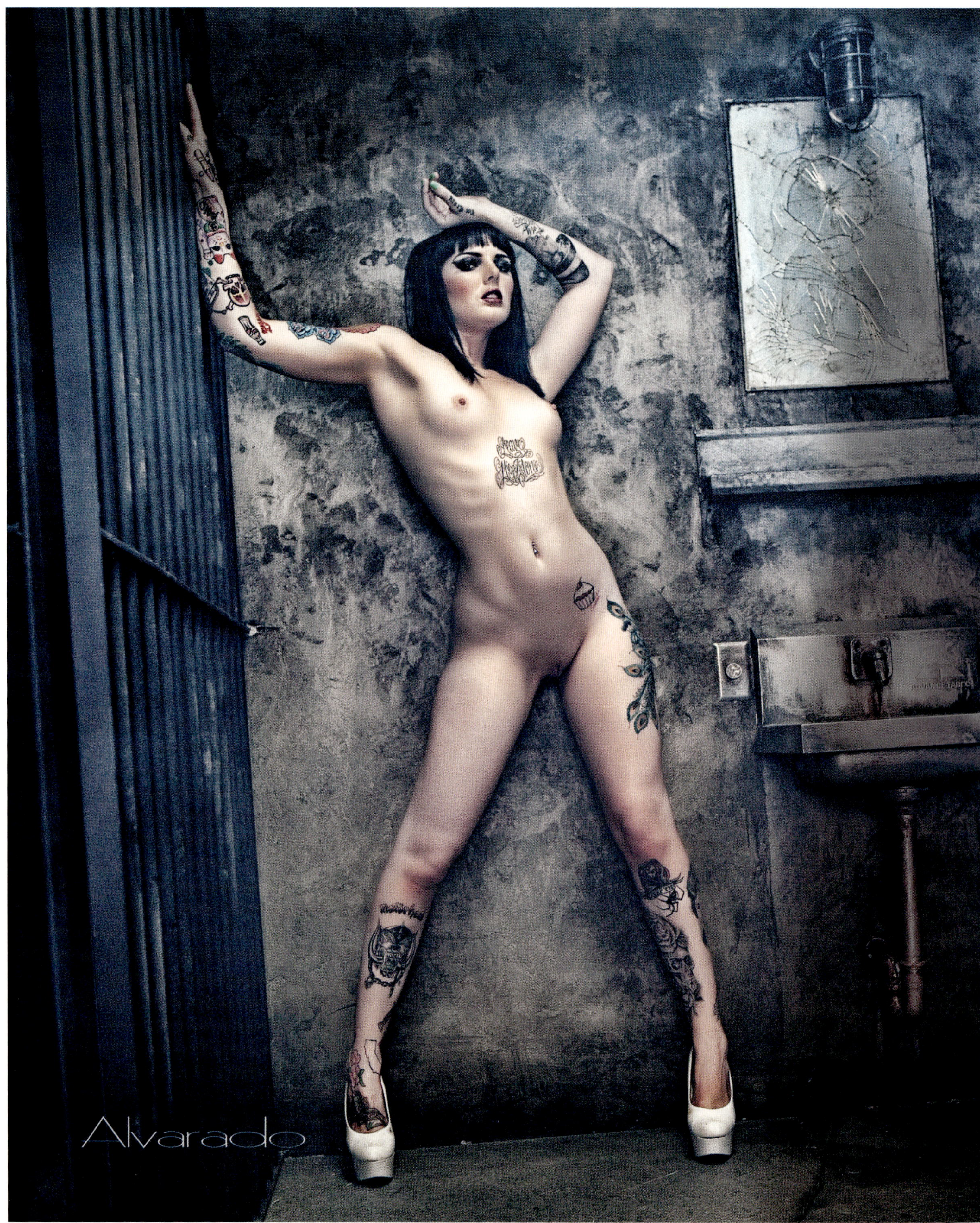
Alvarado

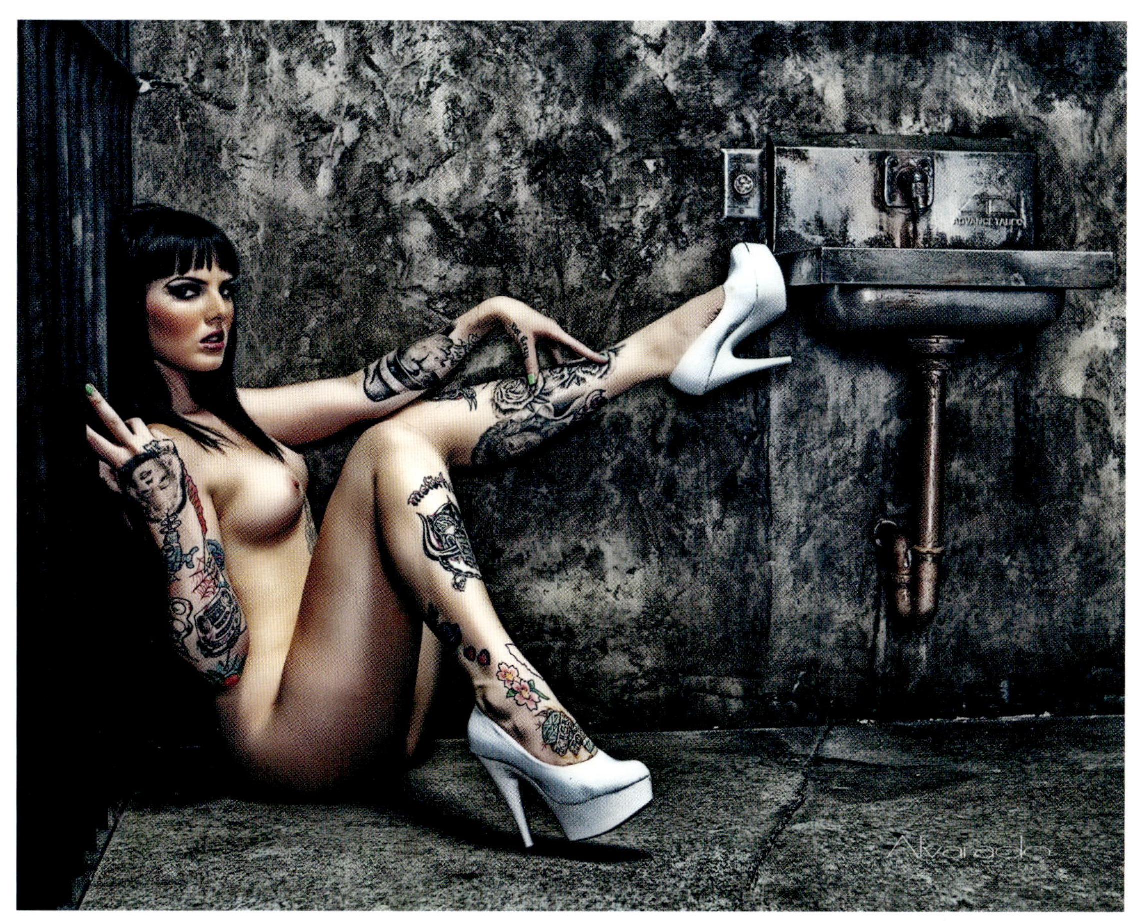
Alvarado

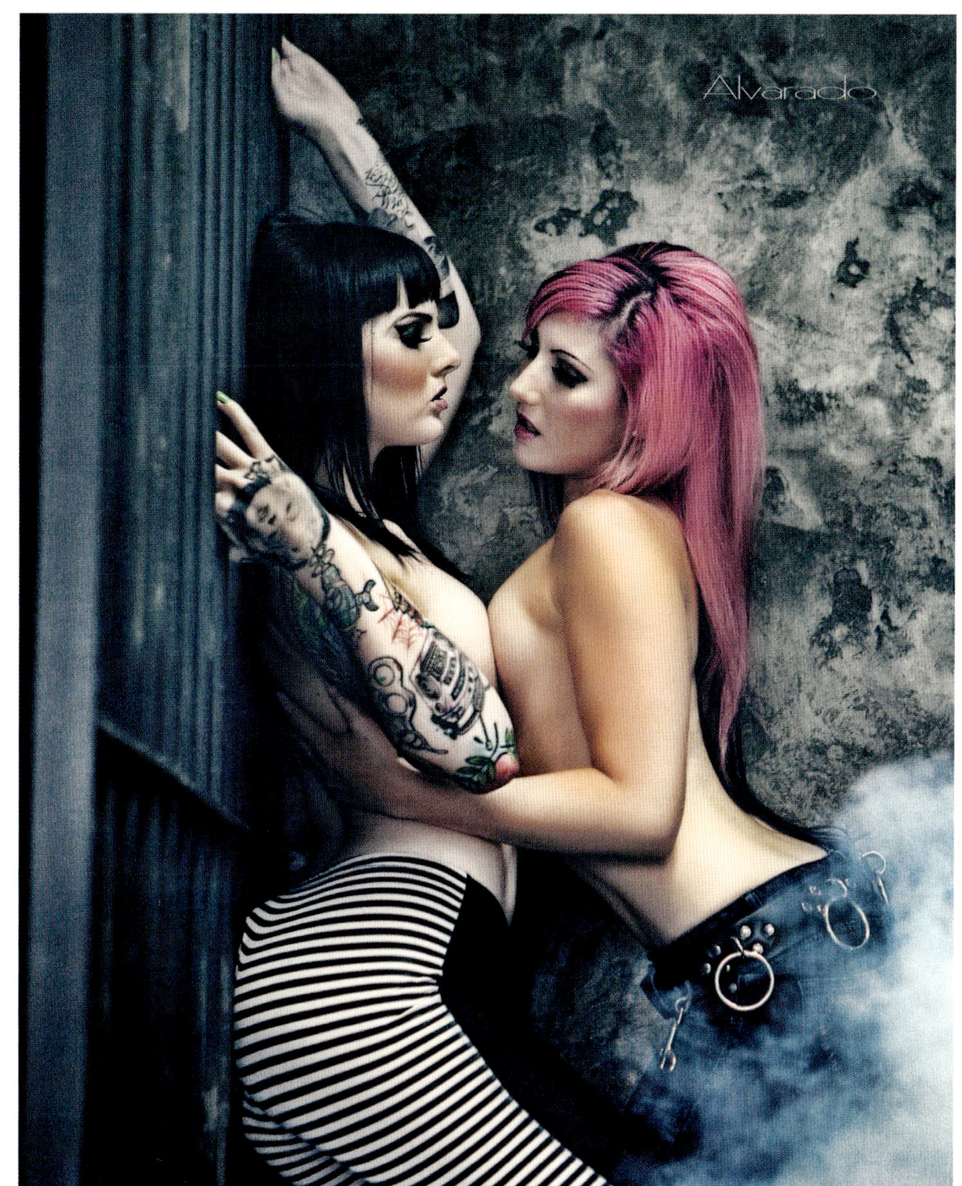
Alvarado

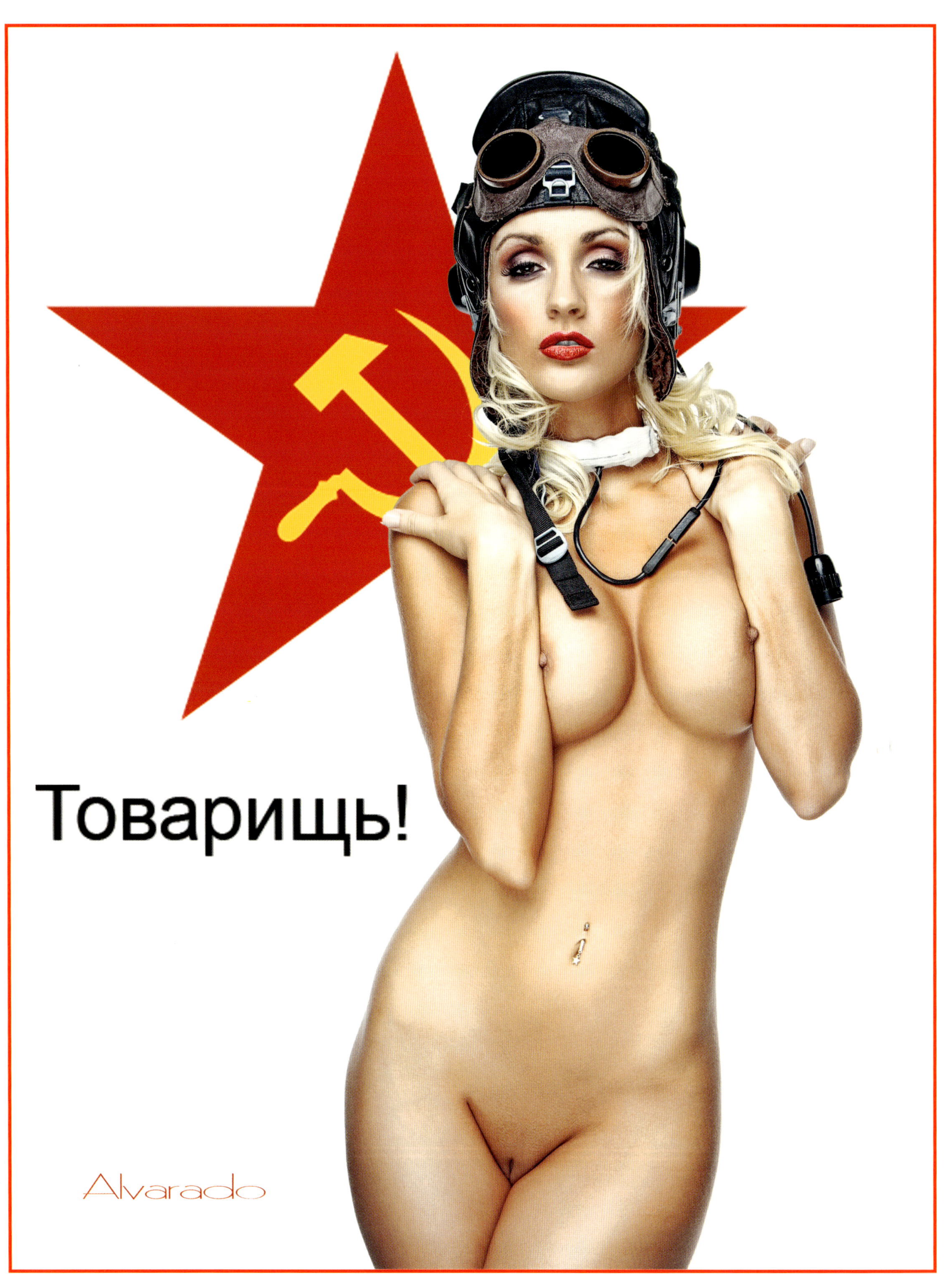
Товарищь!
Alvarado

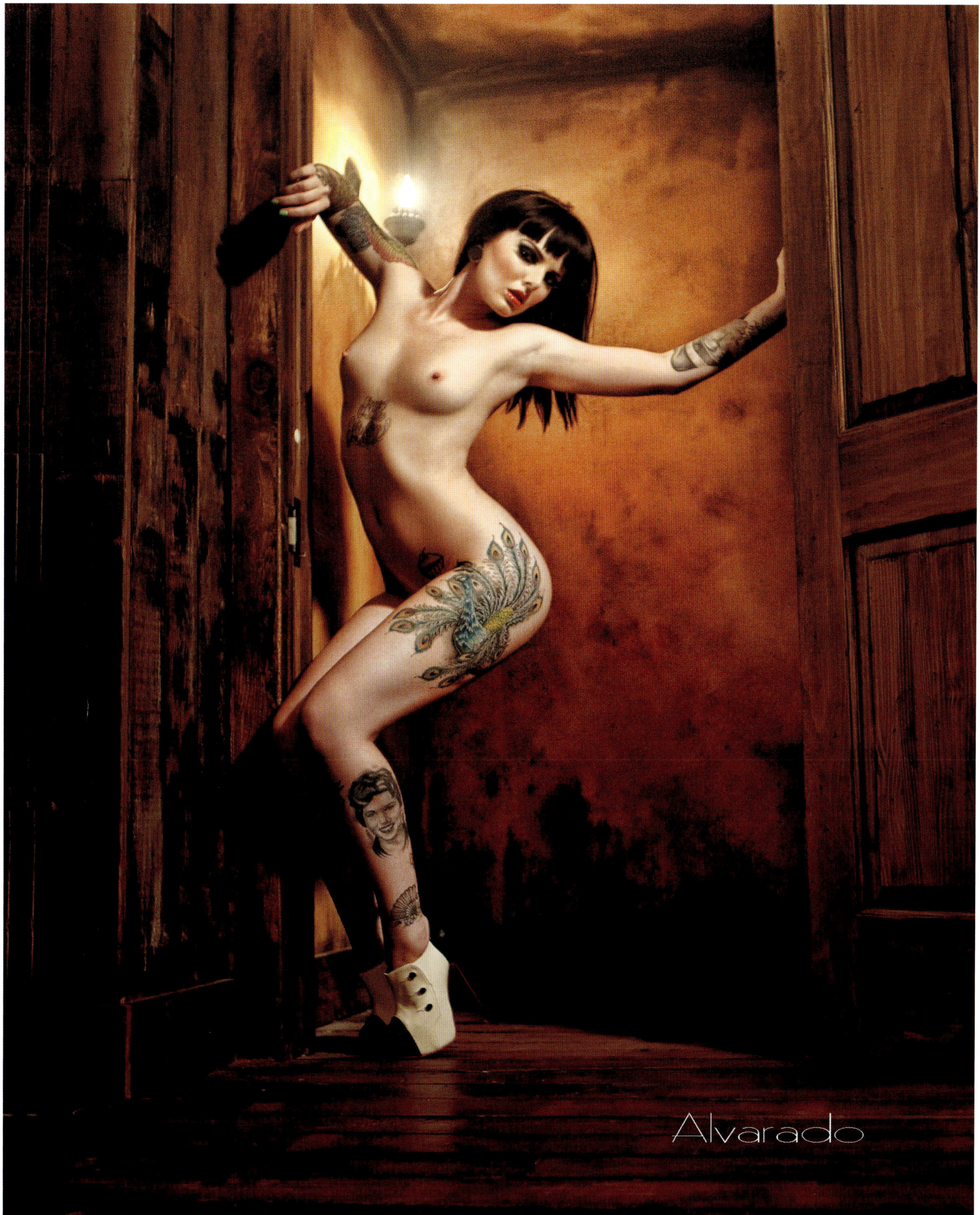
Alvarado

Alvarado

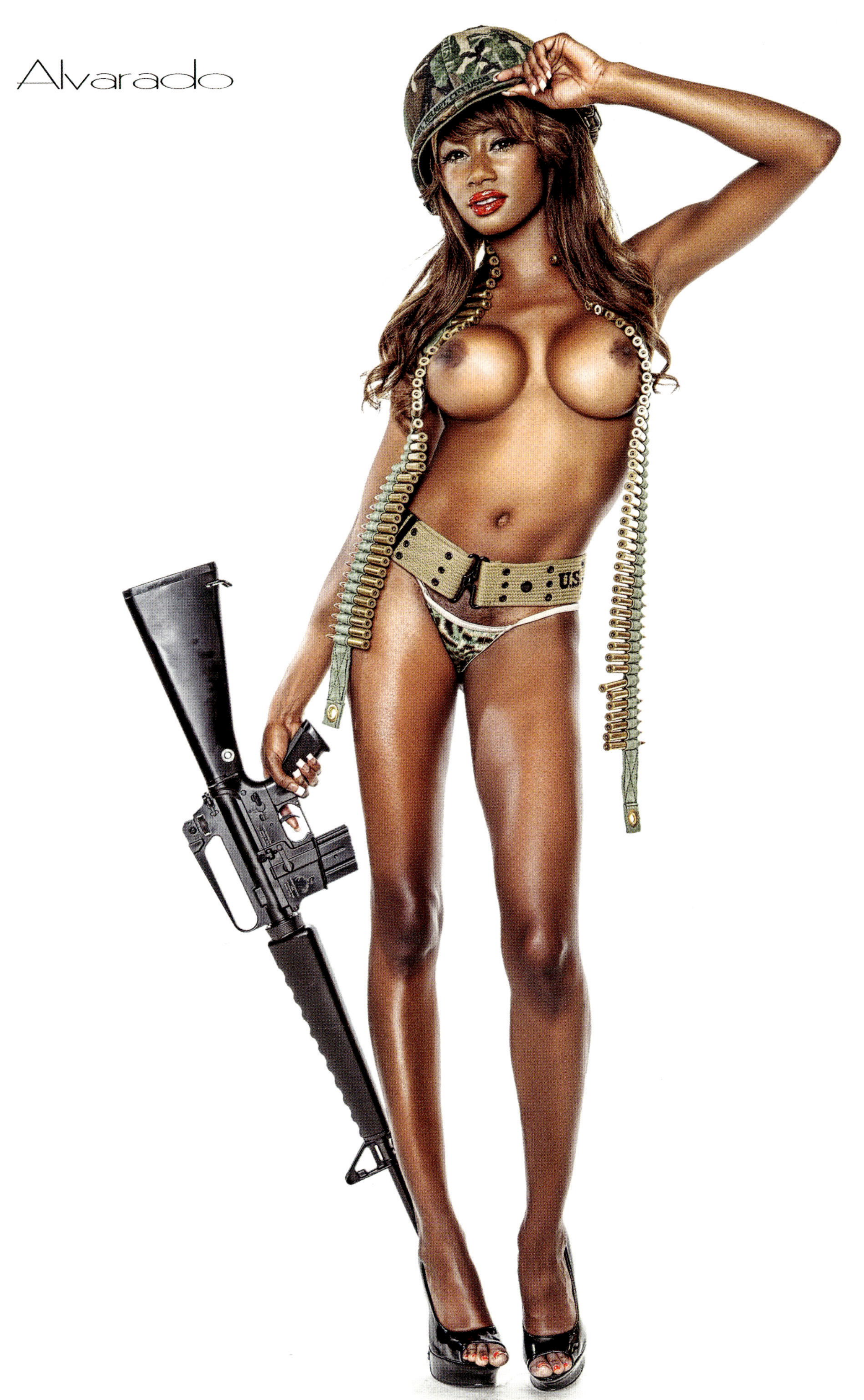

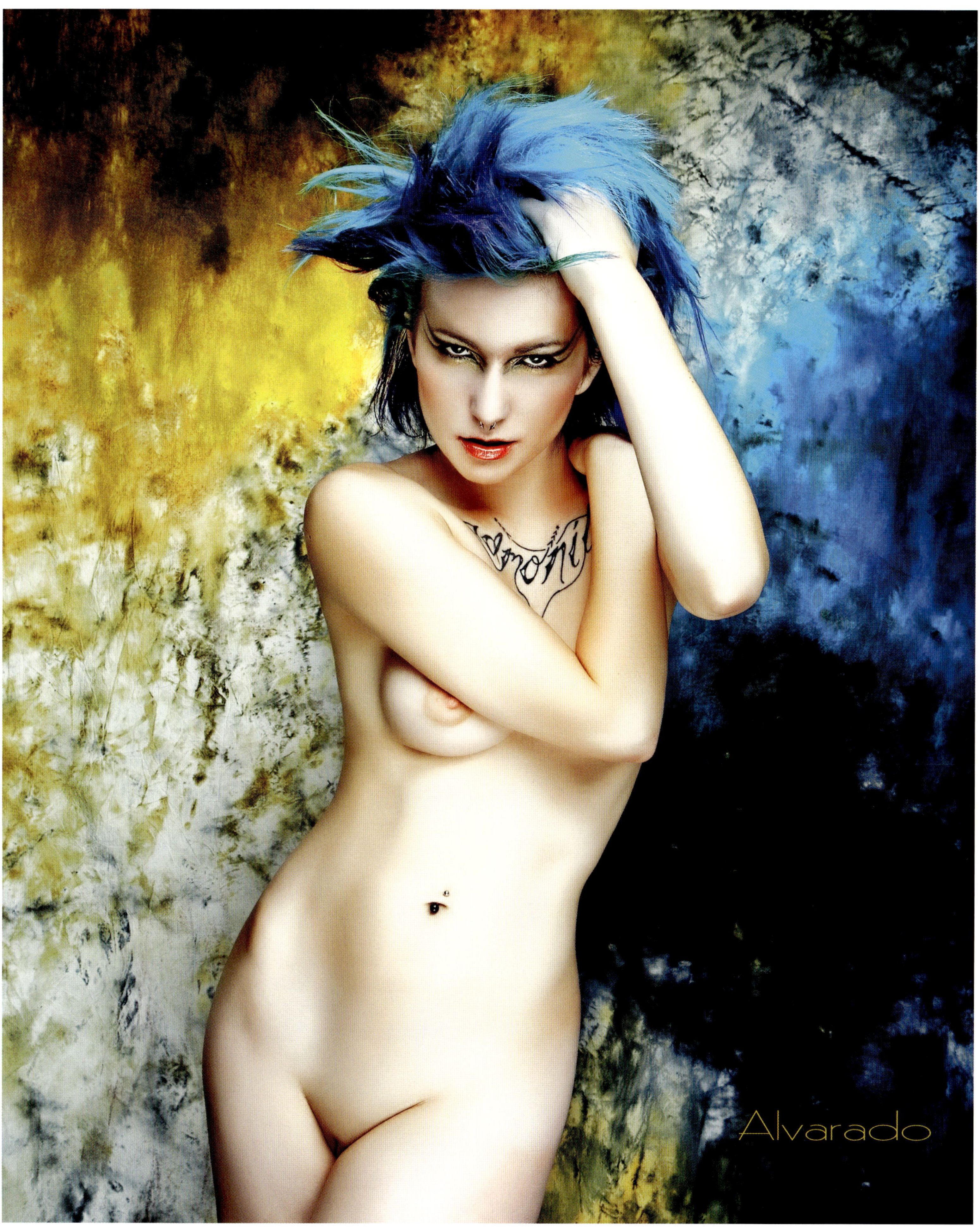
Alvarado

Alvarado

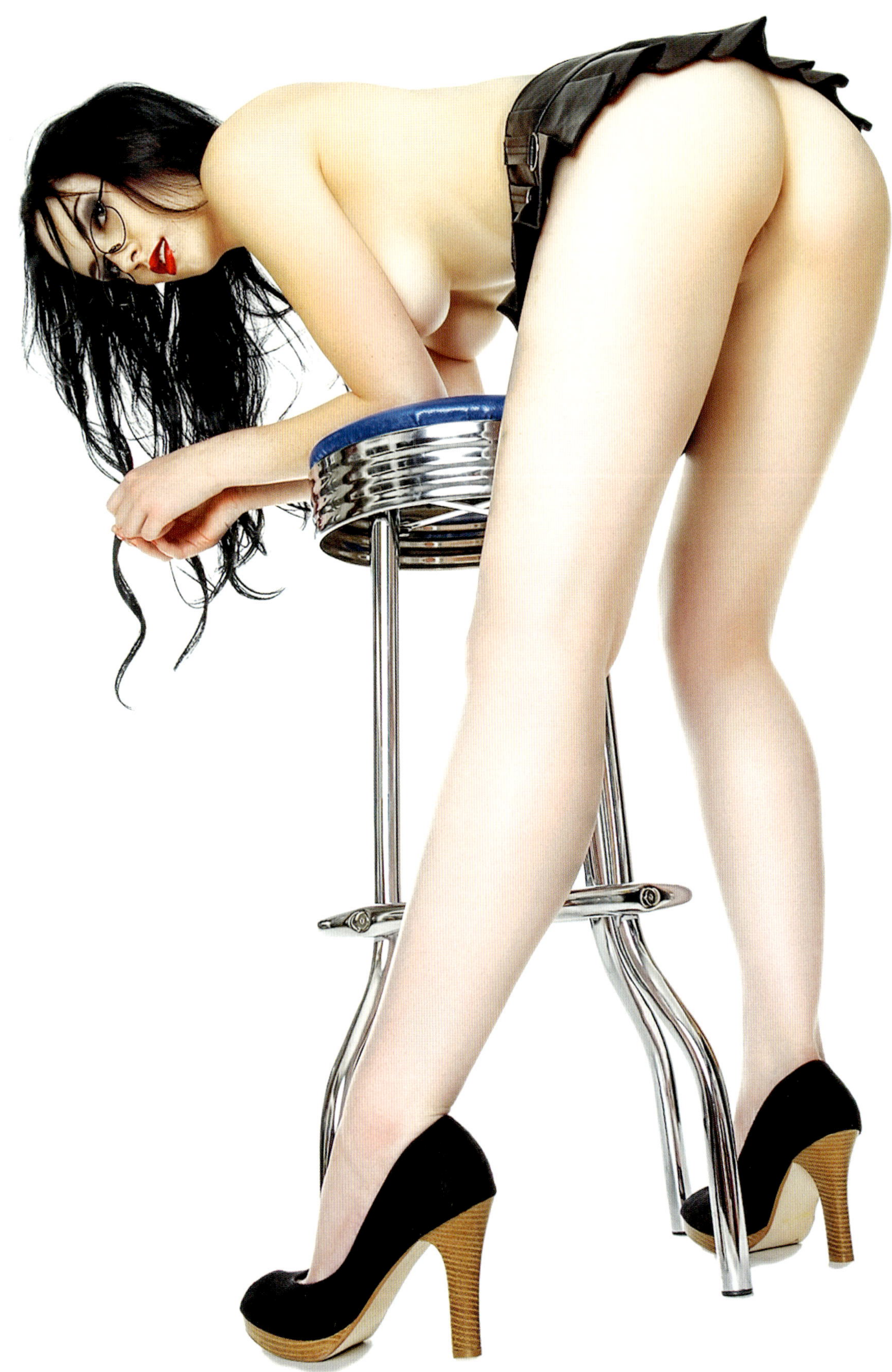

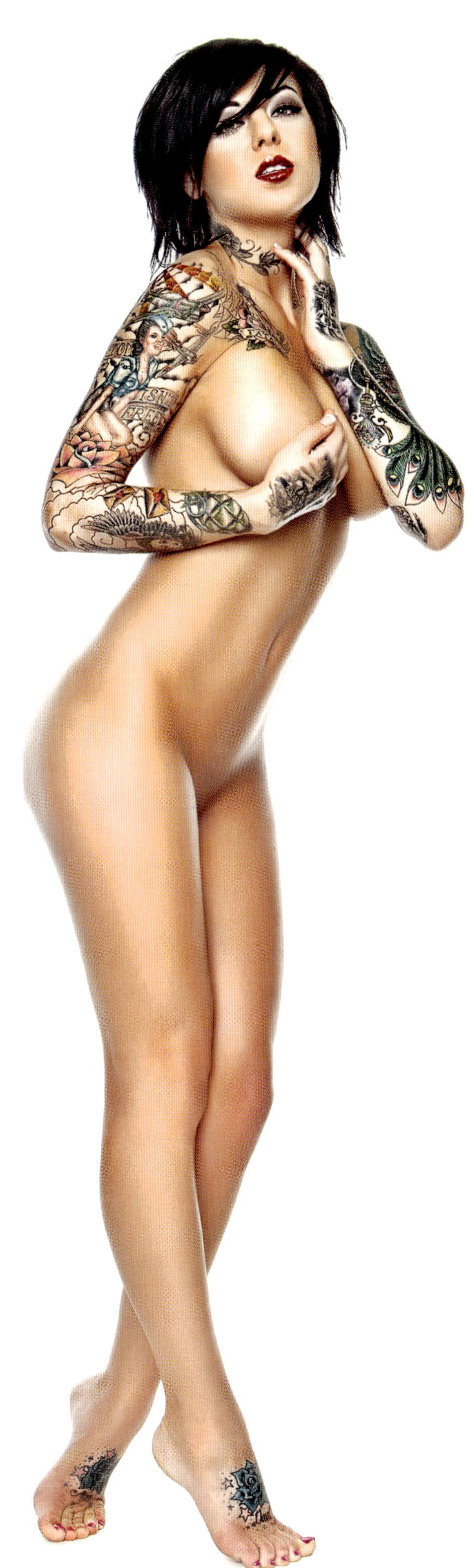

Alvarado

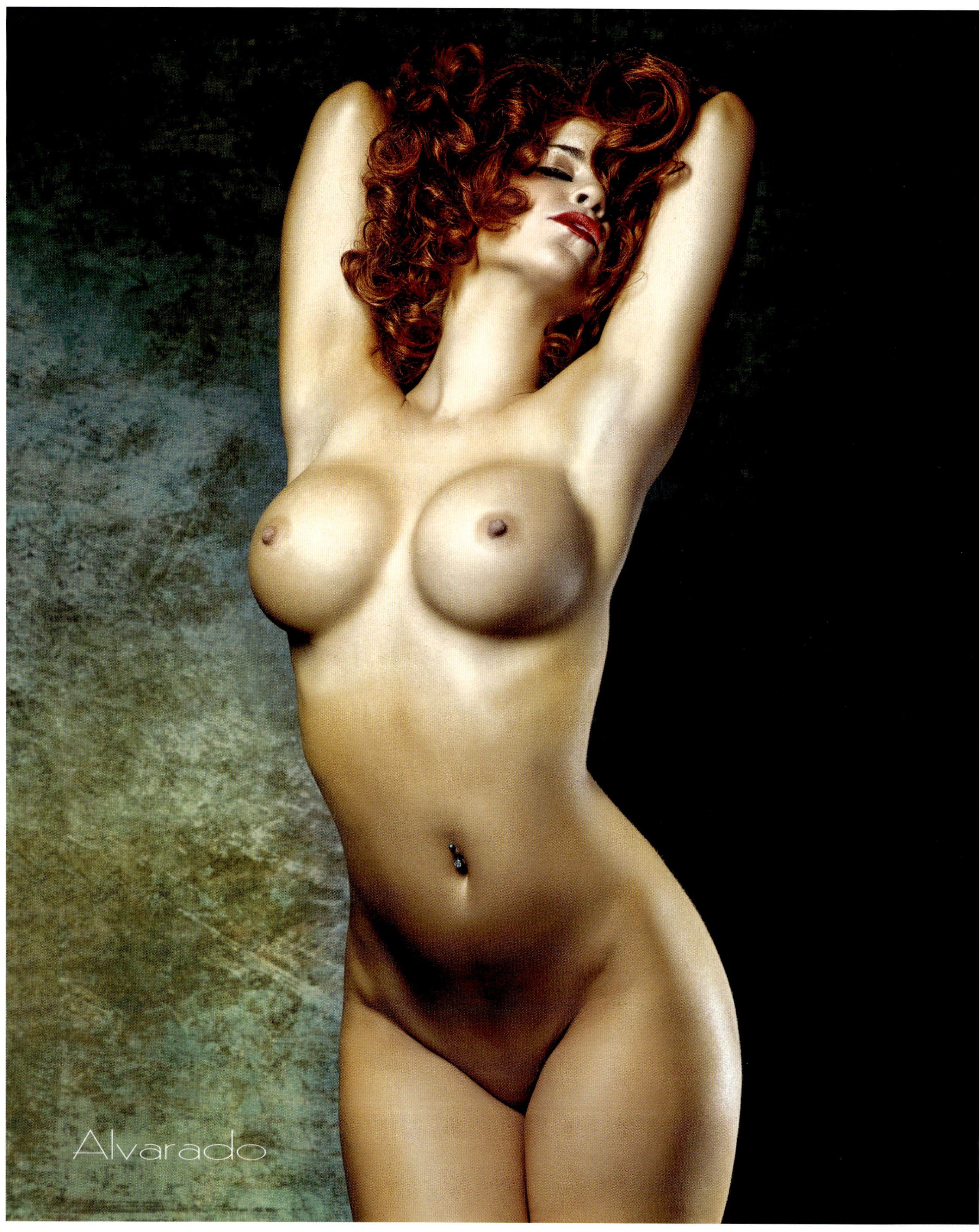
Alvarado

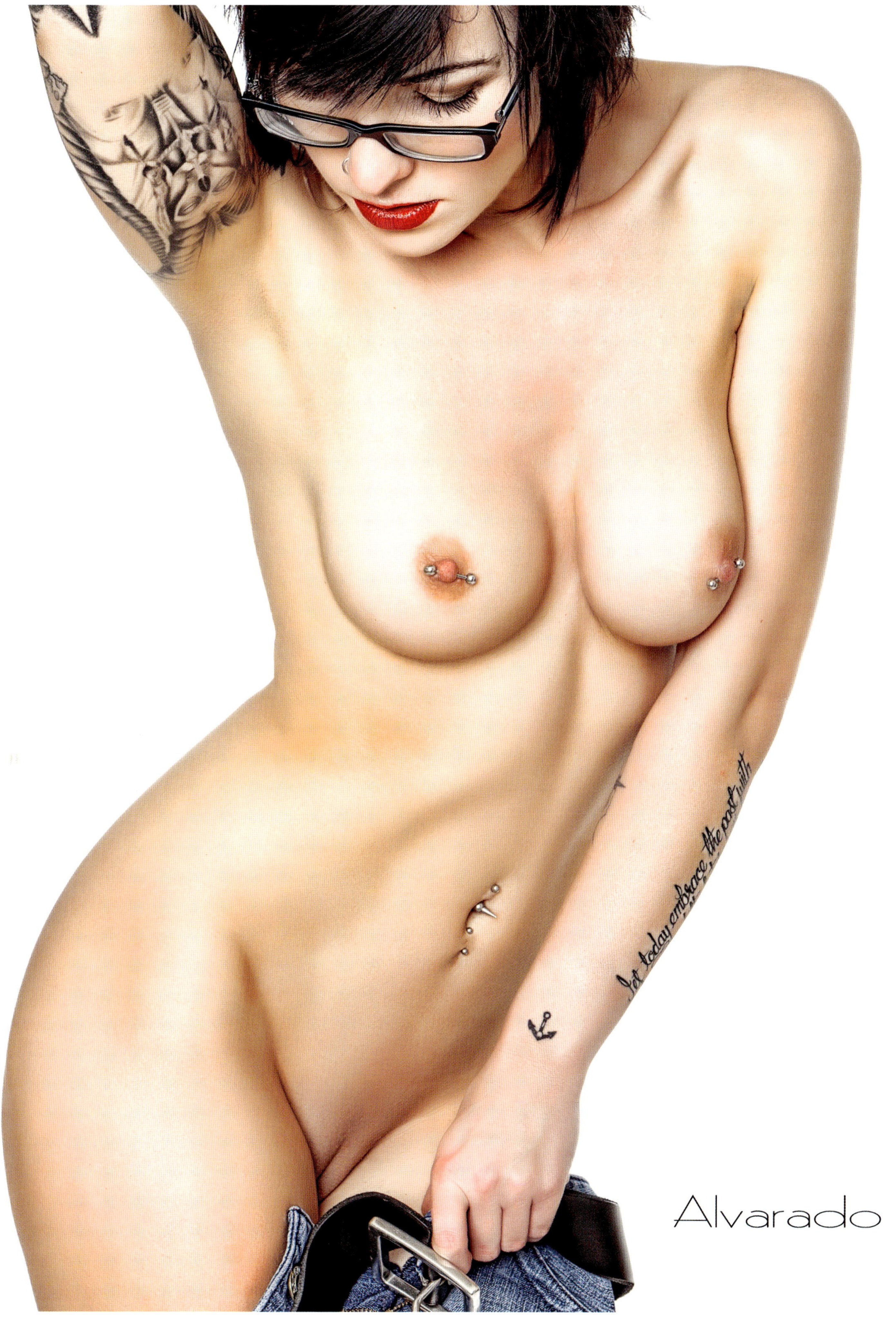

Alvarado

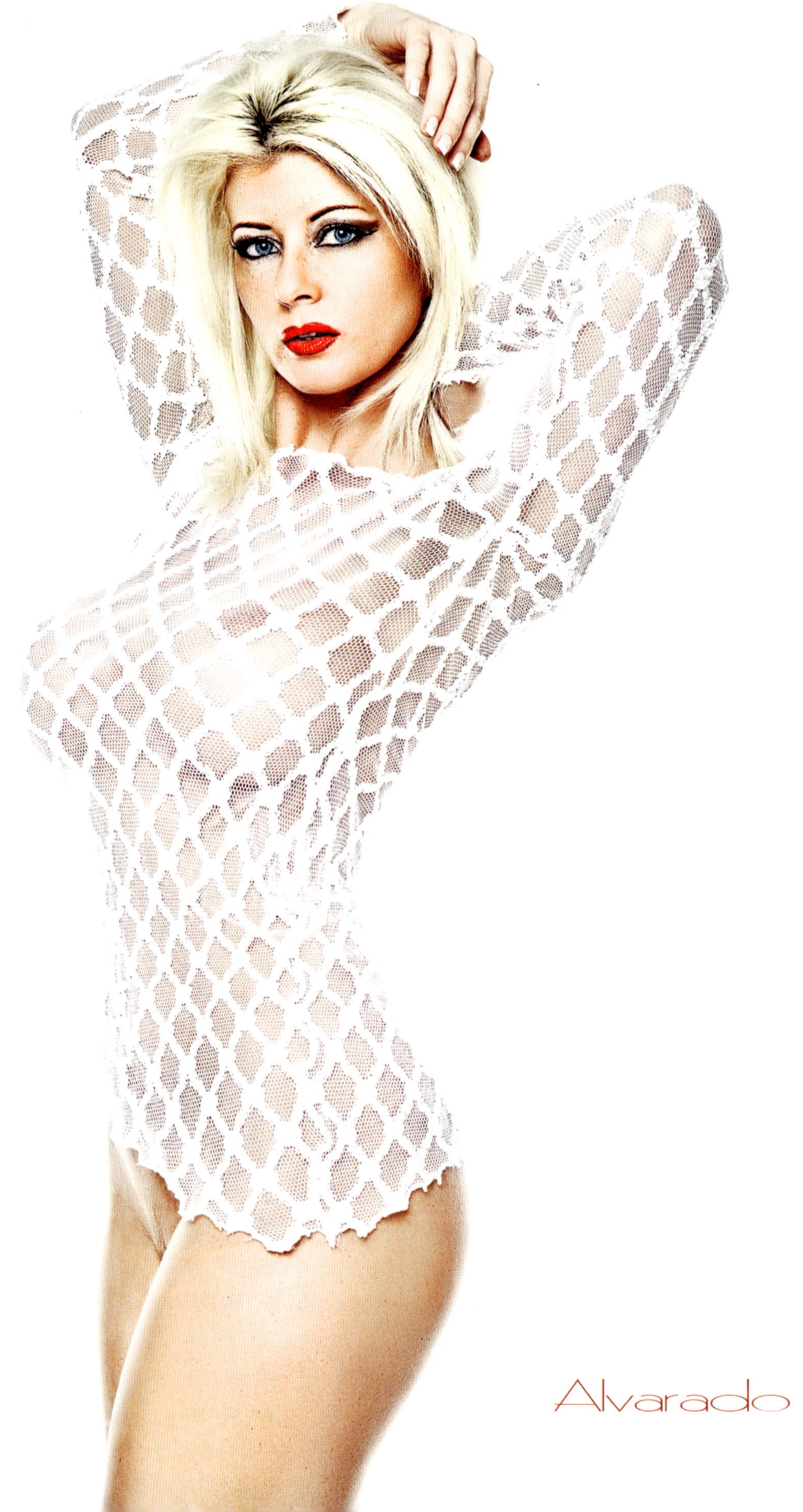
Alvarado

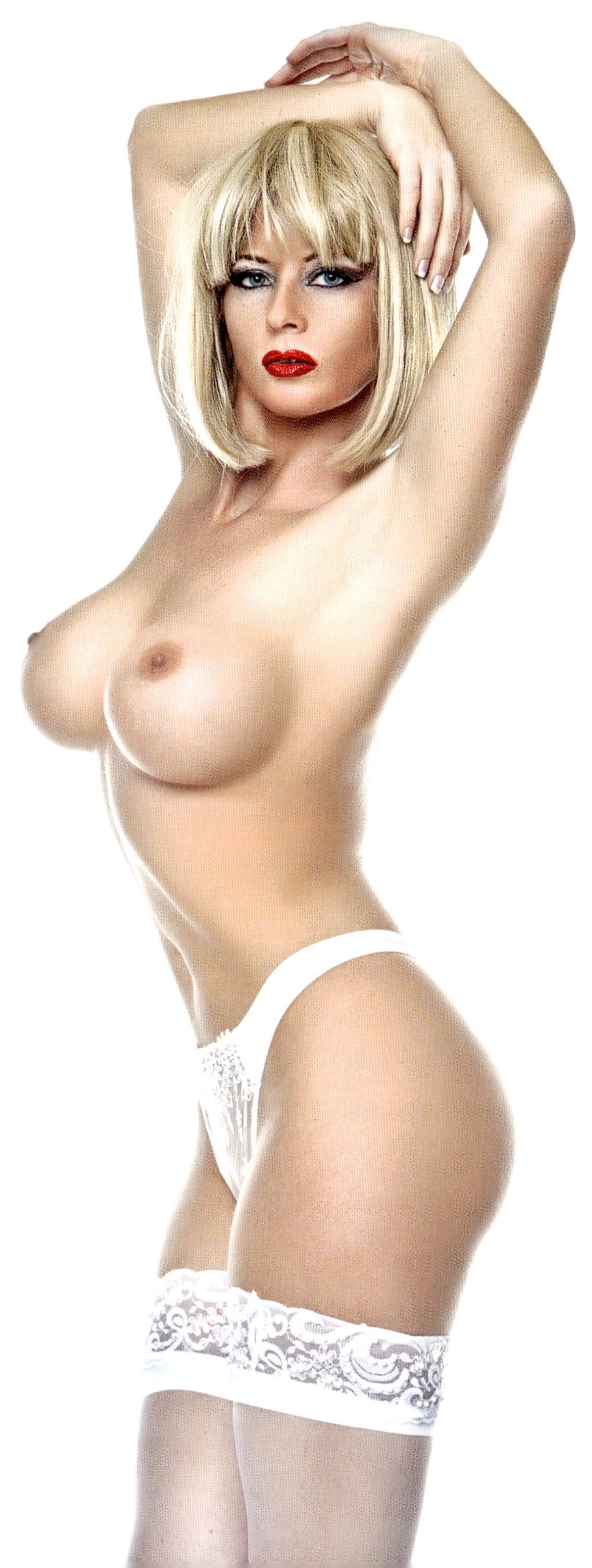

Alvarado

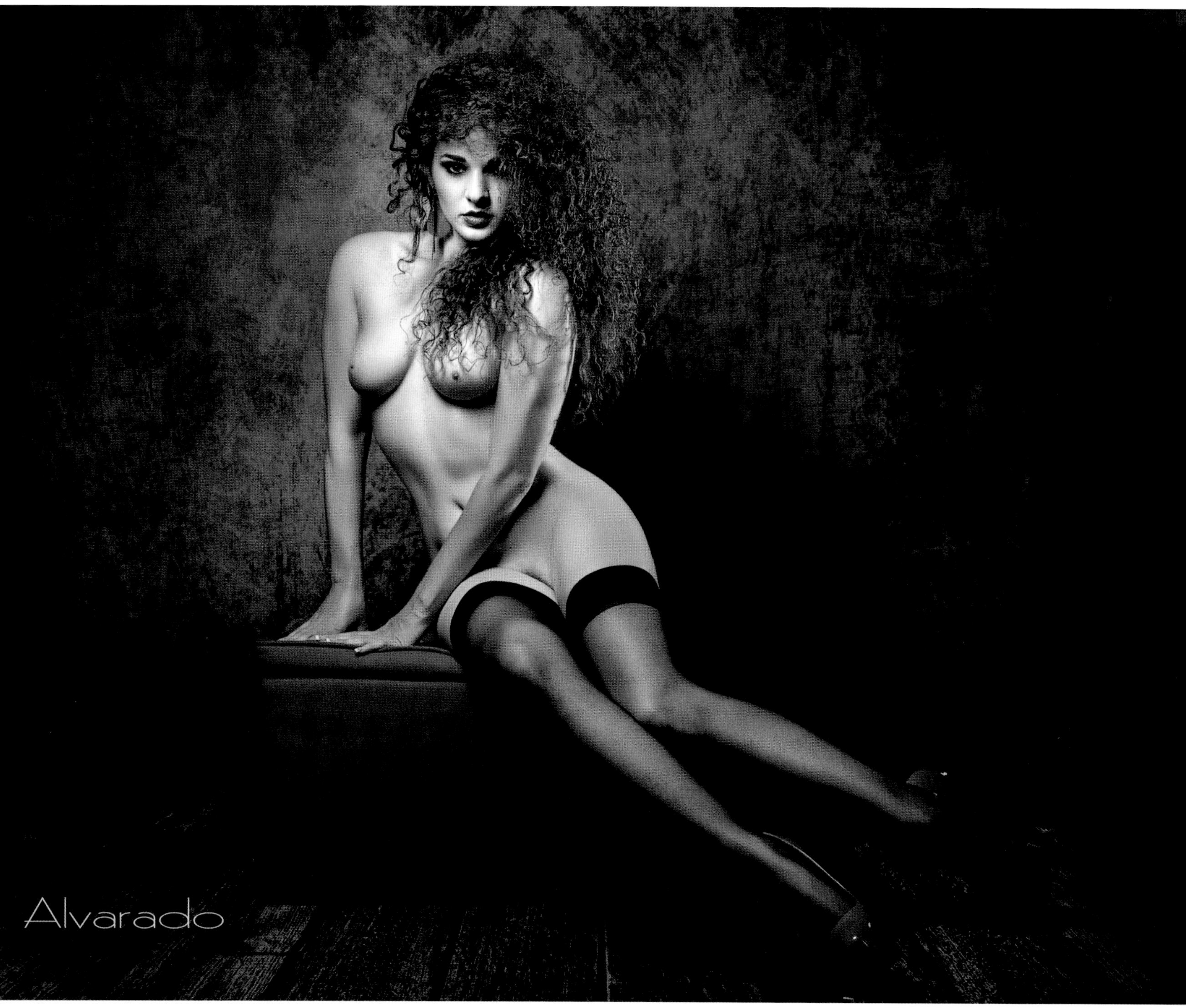
Alvarado

Alvarado

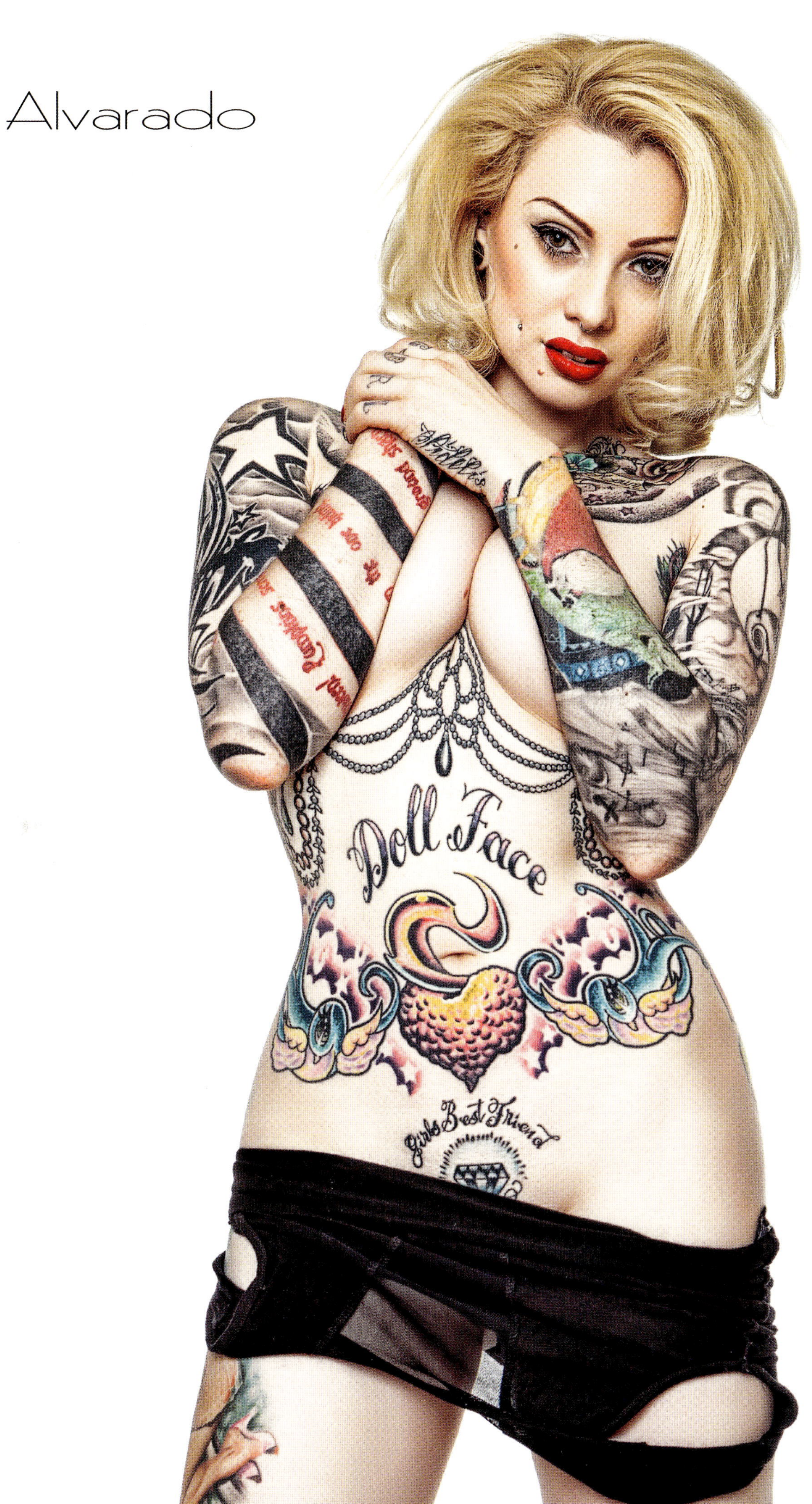

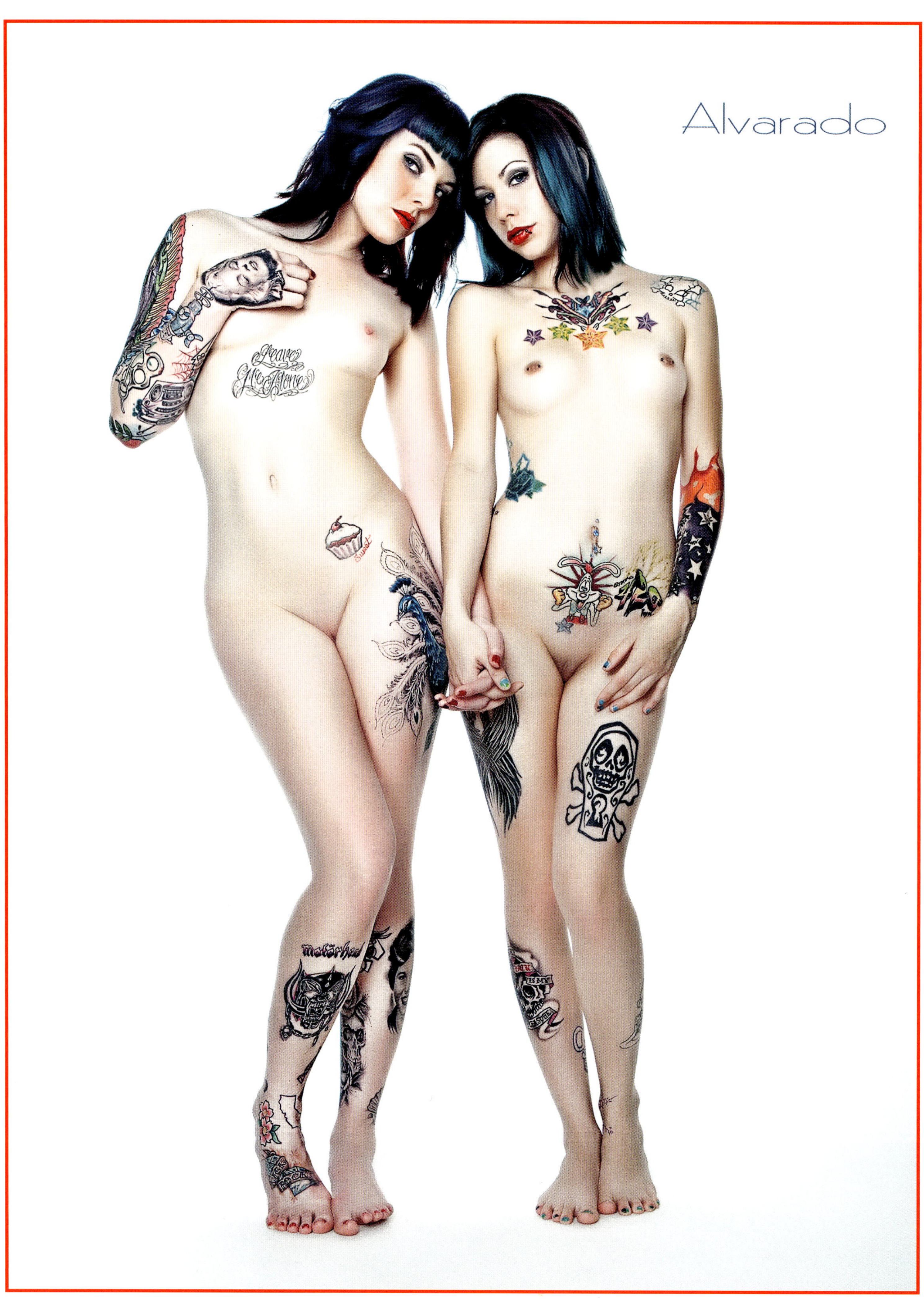

Alvarado

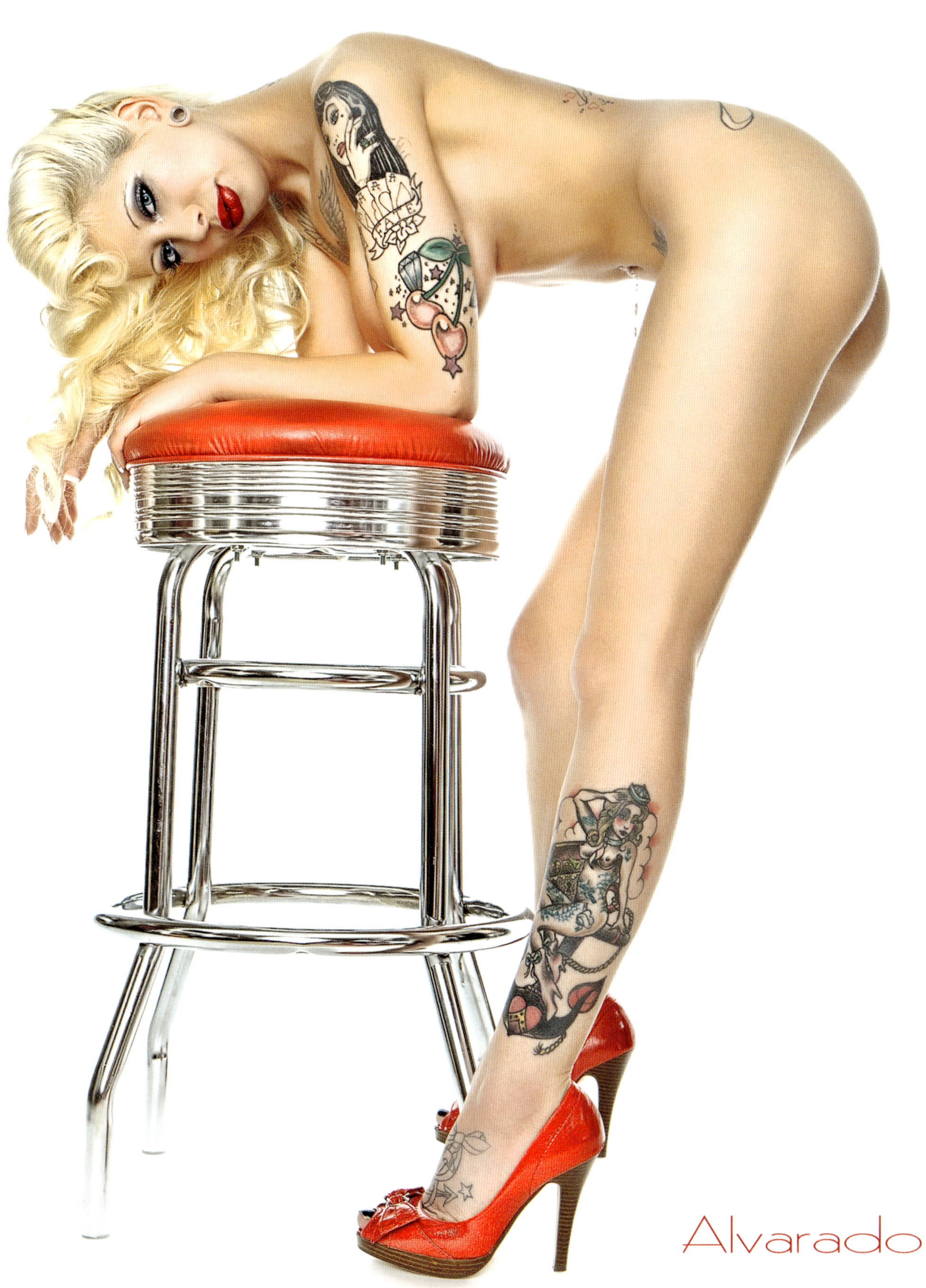

Alvarado

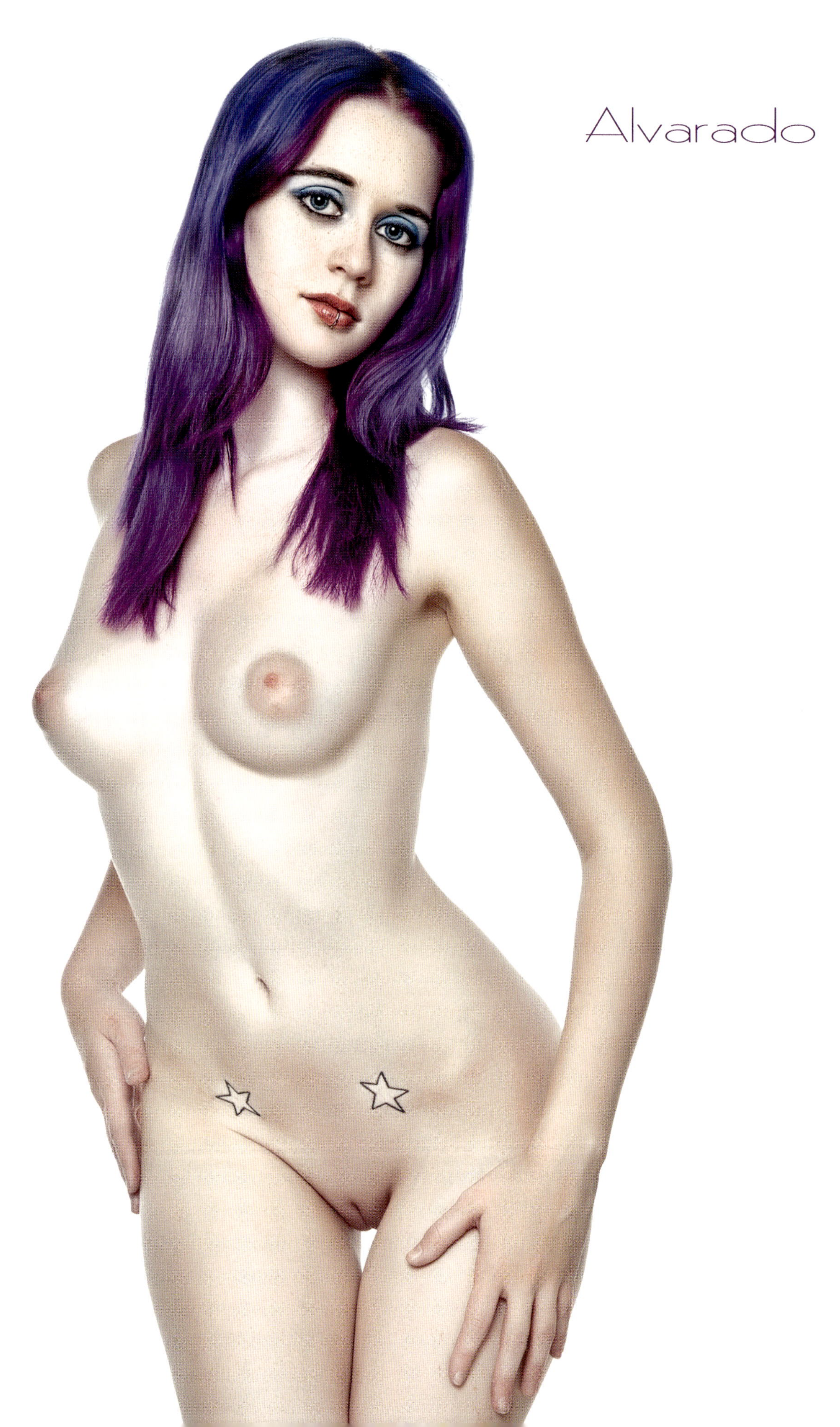

Alvarado

Alvarado

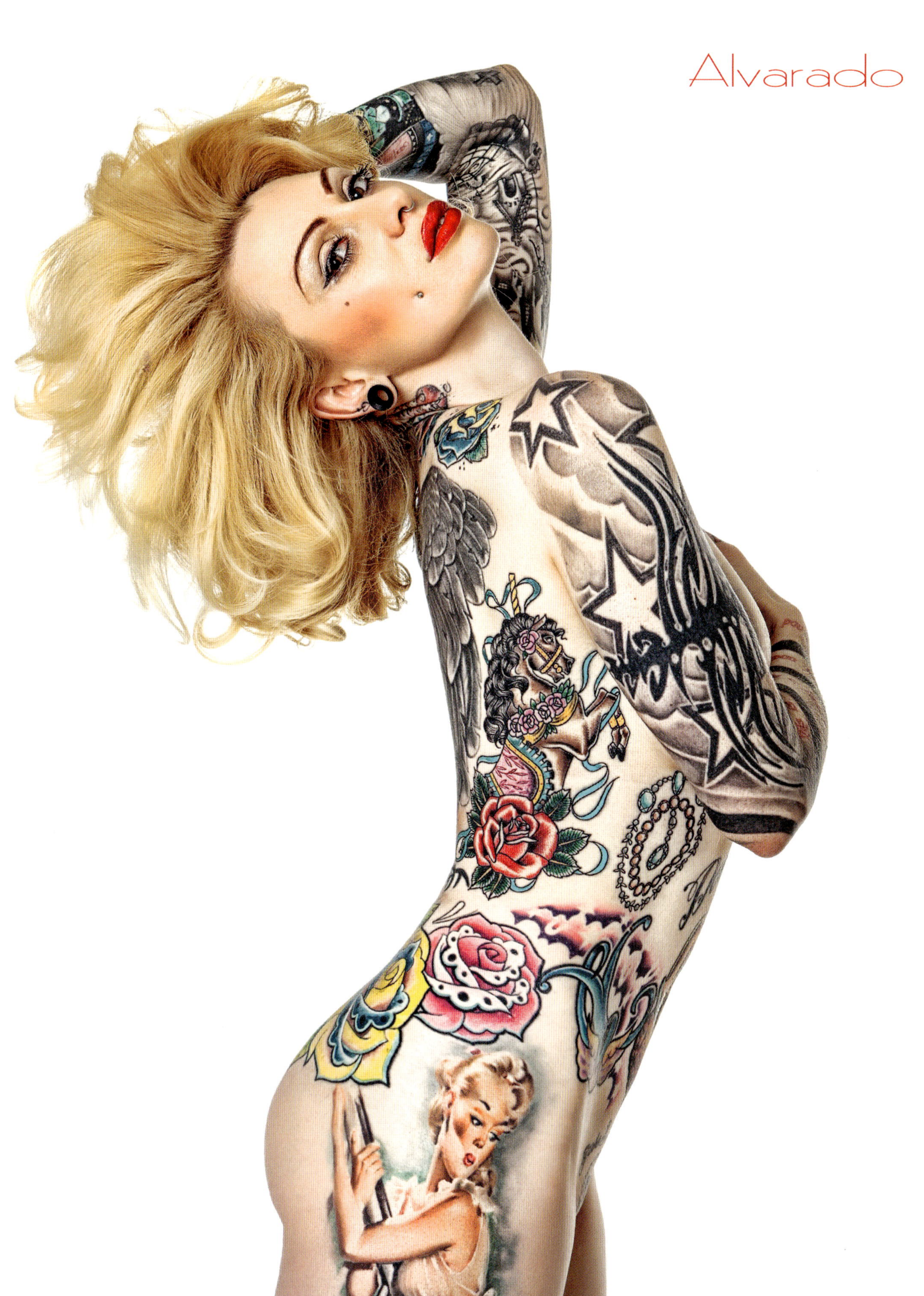

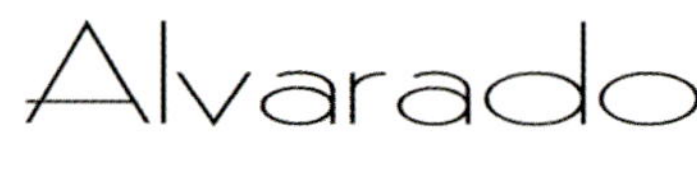
Alvarado

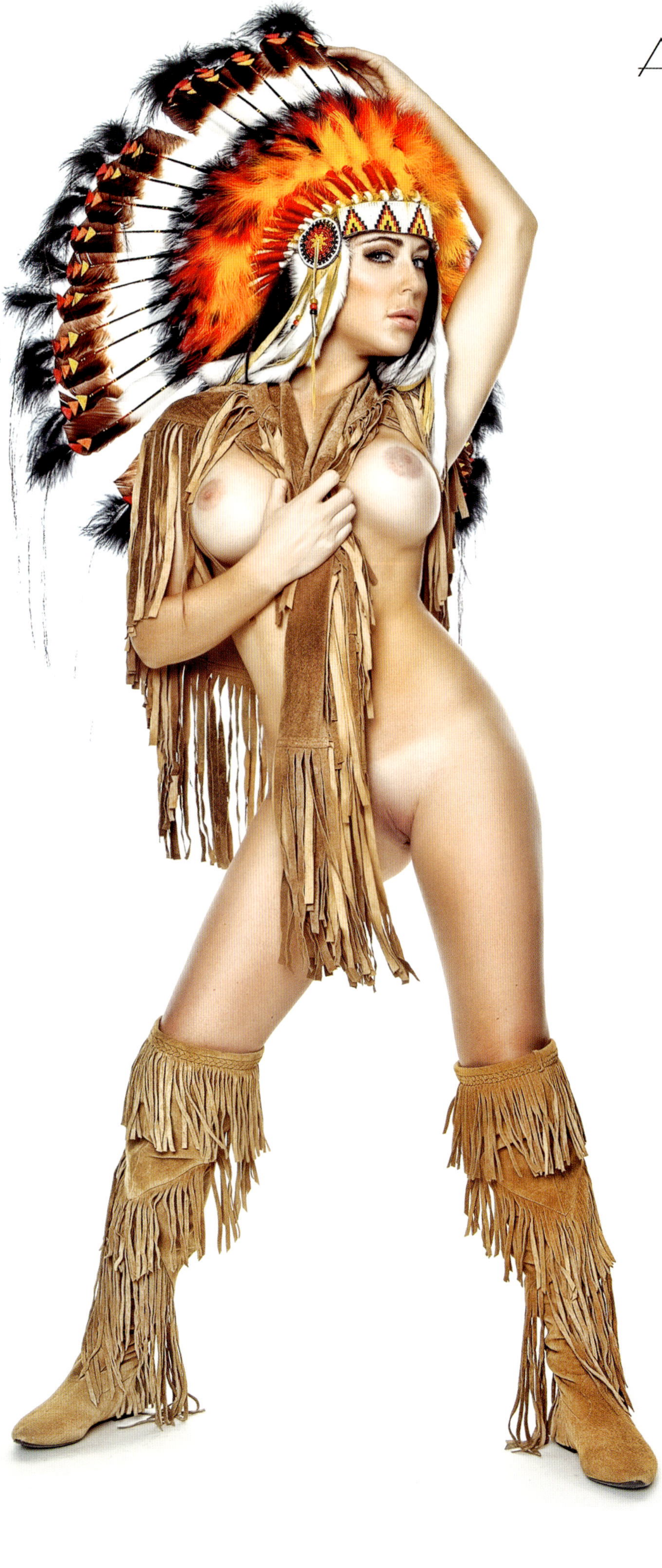

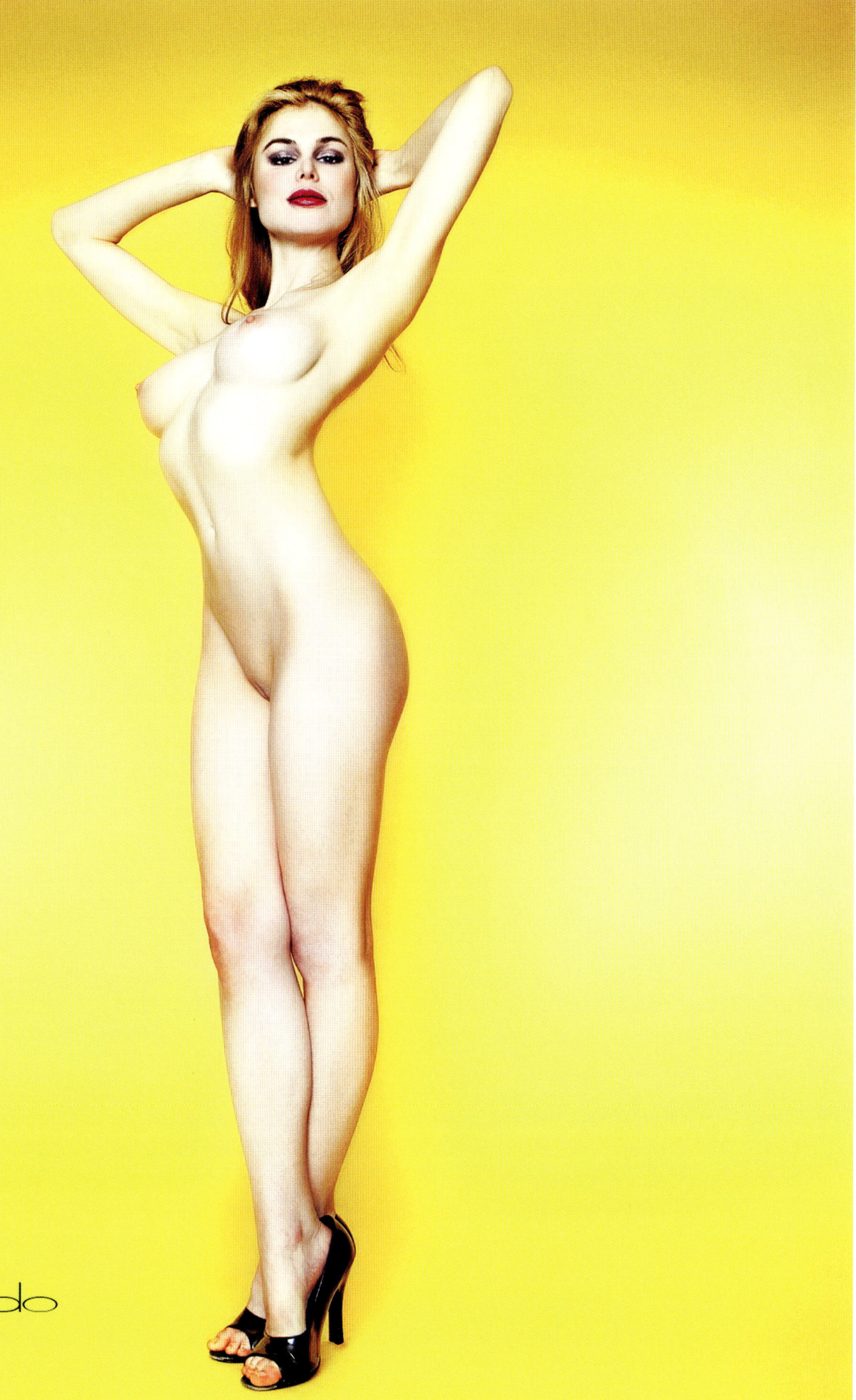
Alvarado

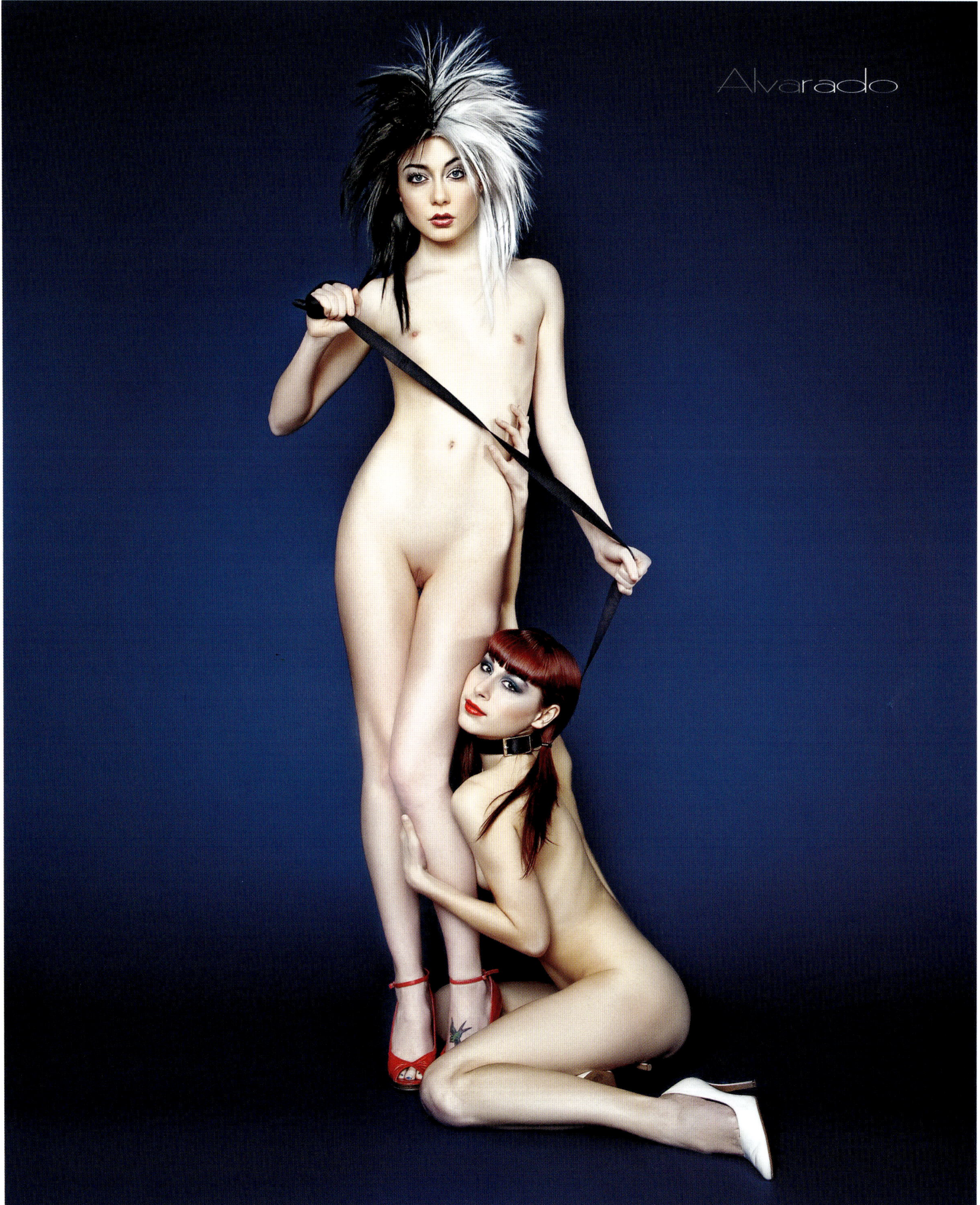
Alvarado

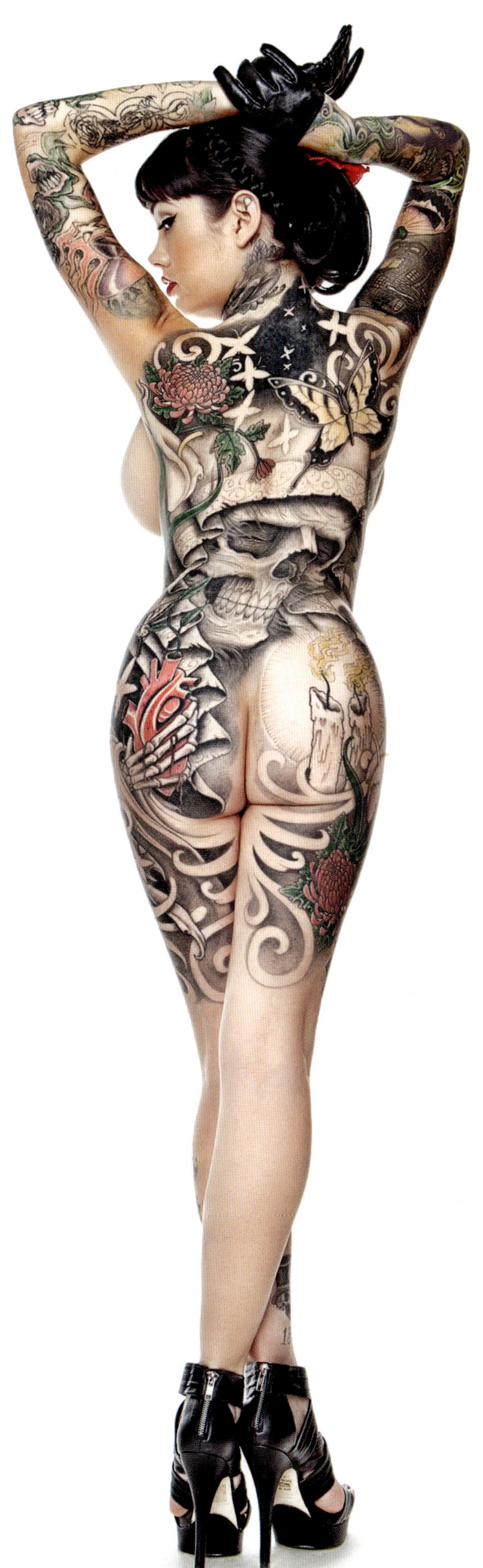

Alvarado

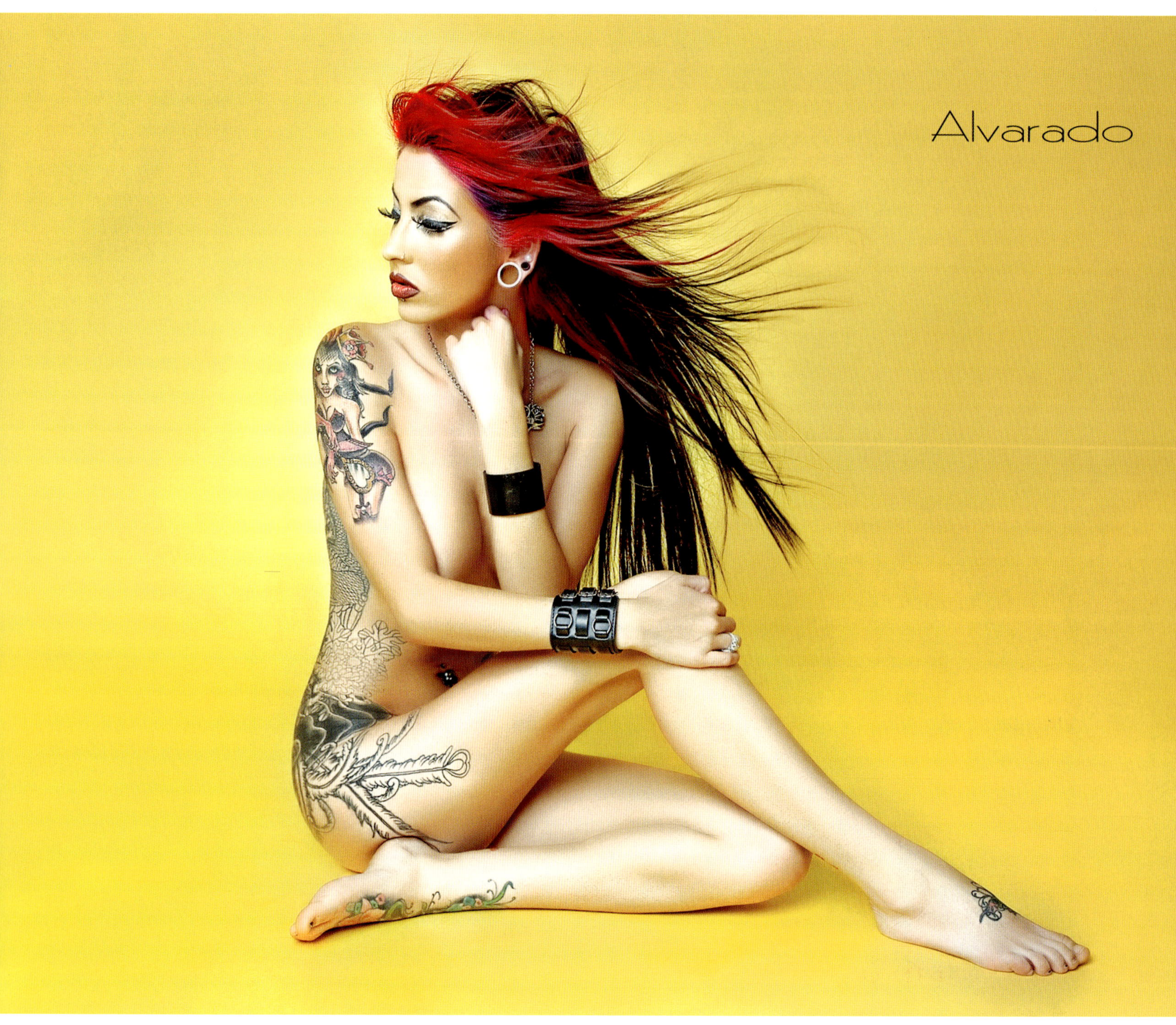
Alvarado

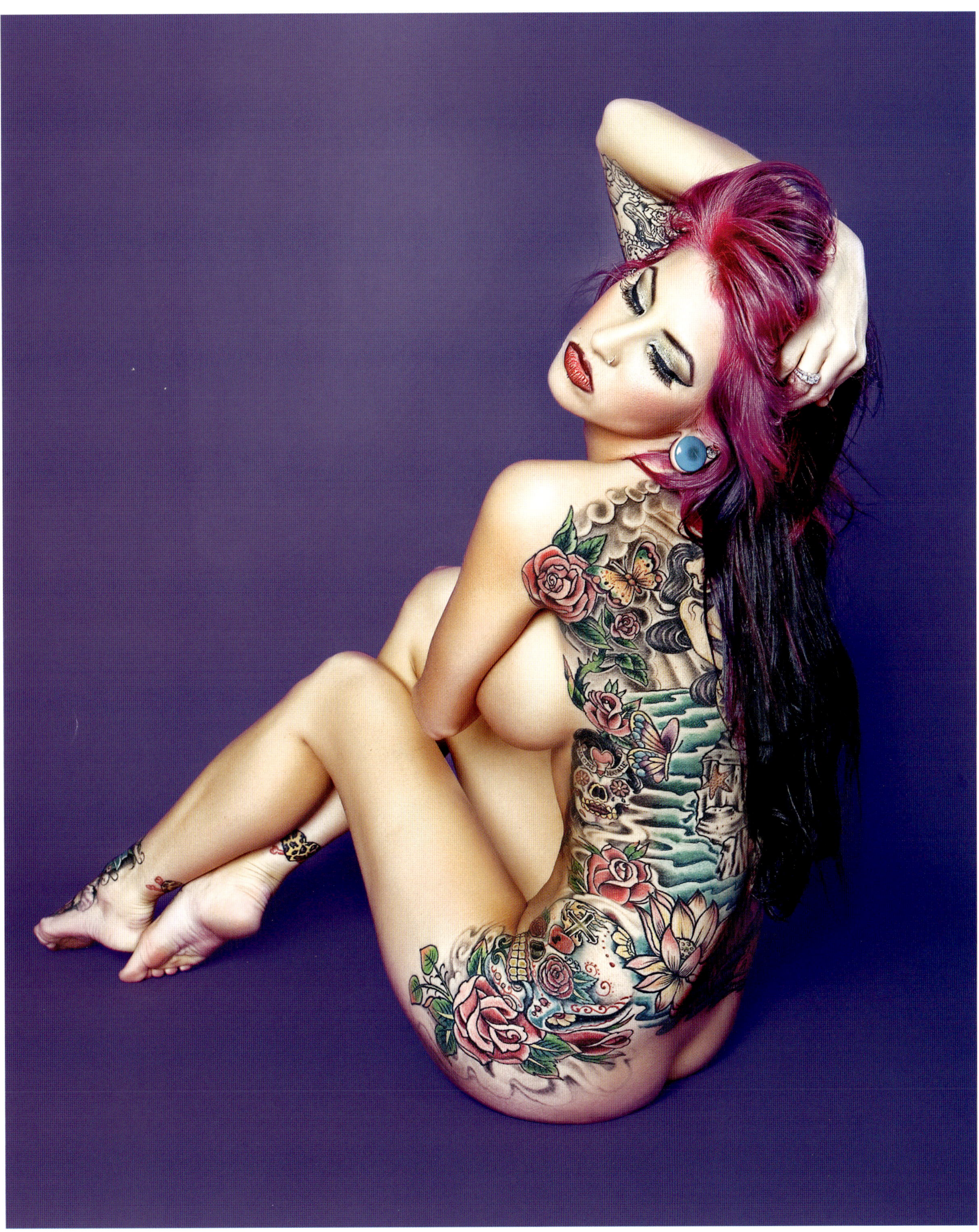

Alvarado

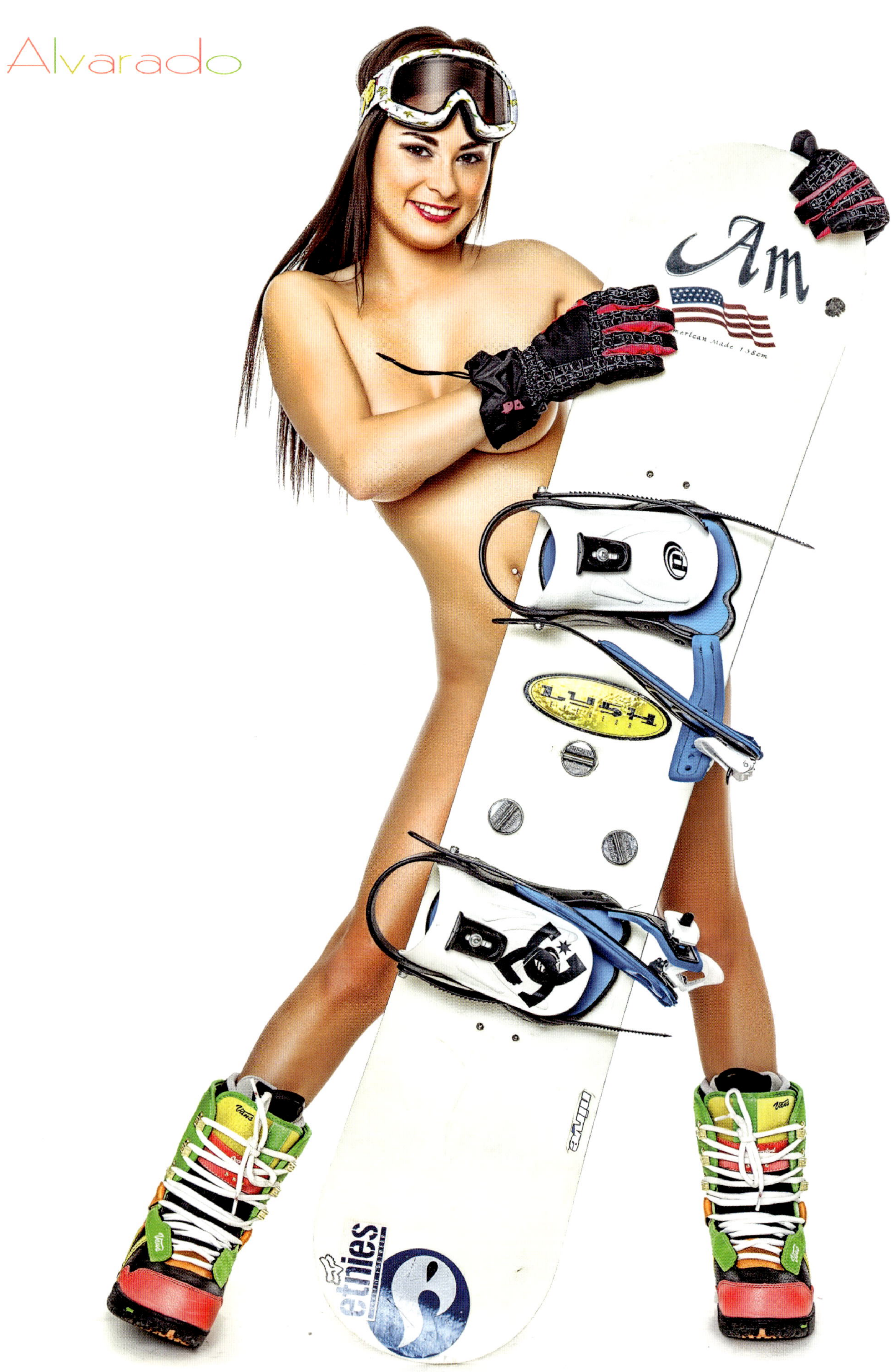

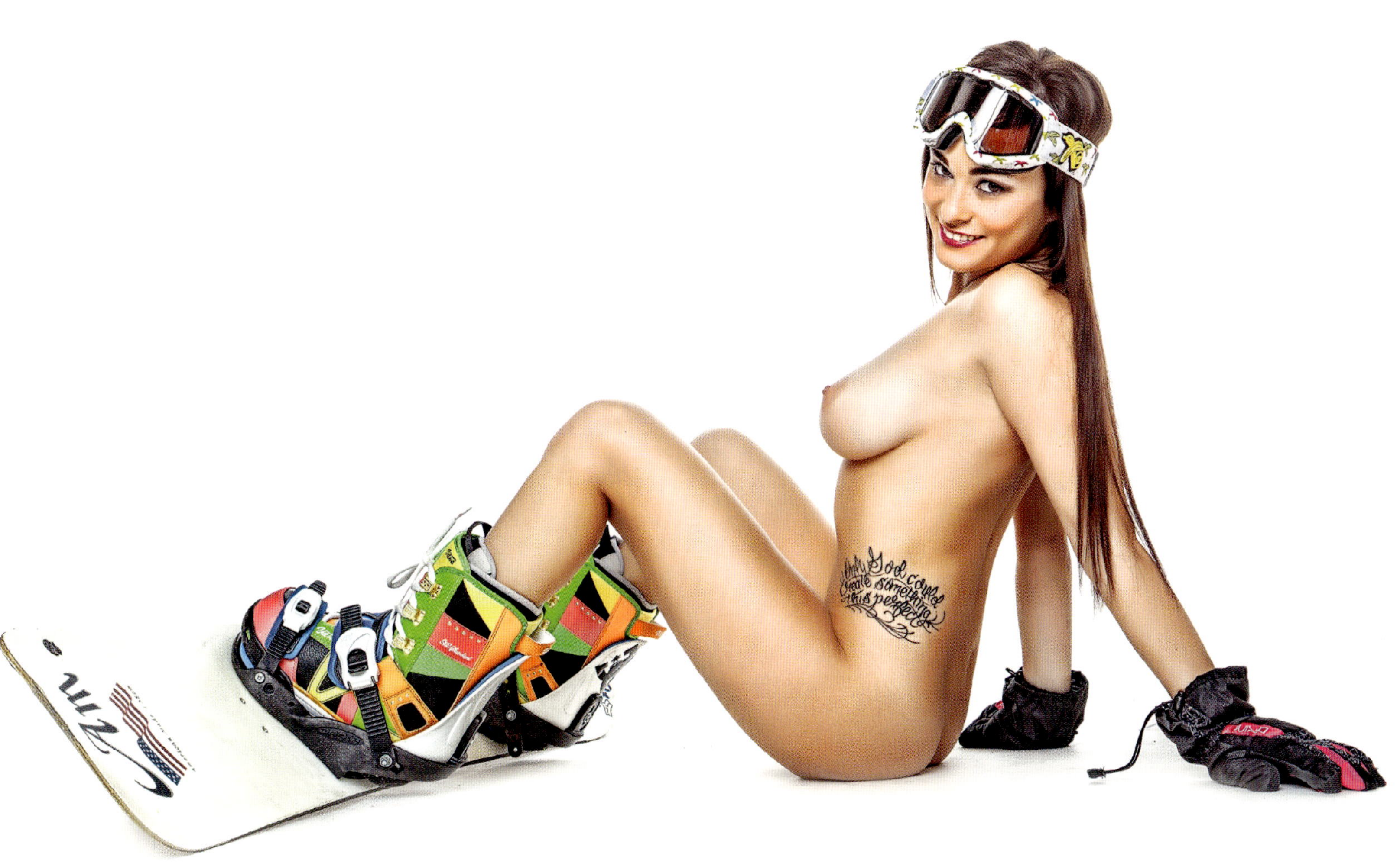

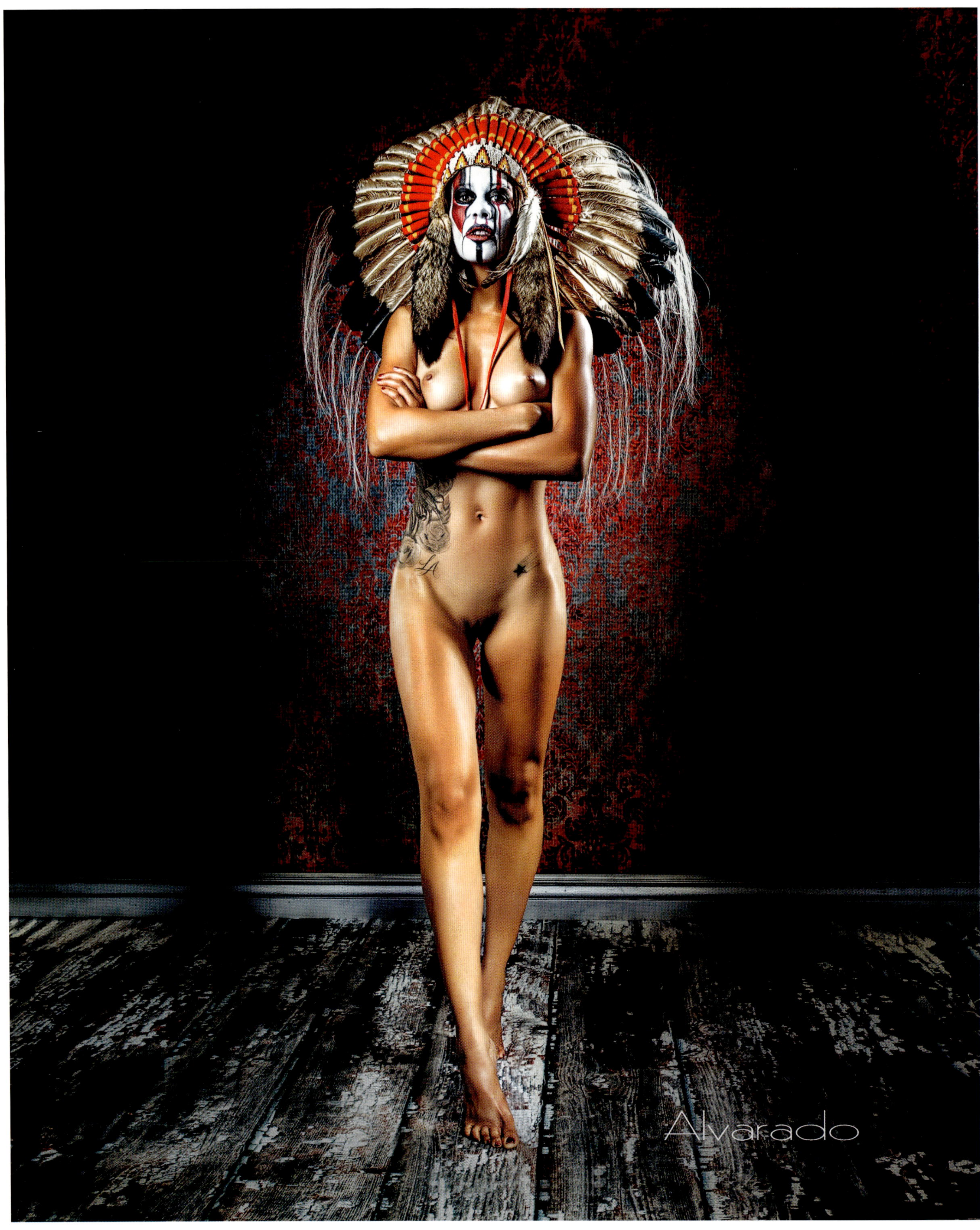
Alvarado

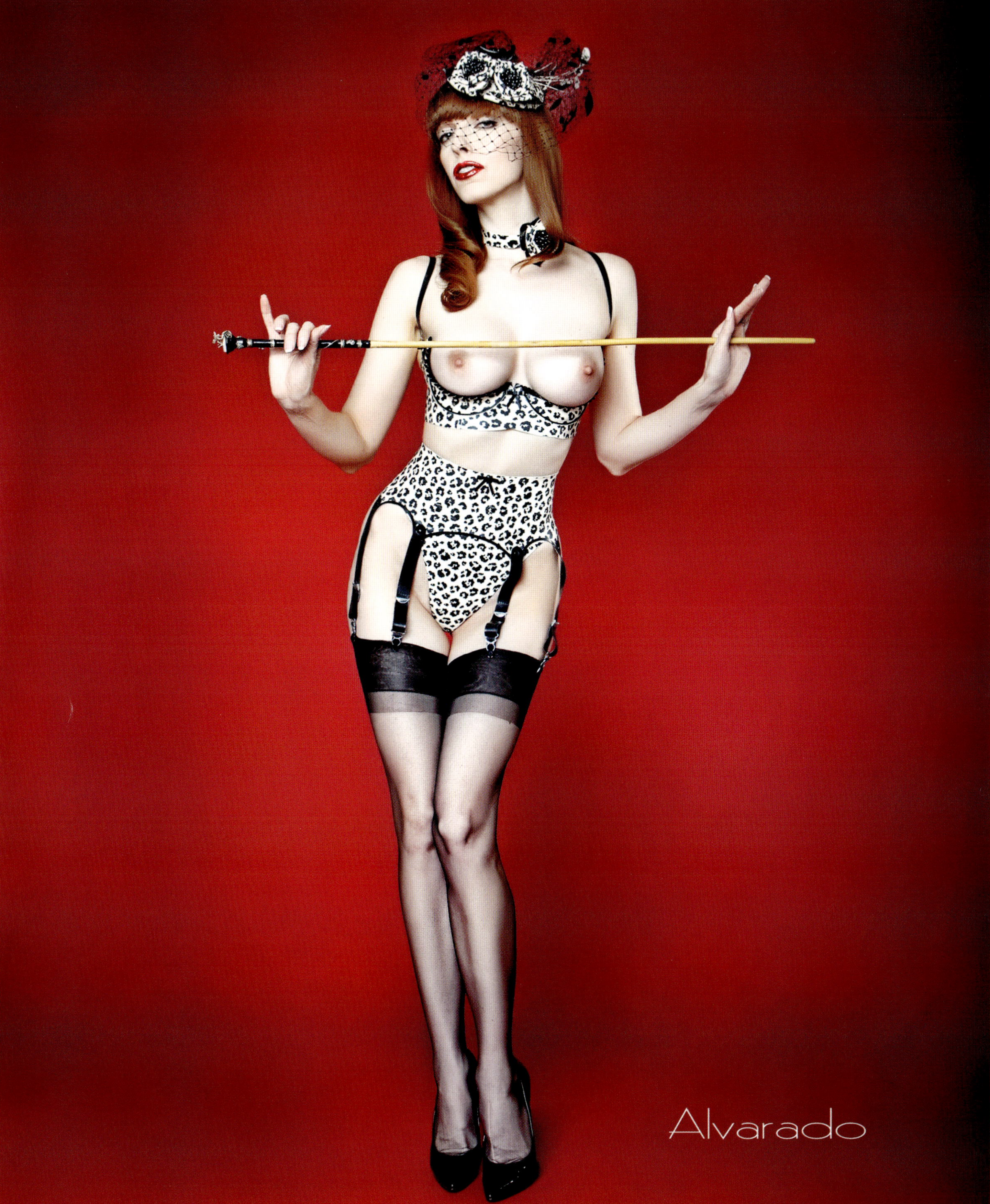

Alvarado

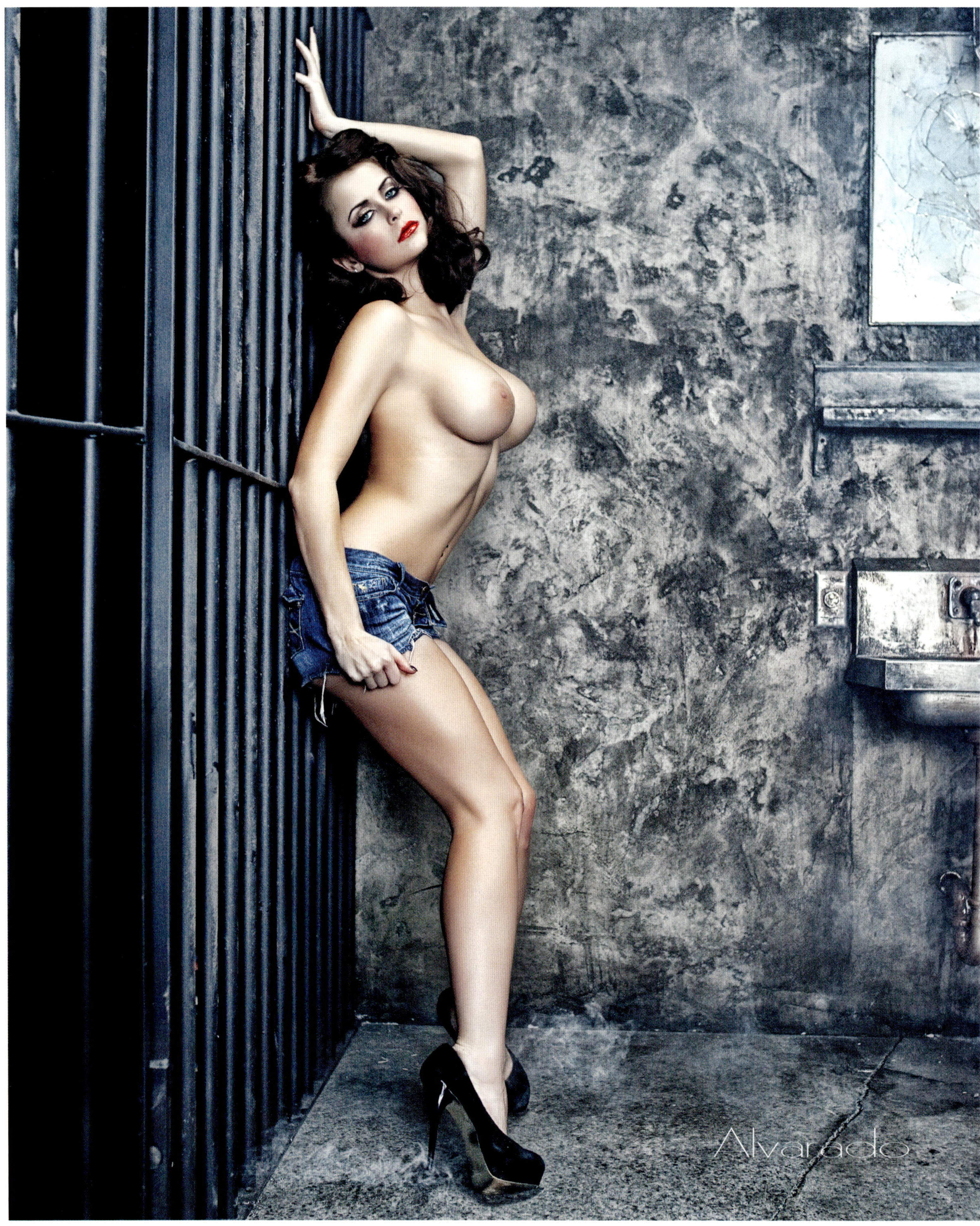
Alvarado

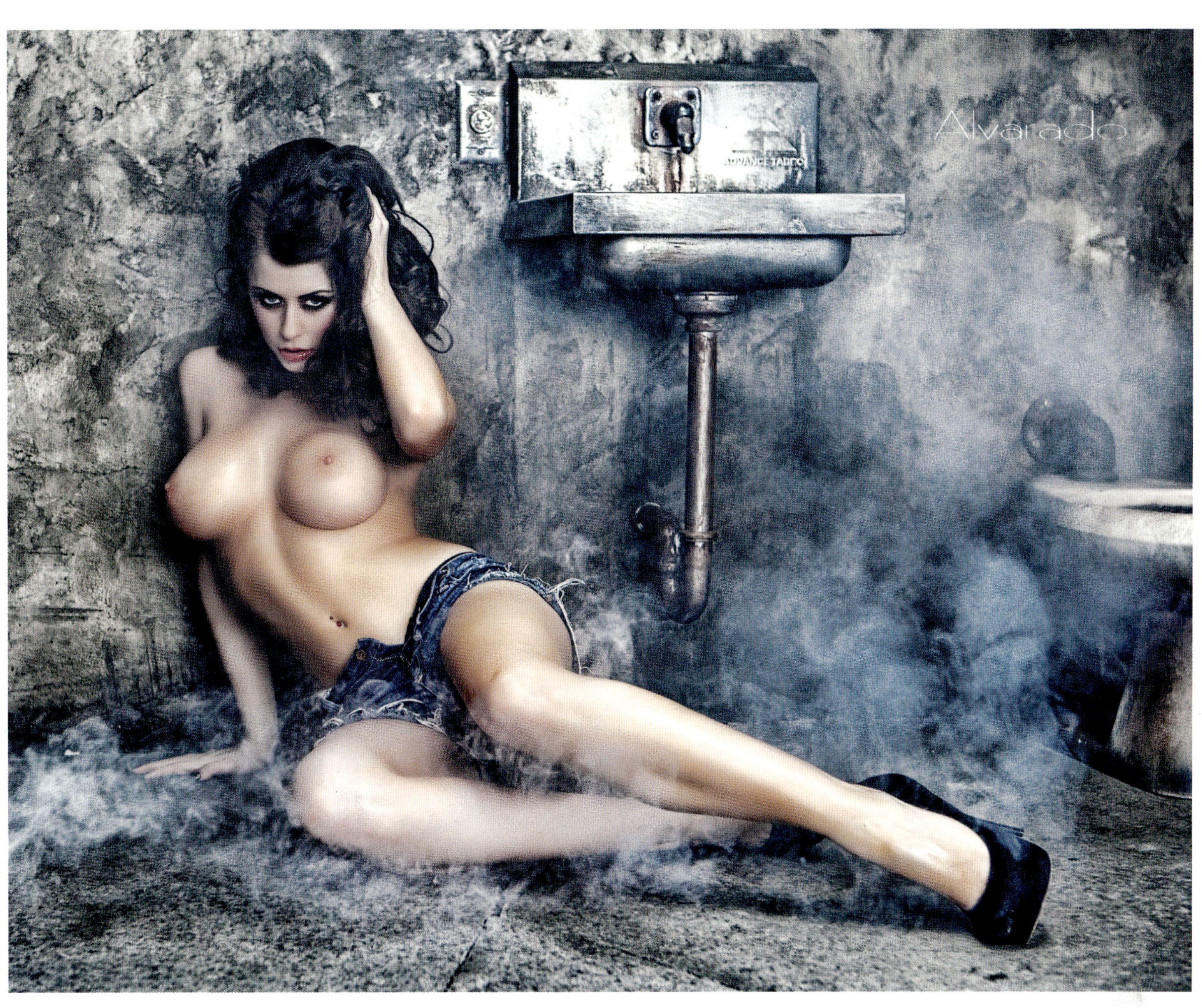
Alvarado

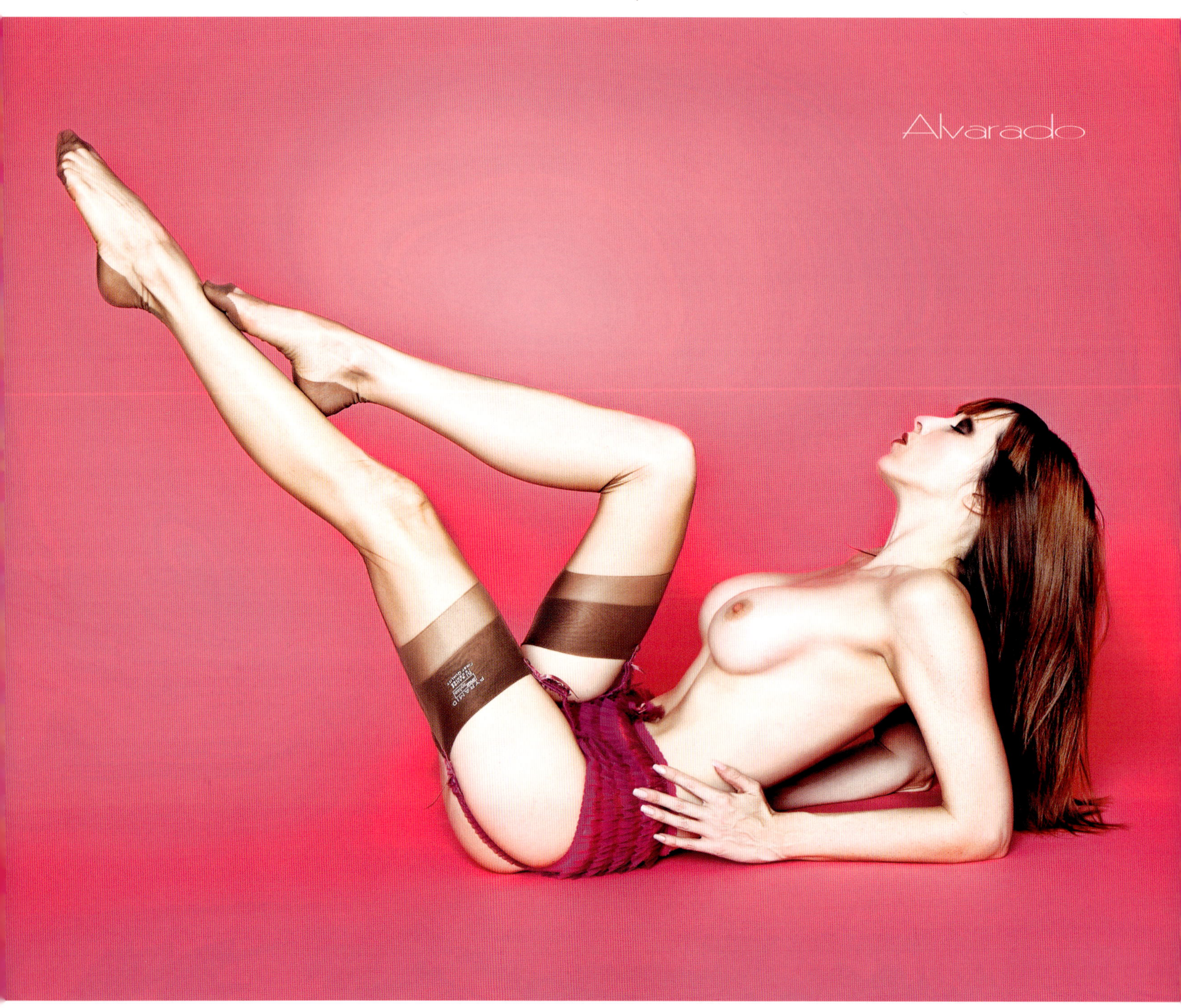
Alvarado

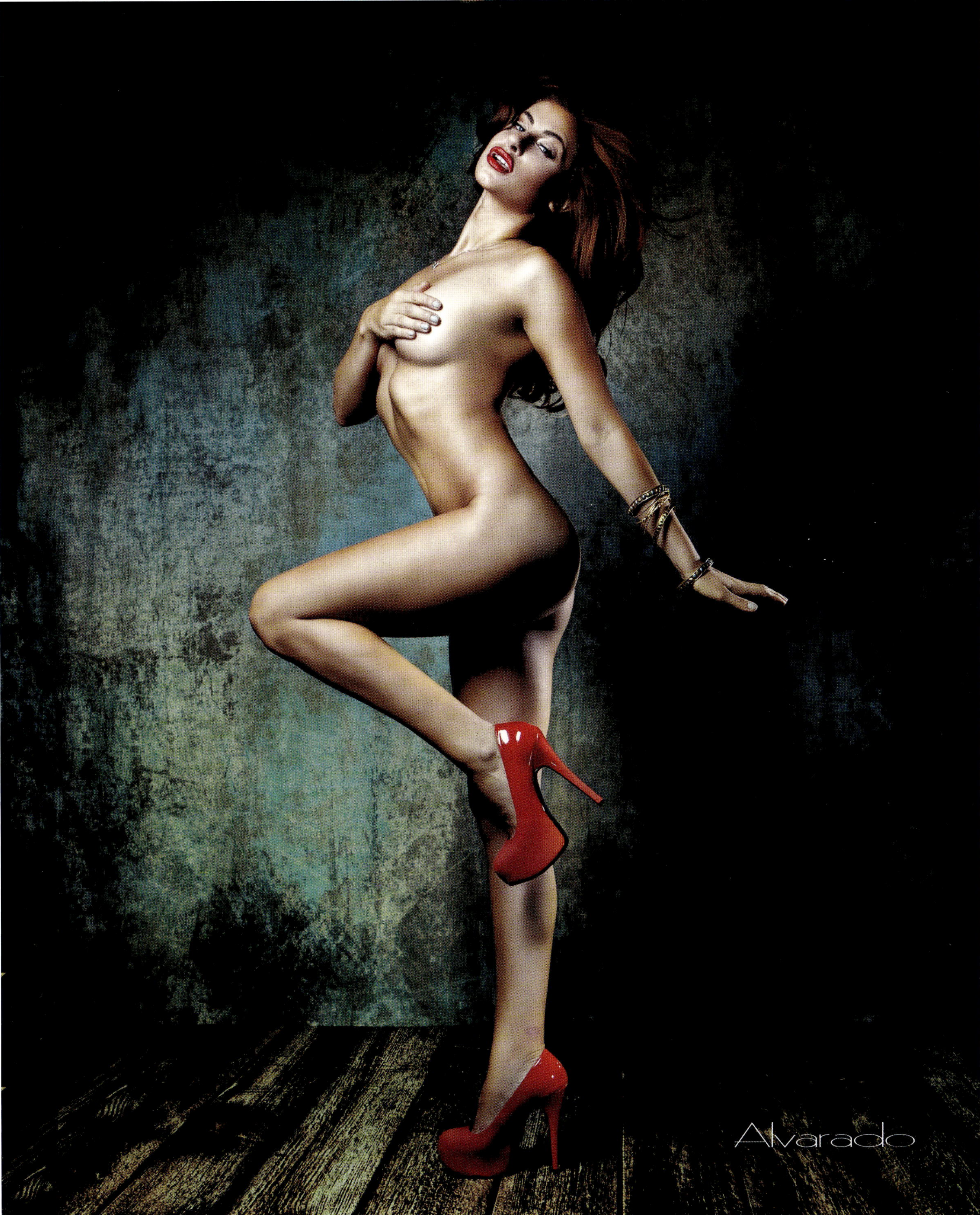
Alvarado

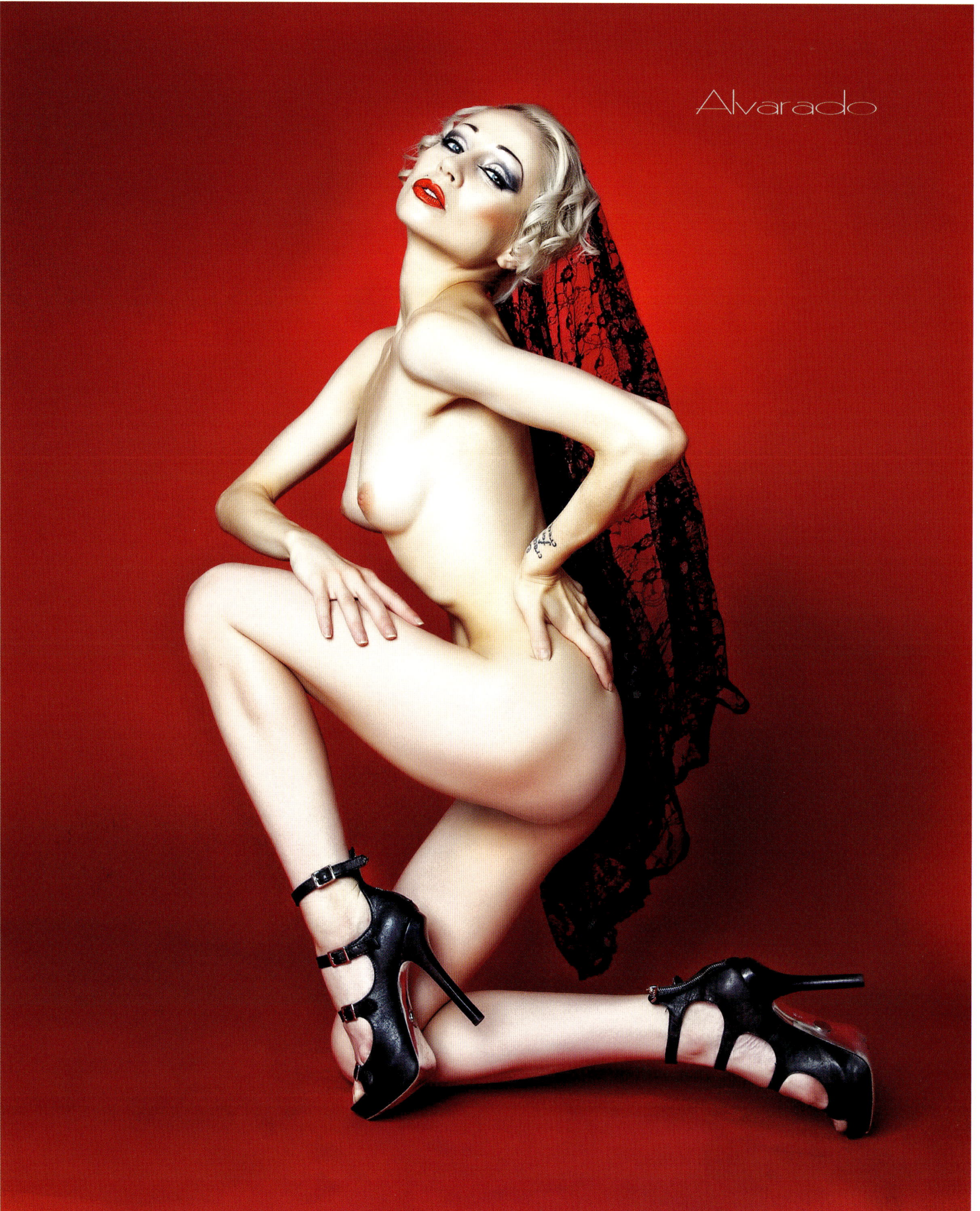
Alvarado

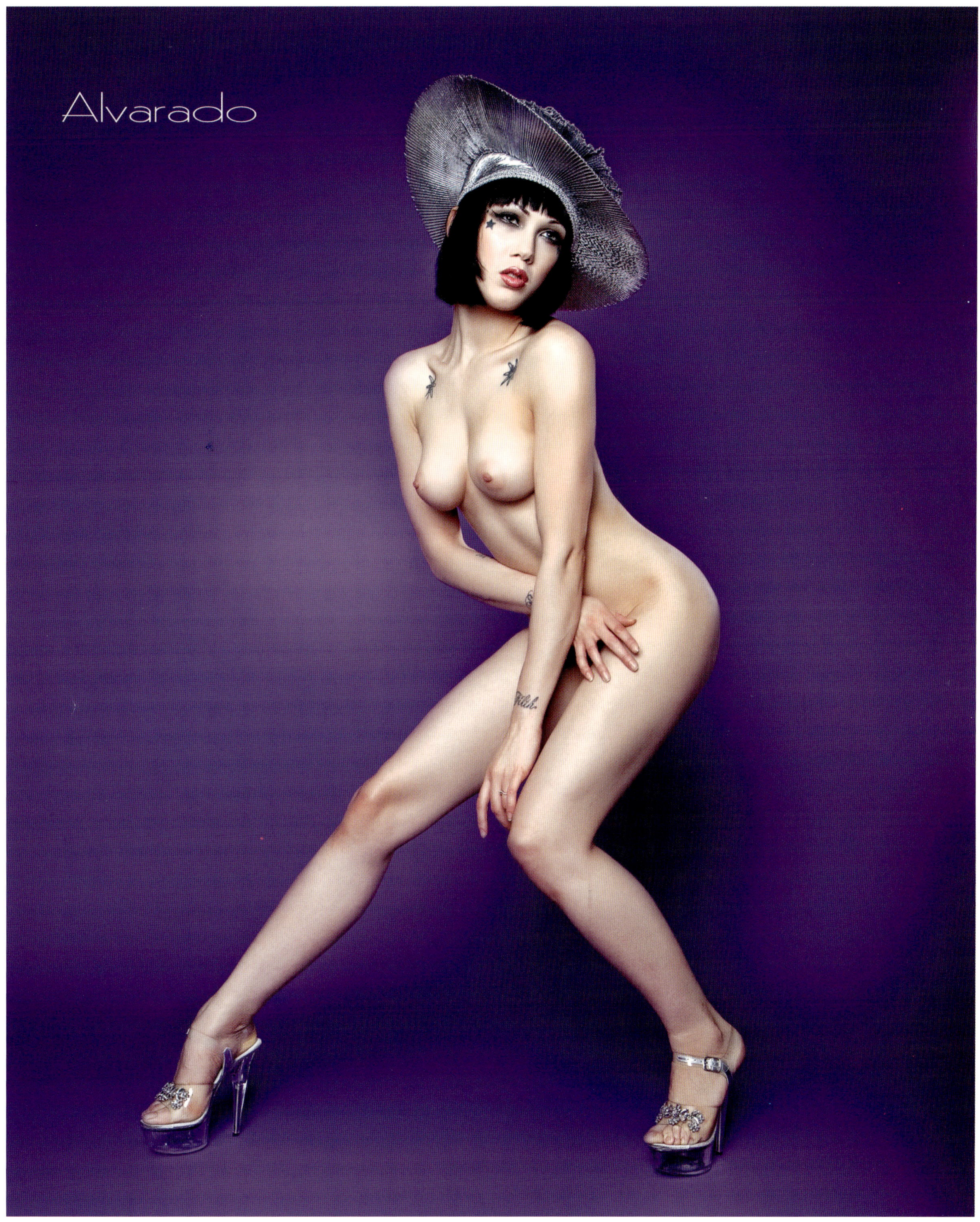
Alvarado

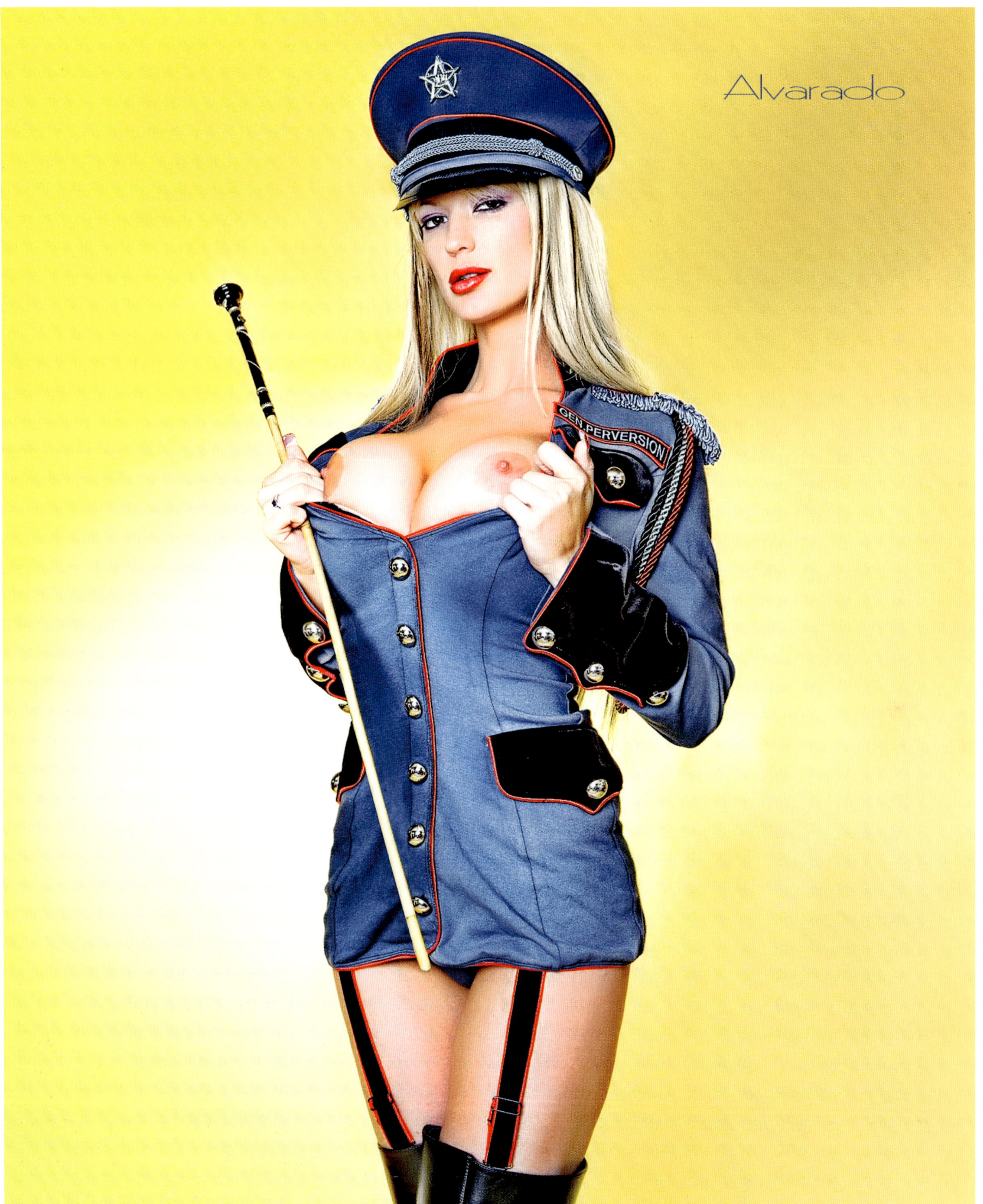
Alvarado
GEN.PERVERSION

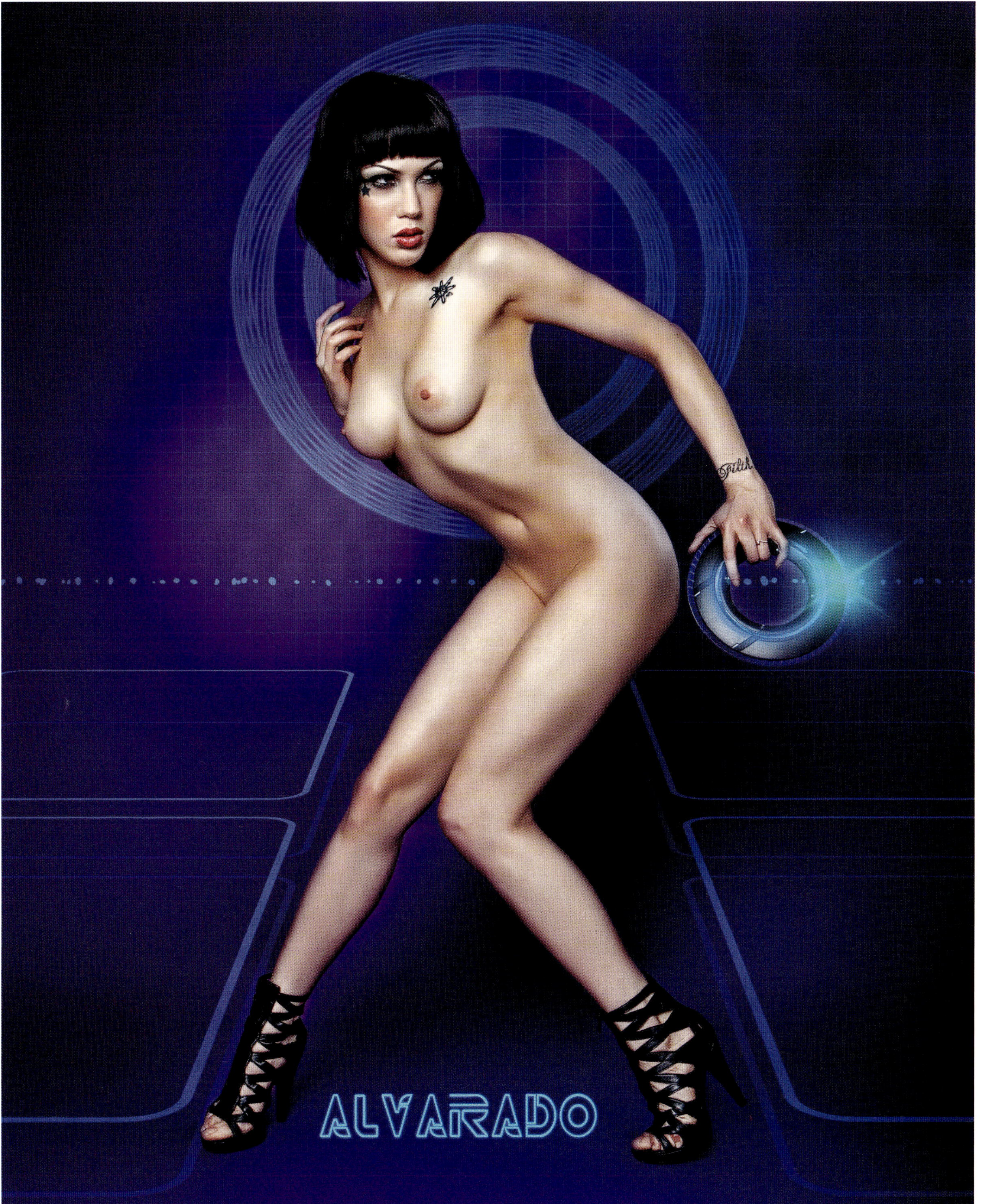
ALVARADO

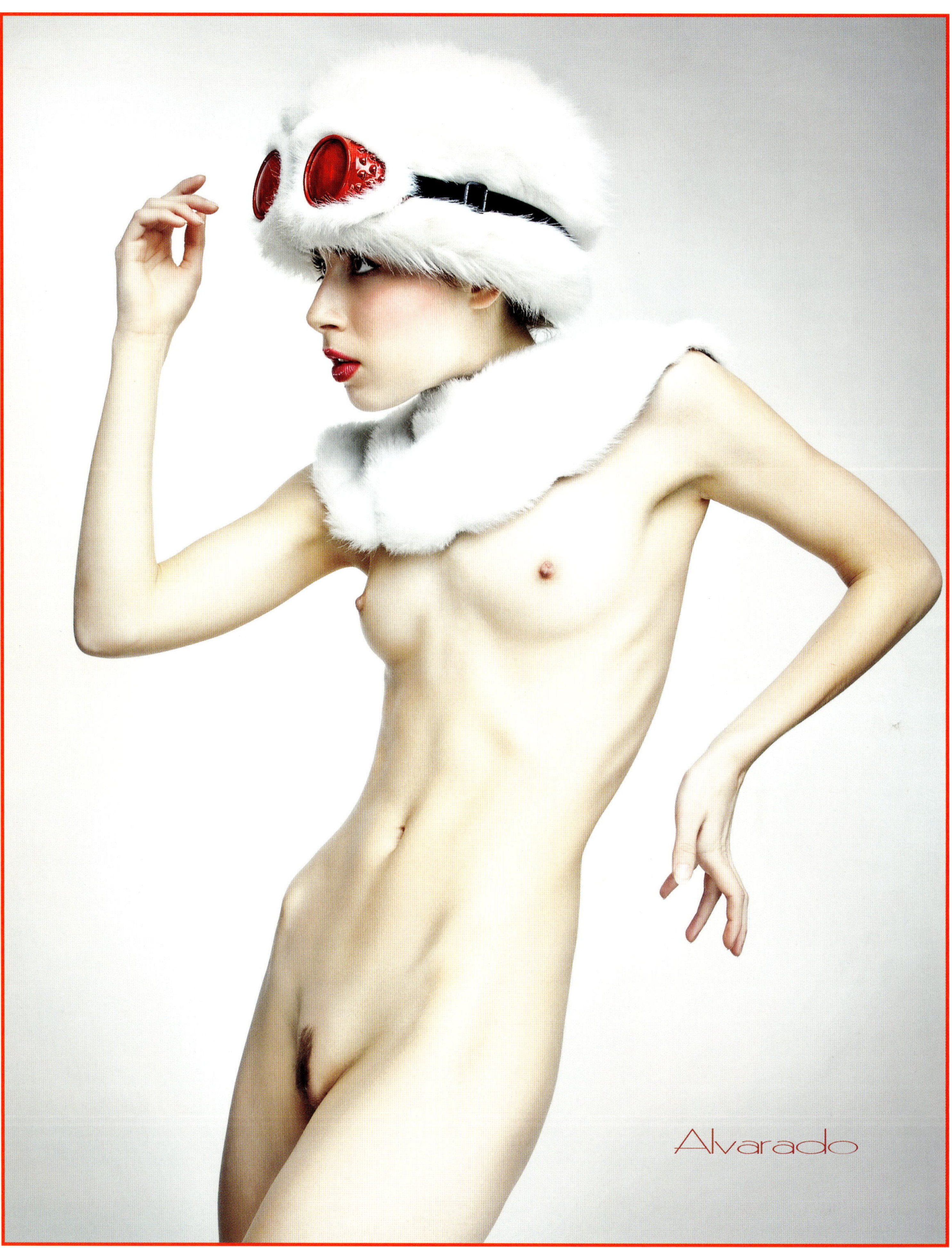
Alvarado

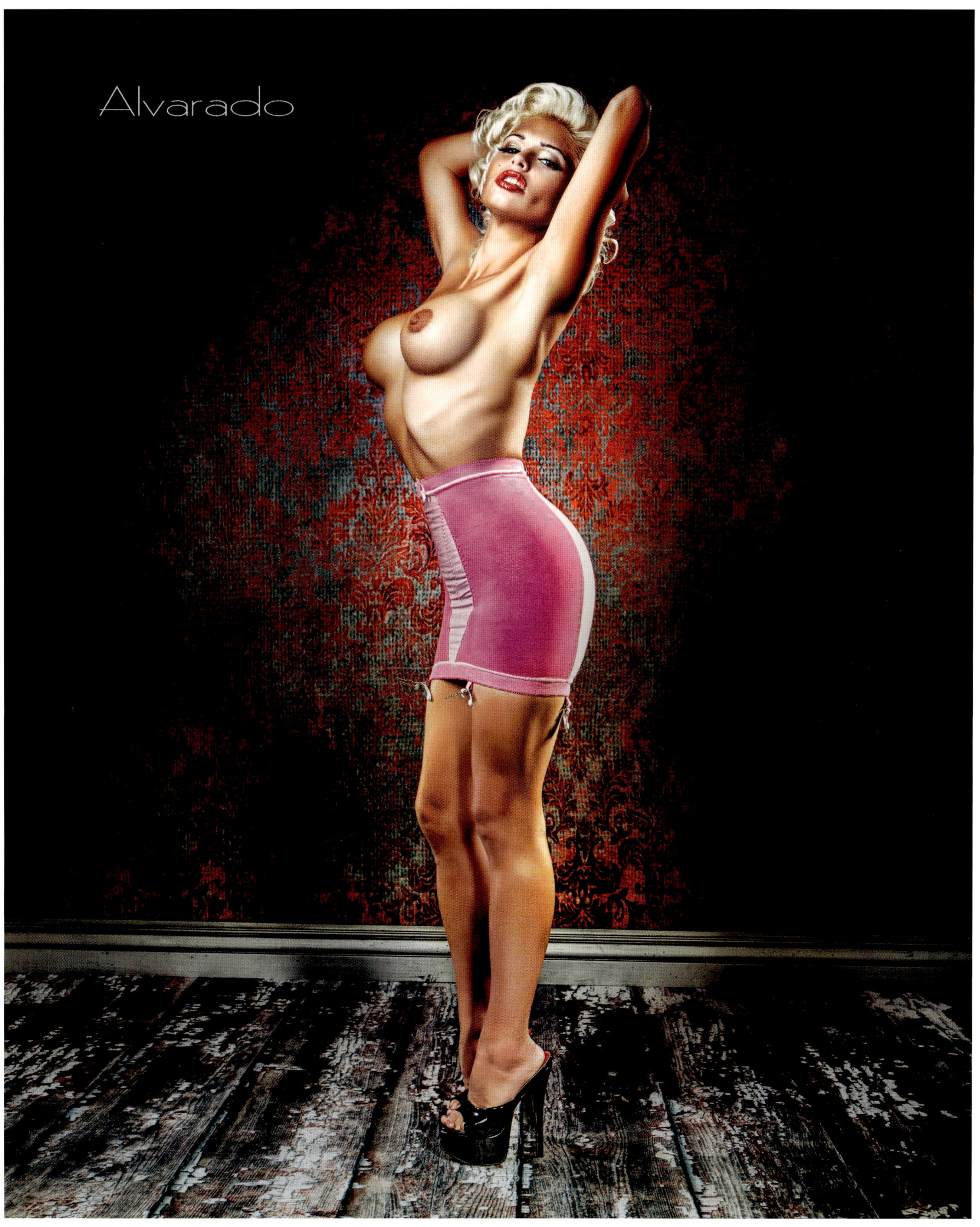
Alvarado

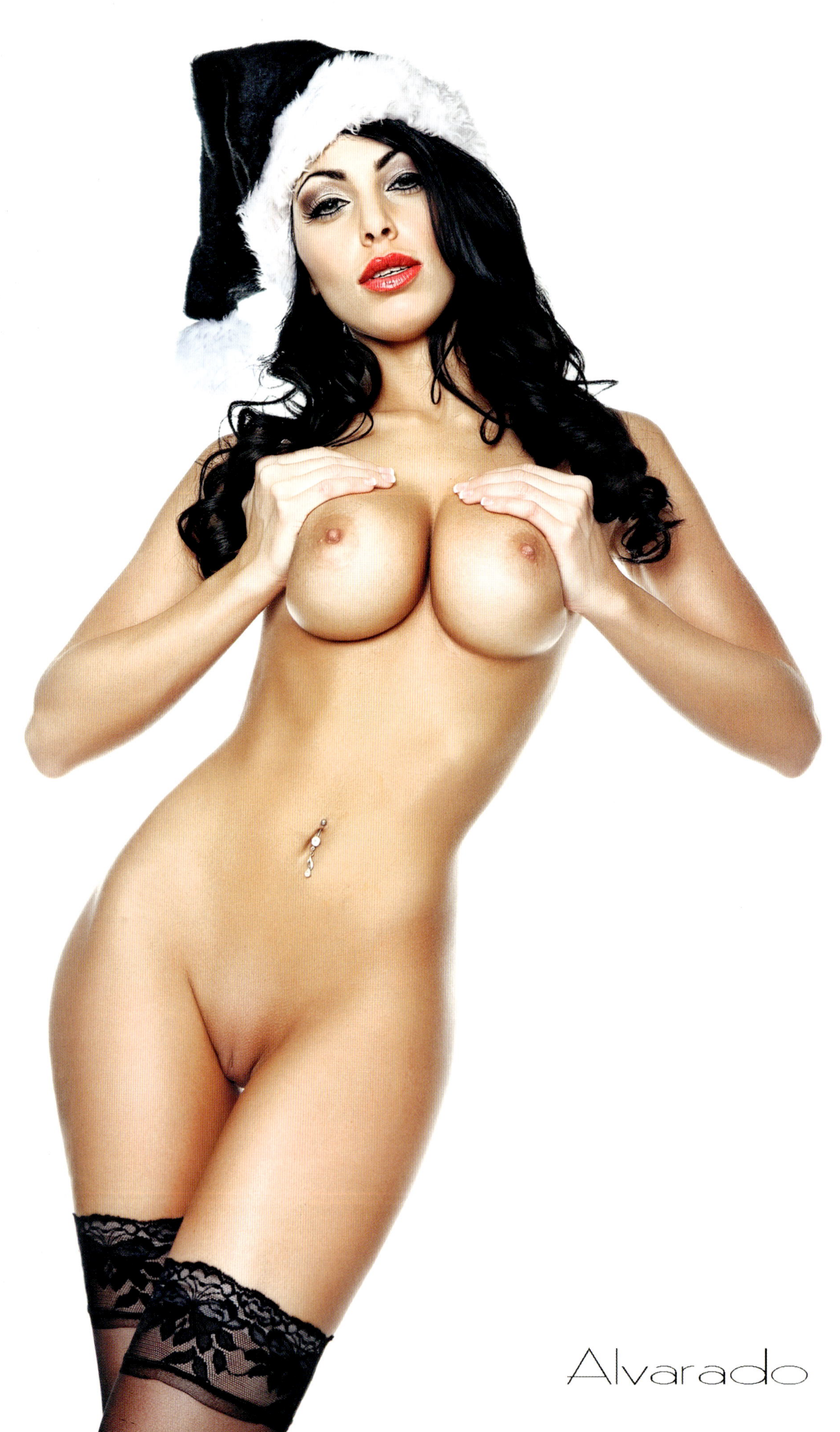

Alvarado

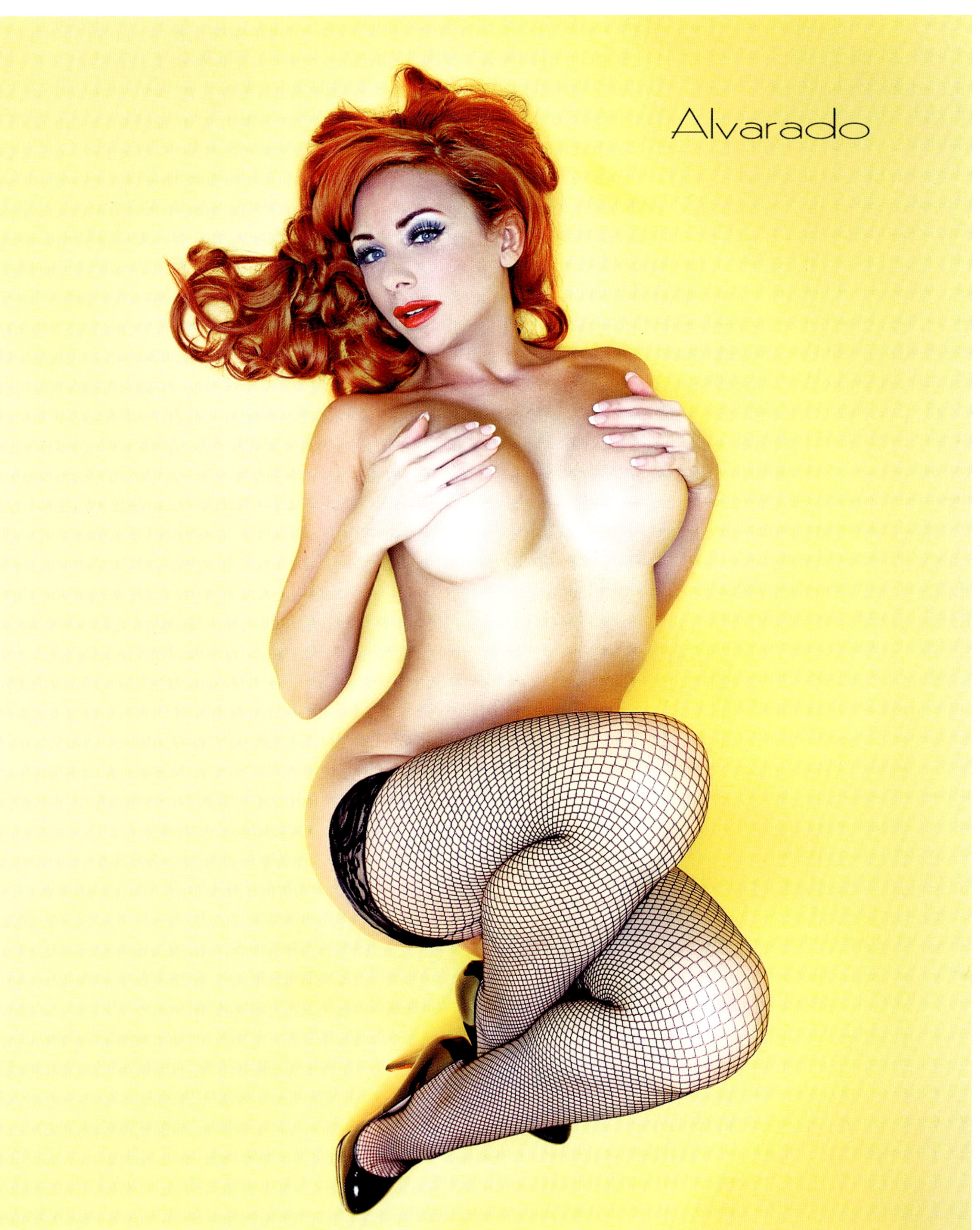
Alvarado

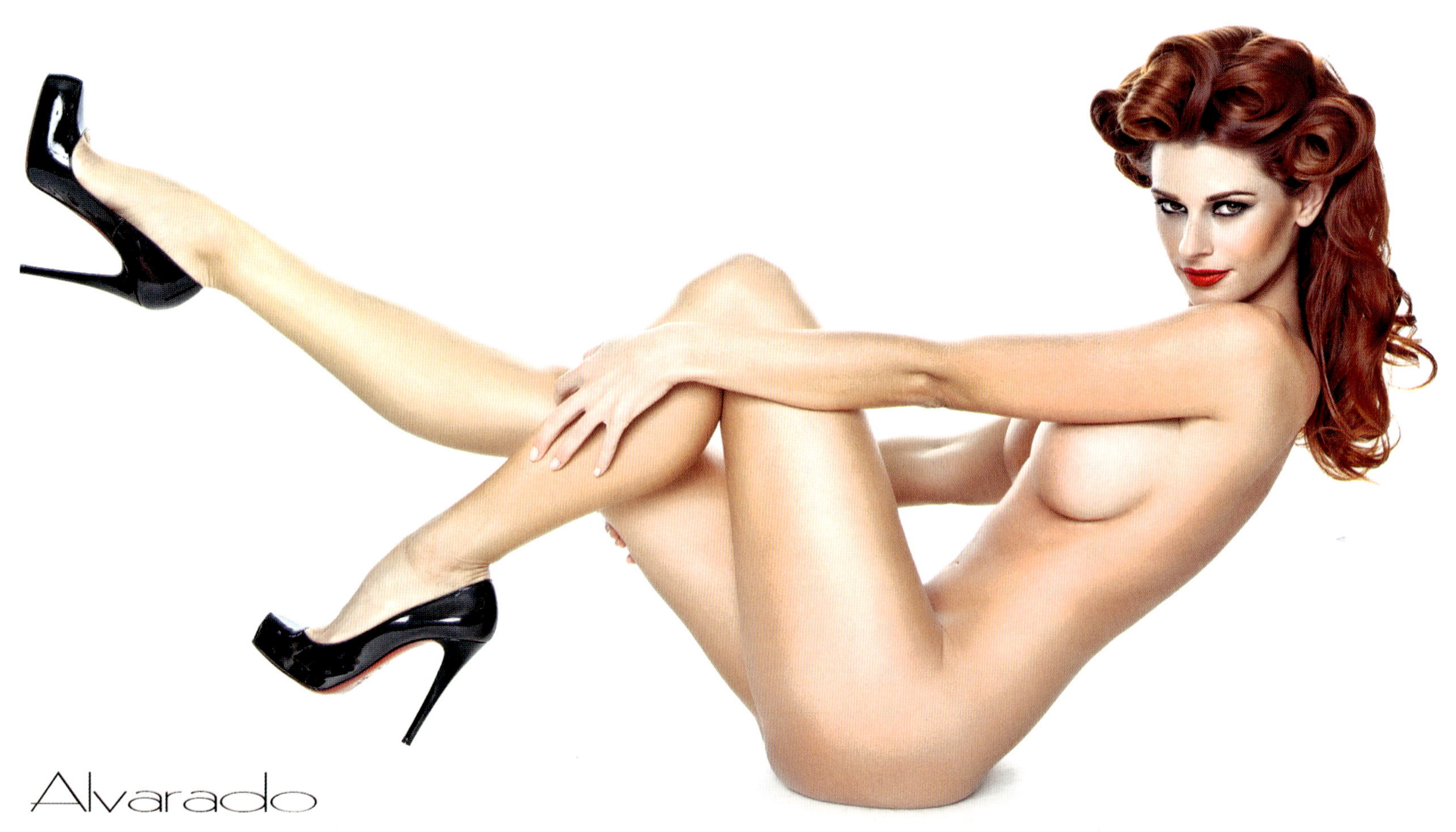
Alvarado

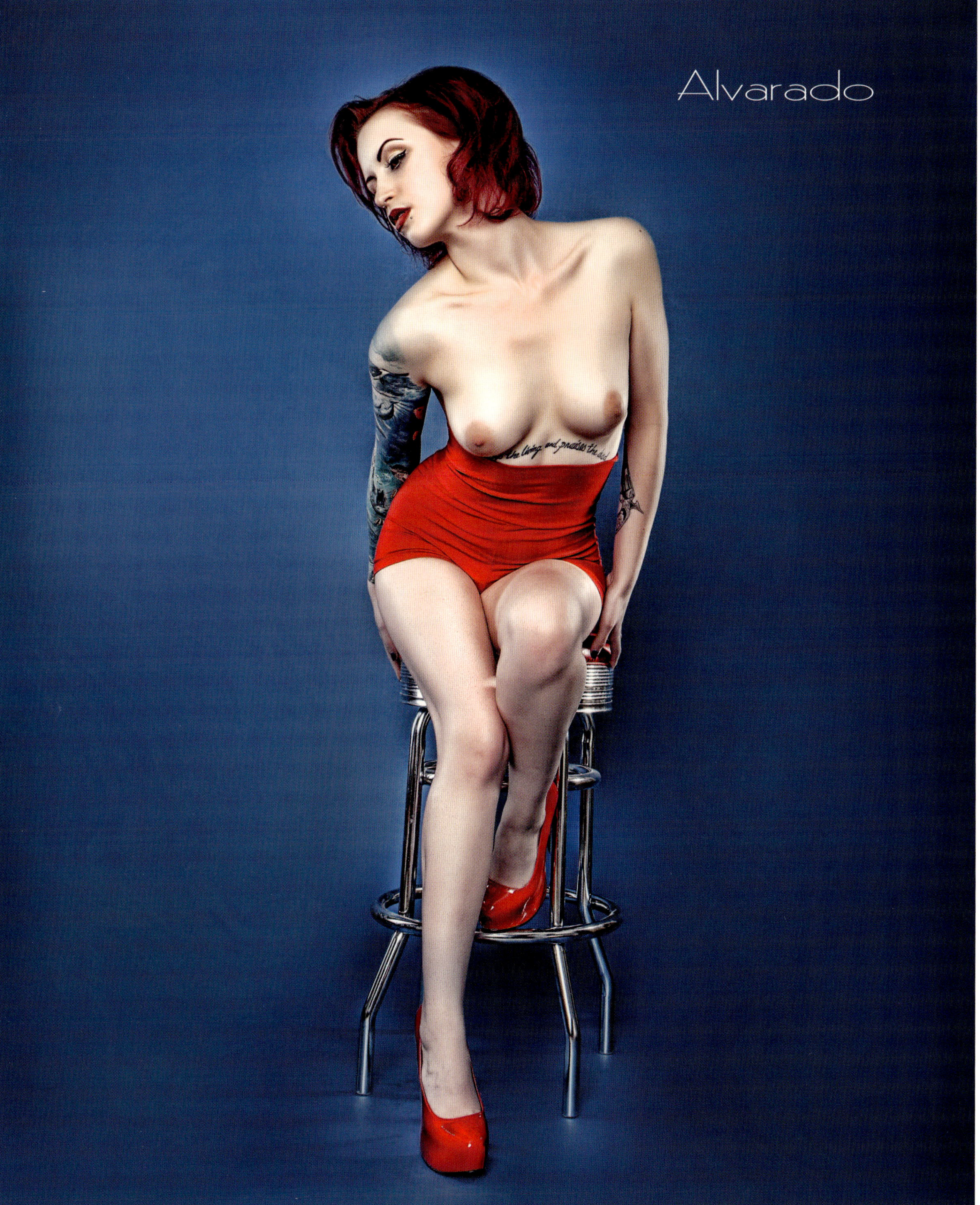
Alvarado

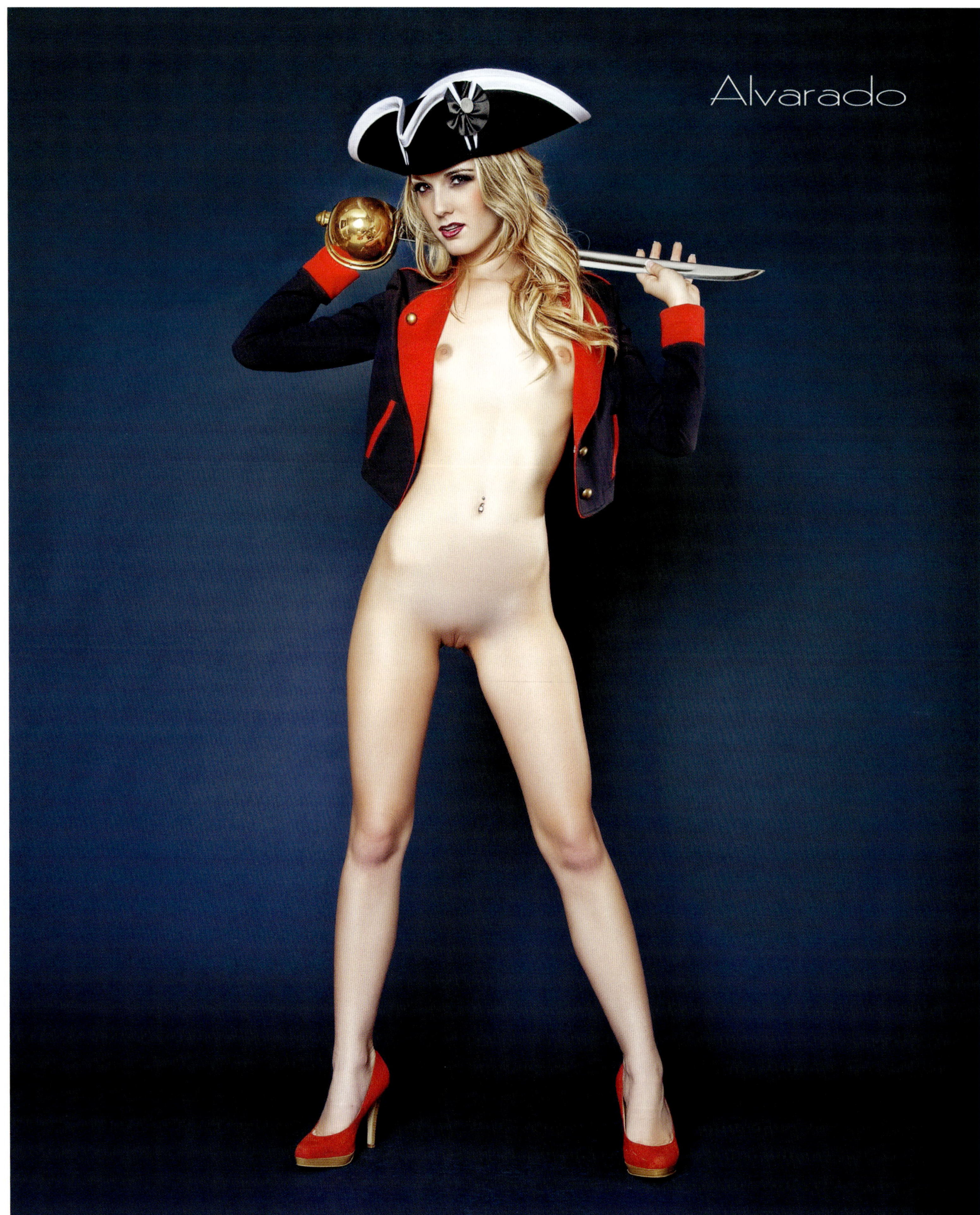
Alvarado

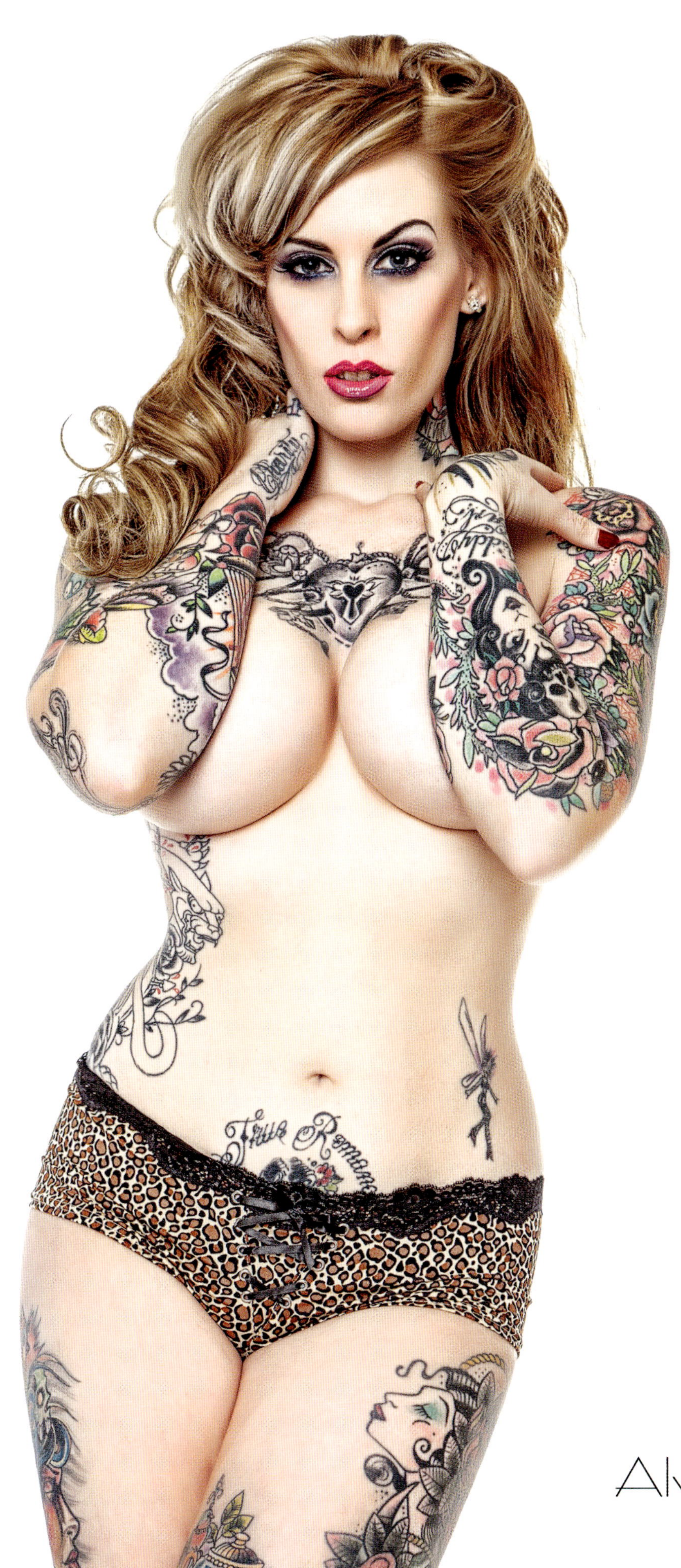

Alvarado

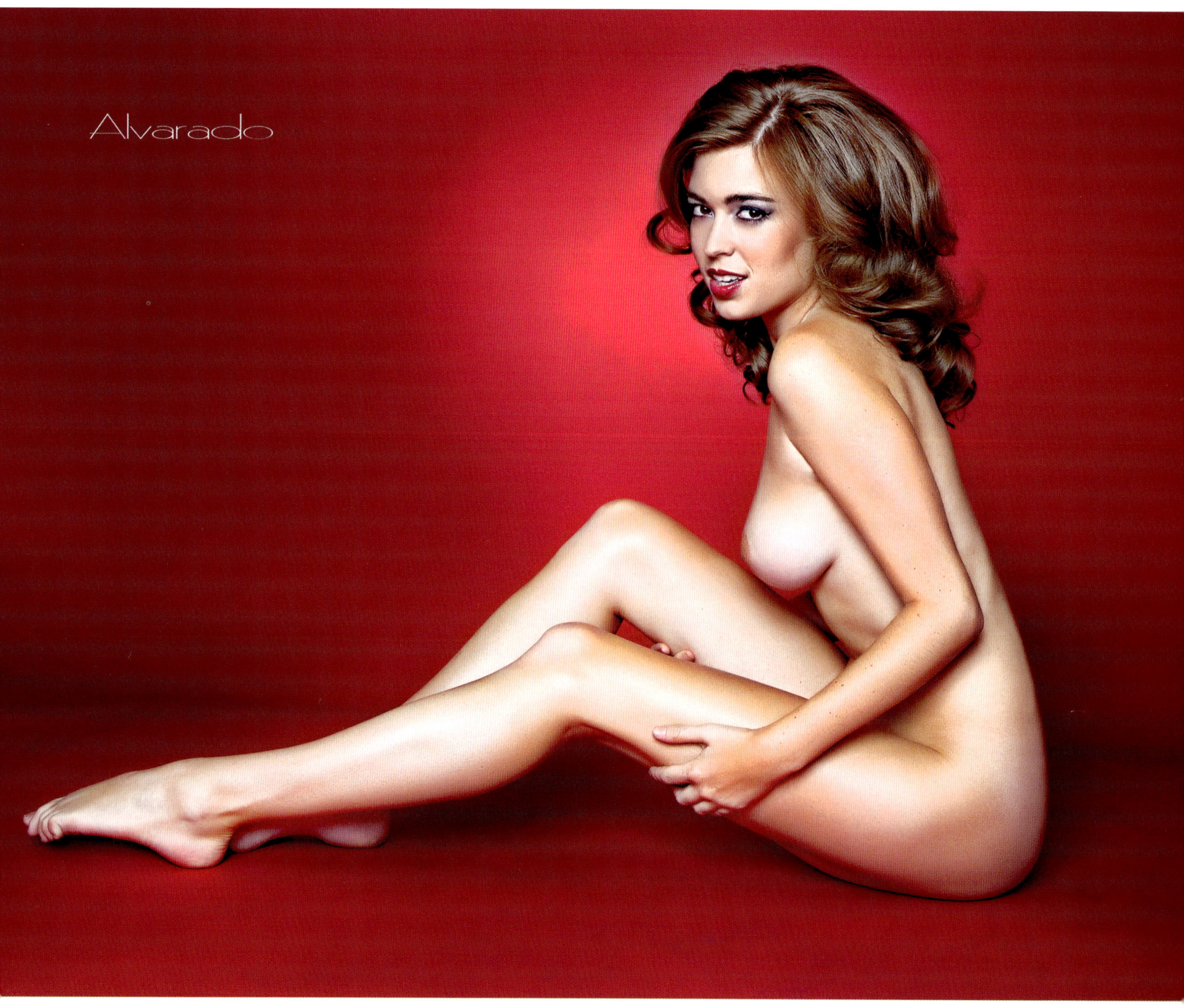
Alvarado

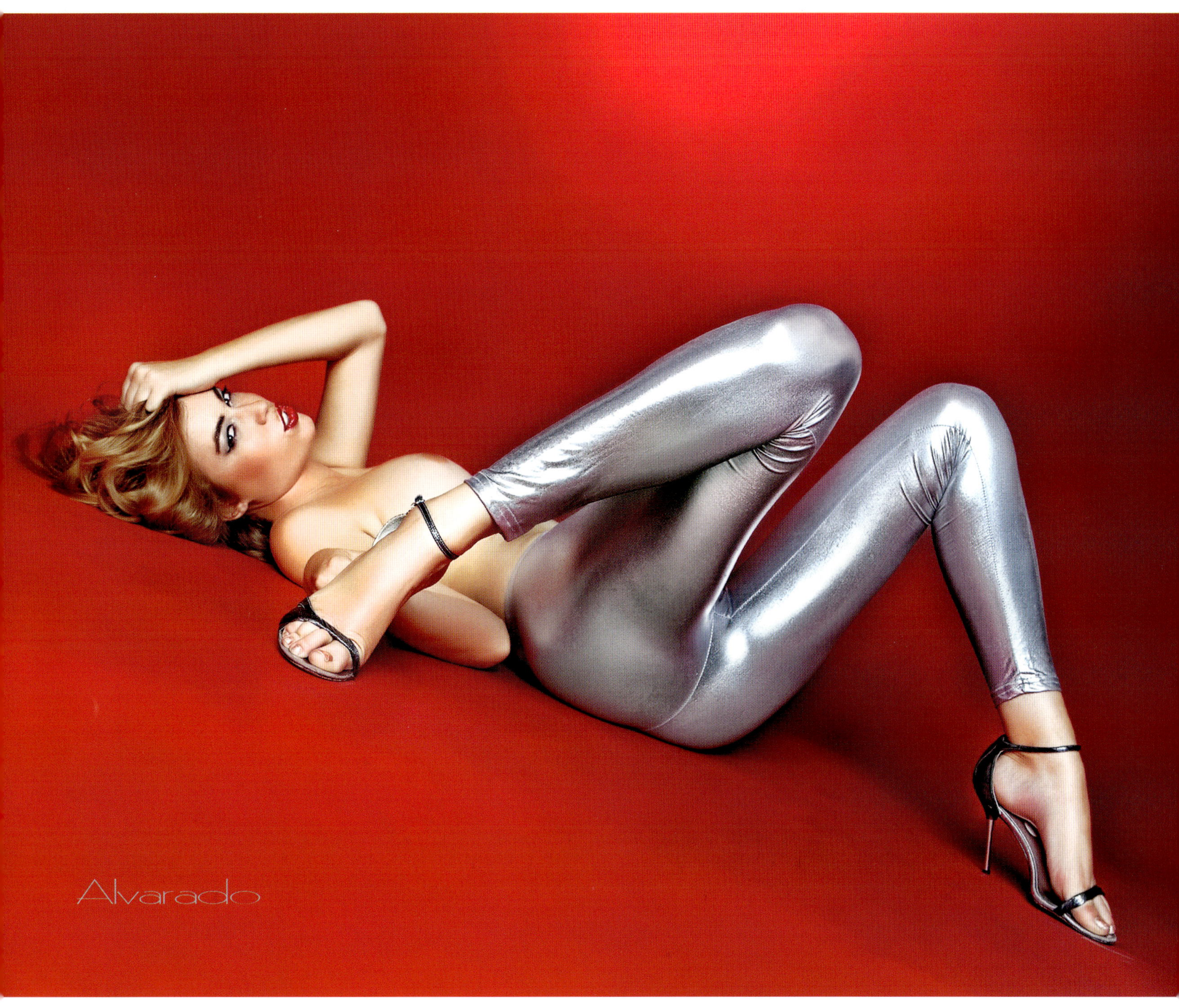
Alvarado

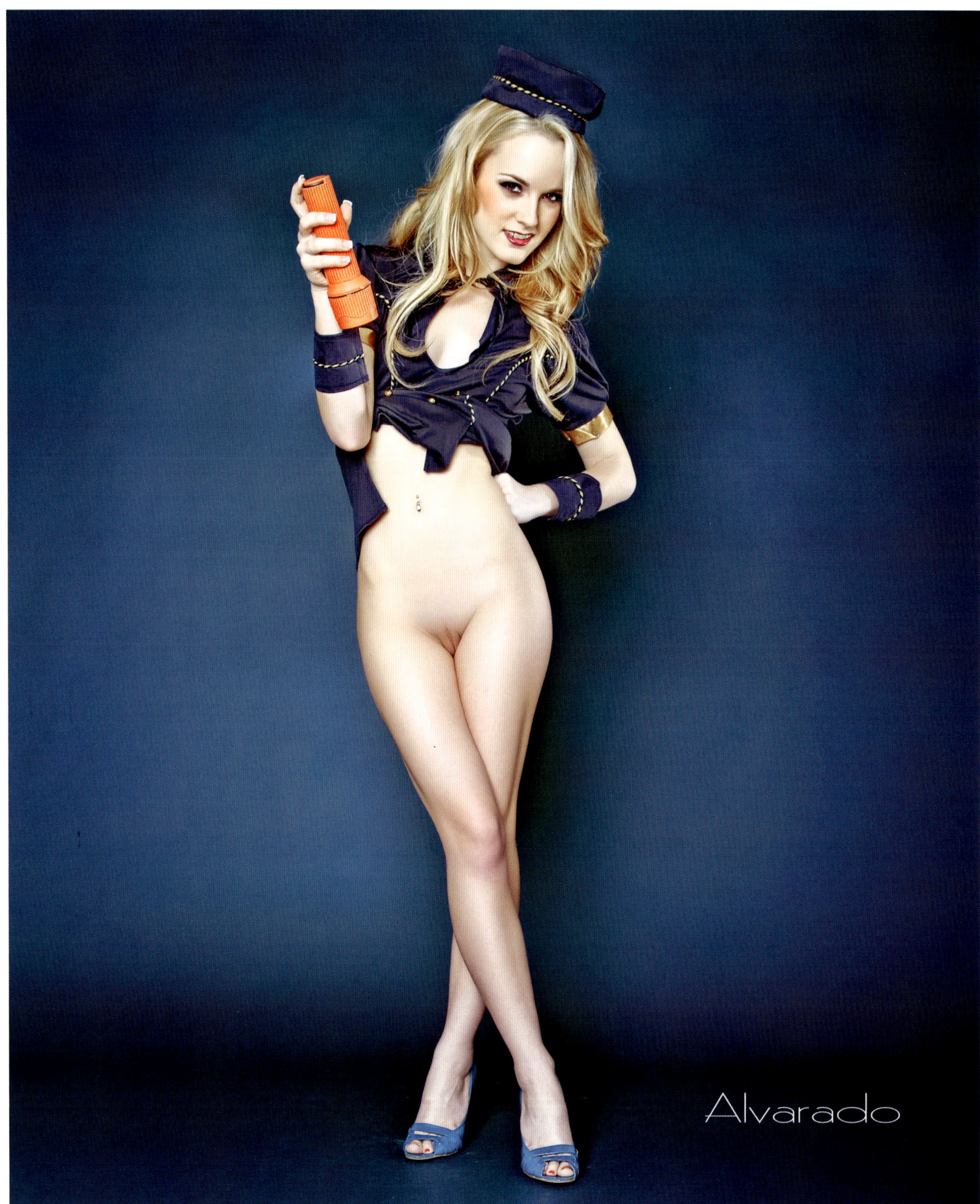
Alvarado

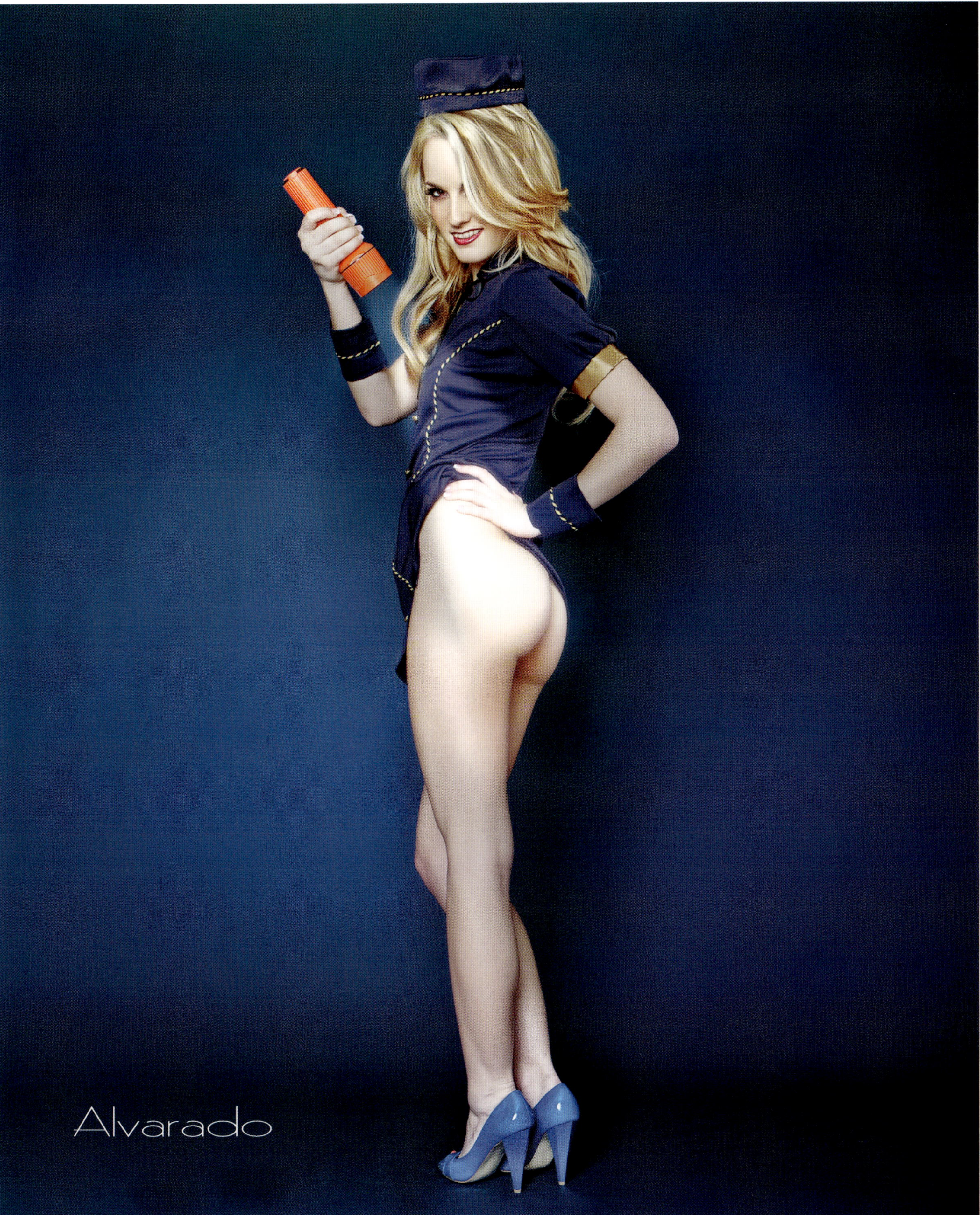
Alvarado

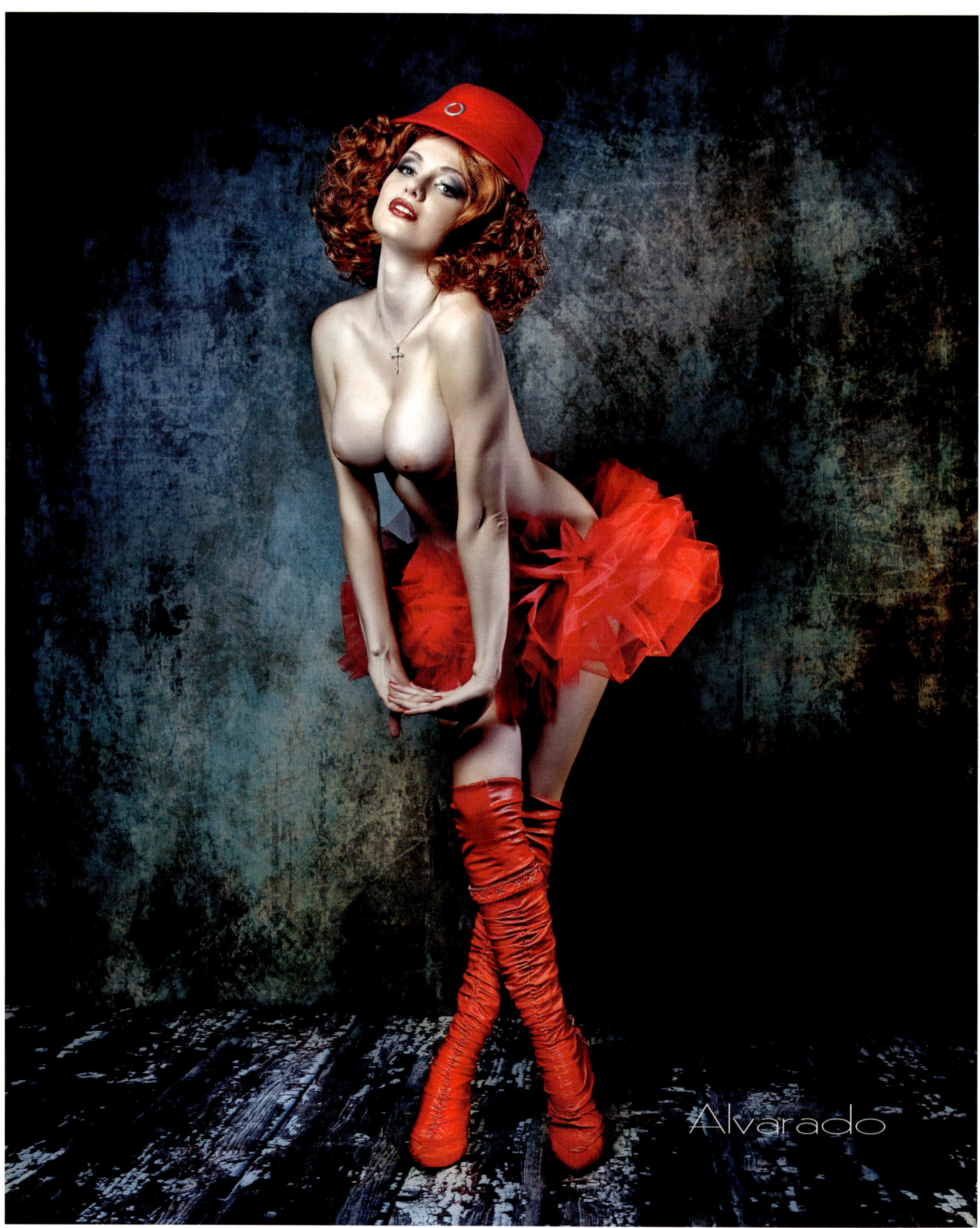
Alvarado

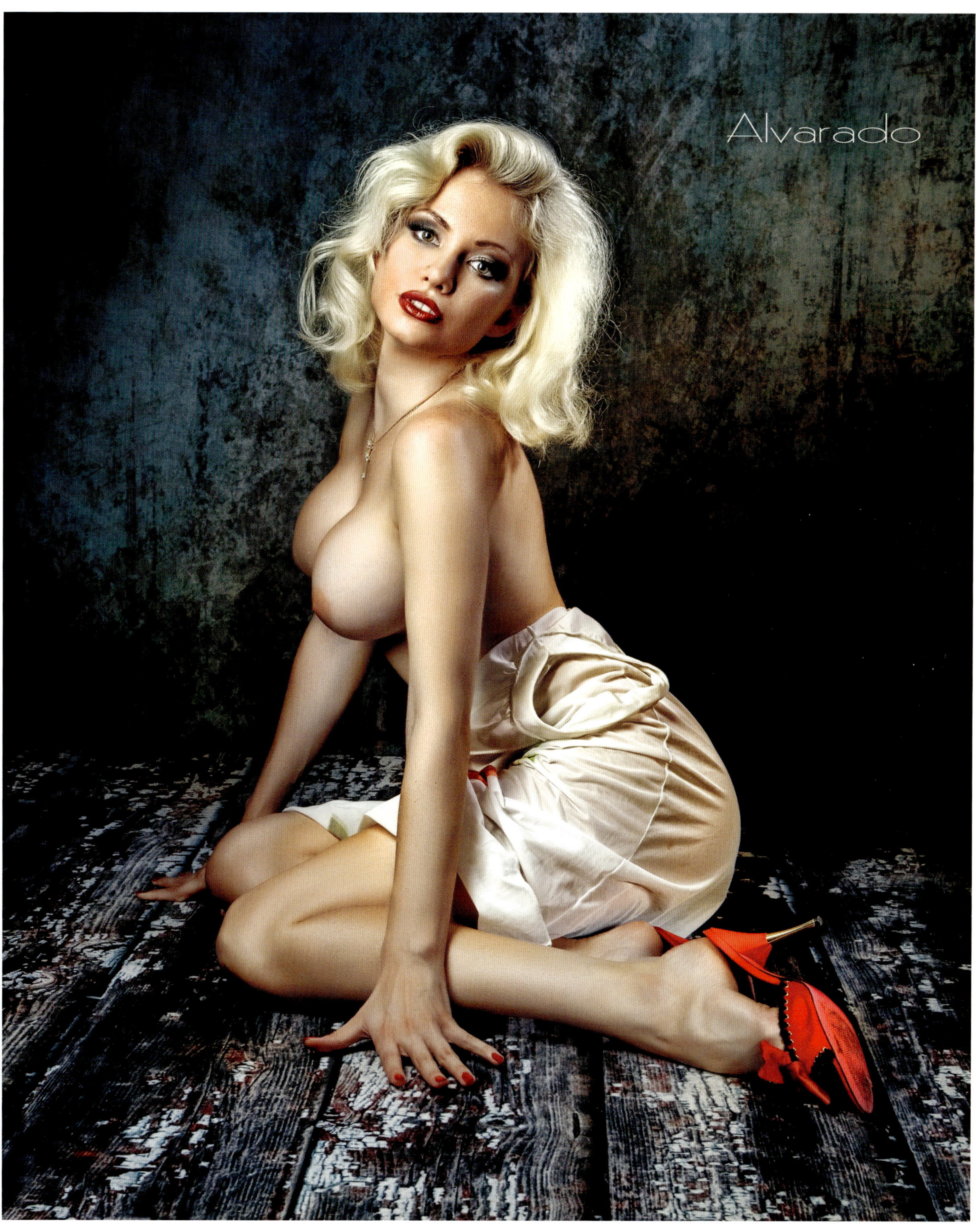
Alvarado

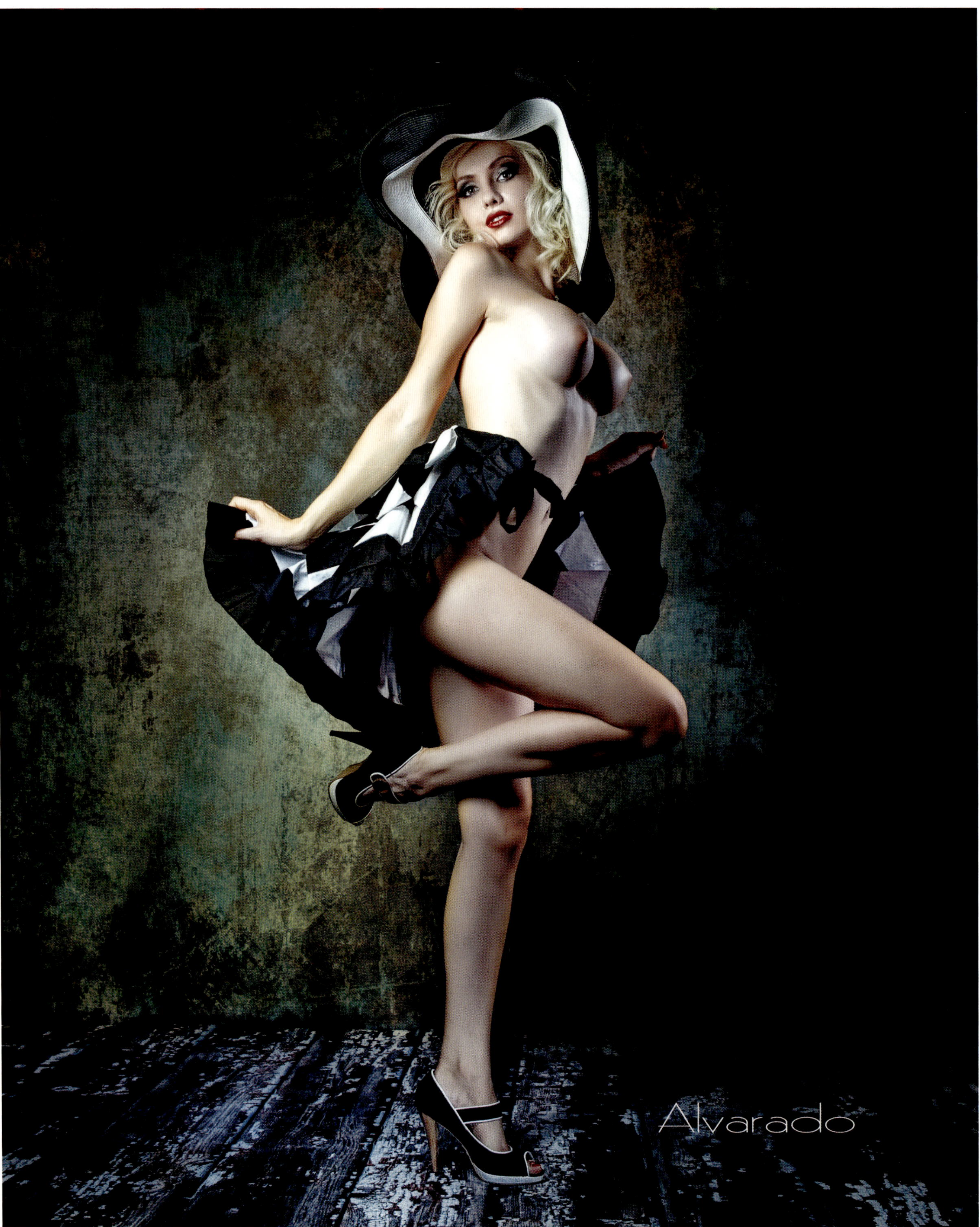
Alvarado

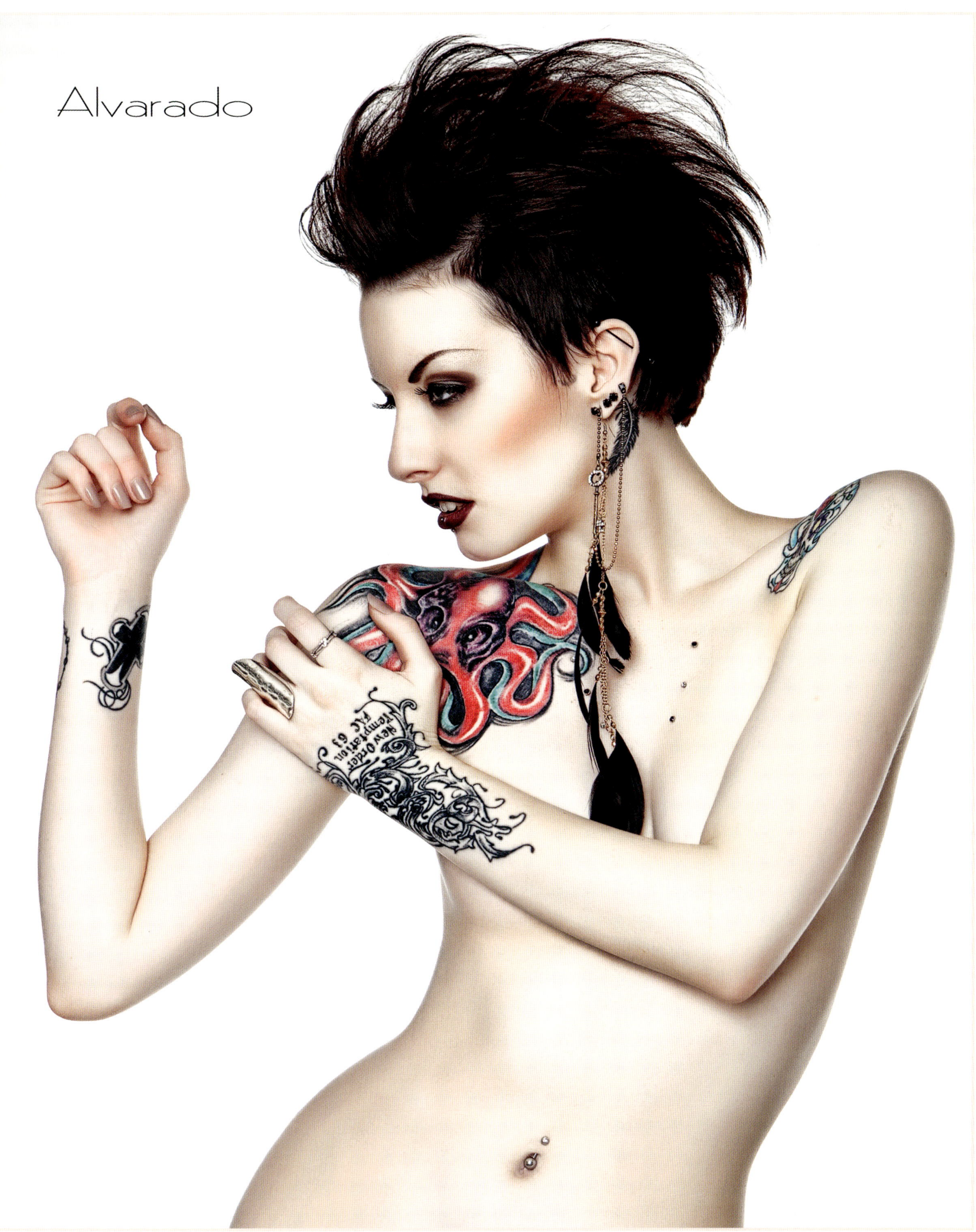
Alvarado
New Order
Temptation
FAC 63

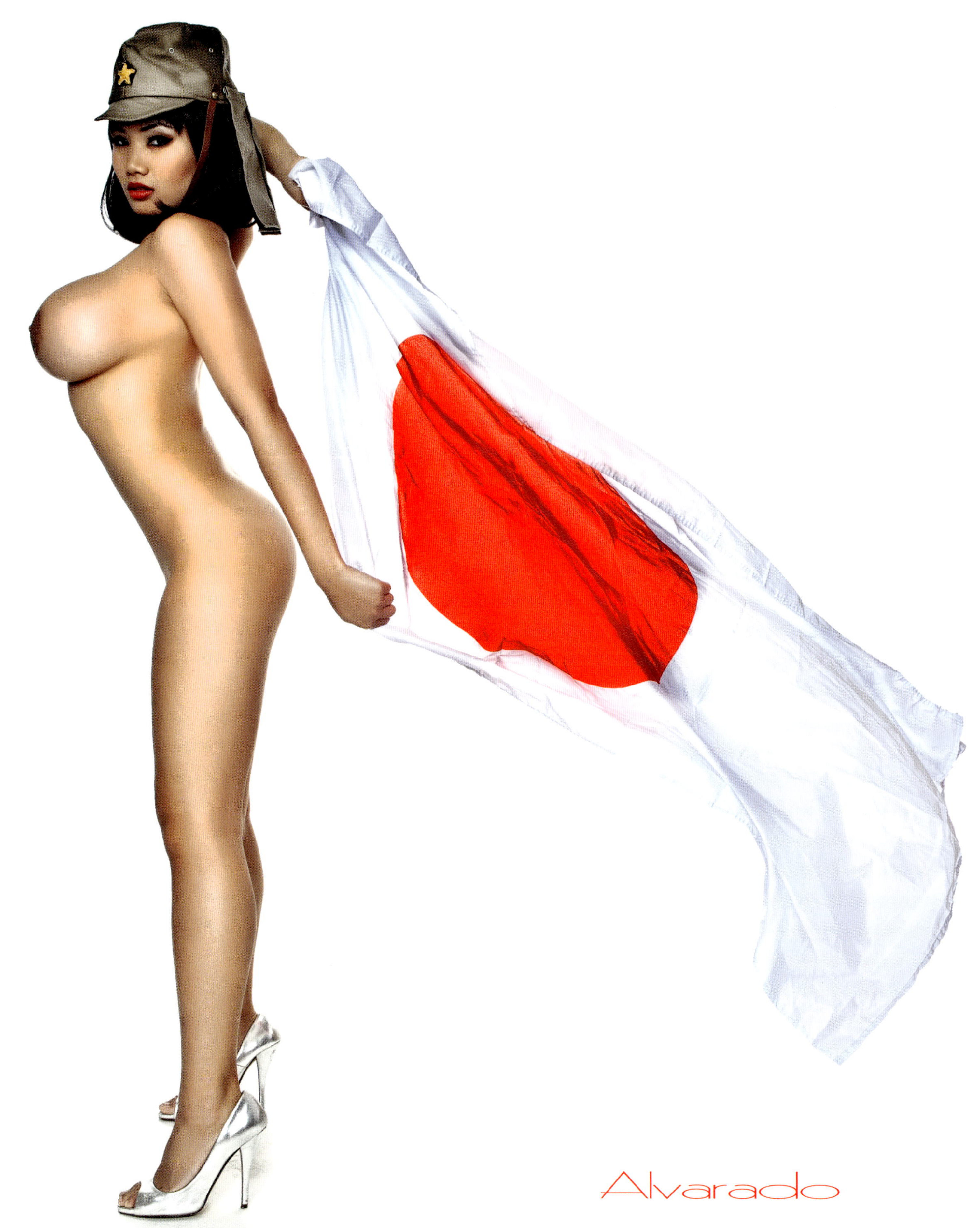
Alvarado

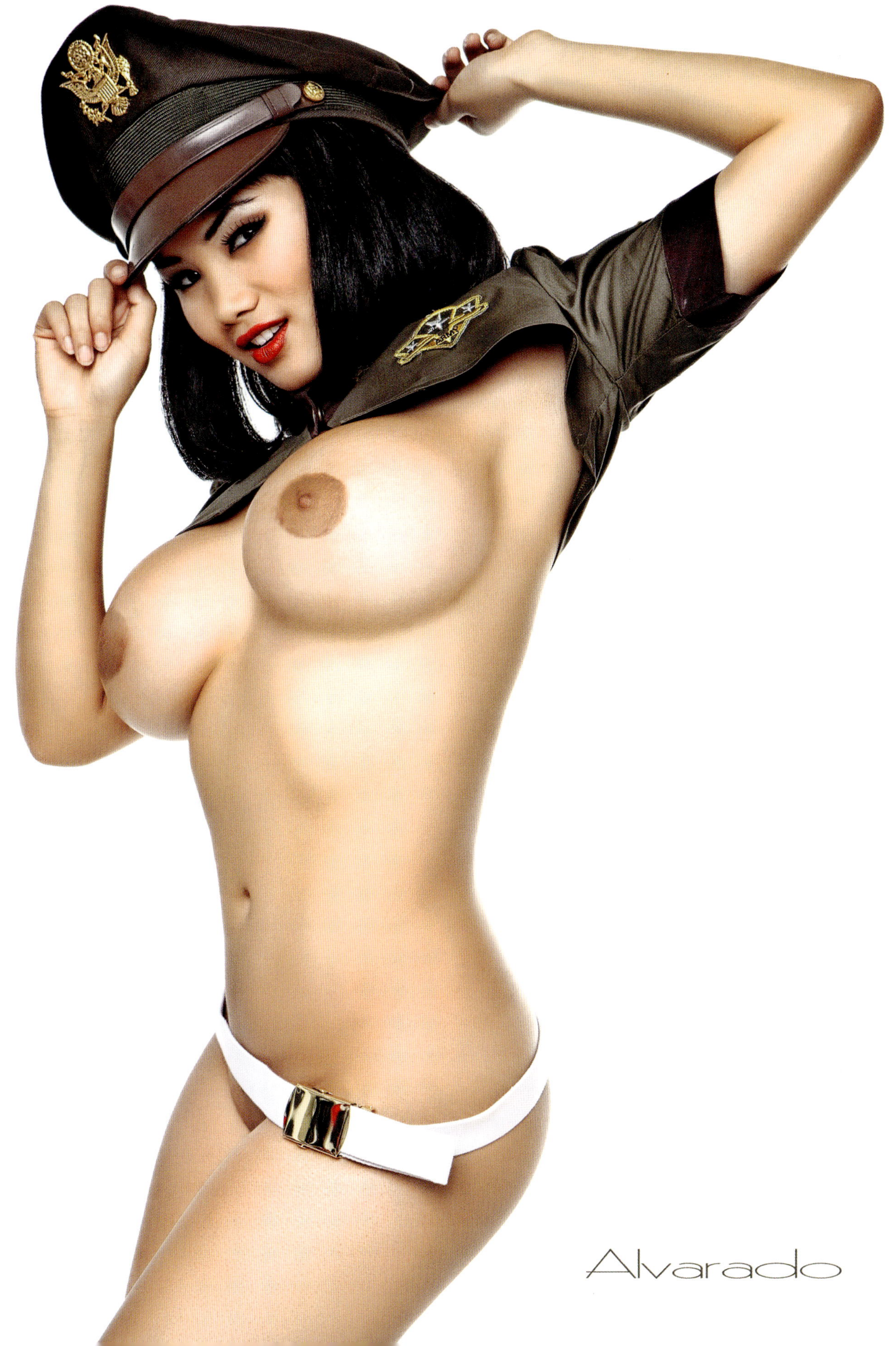
Alvarado

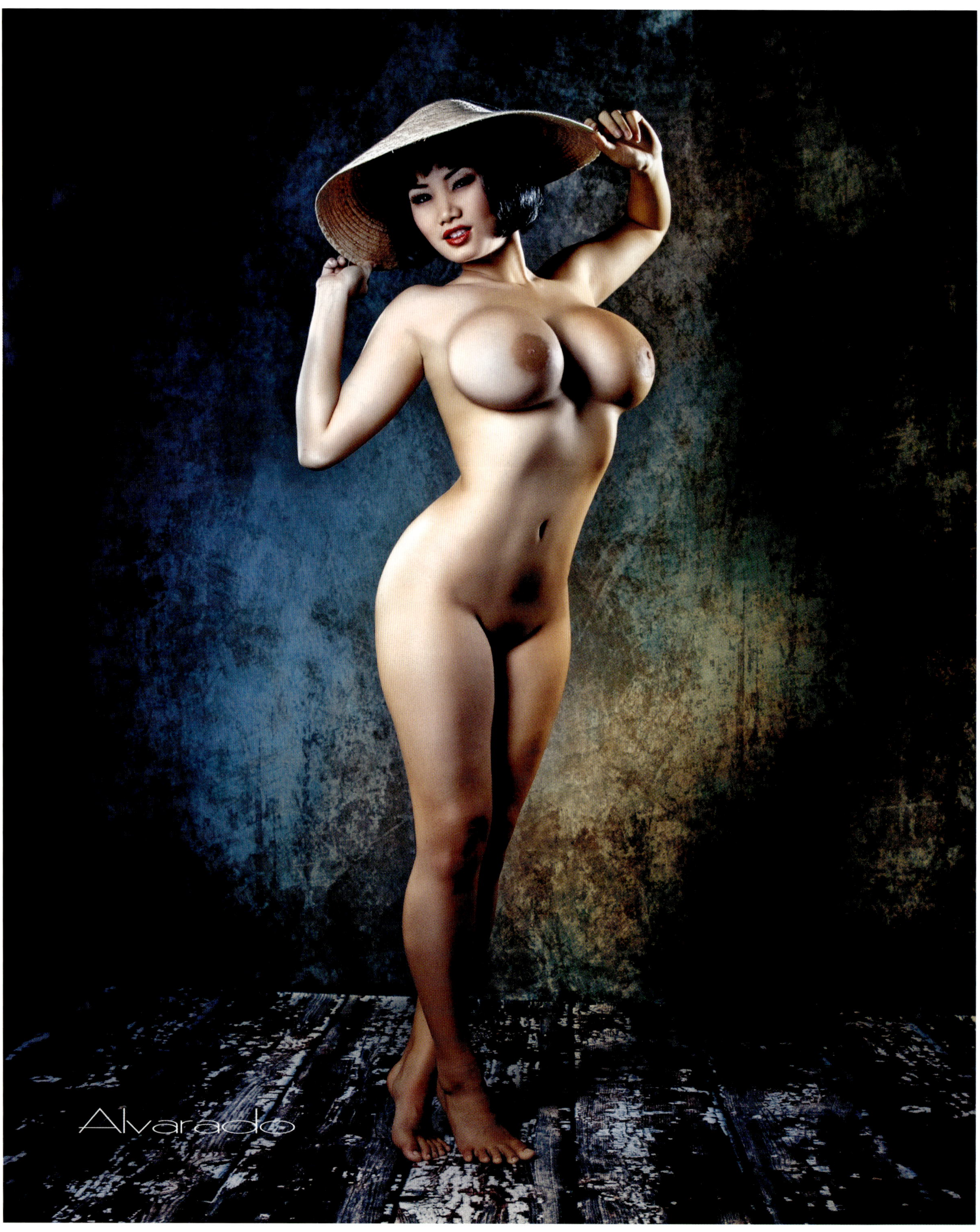
Alvarado

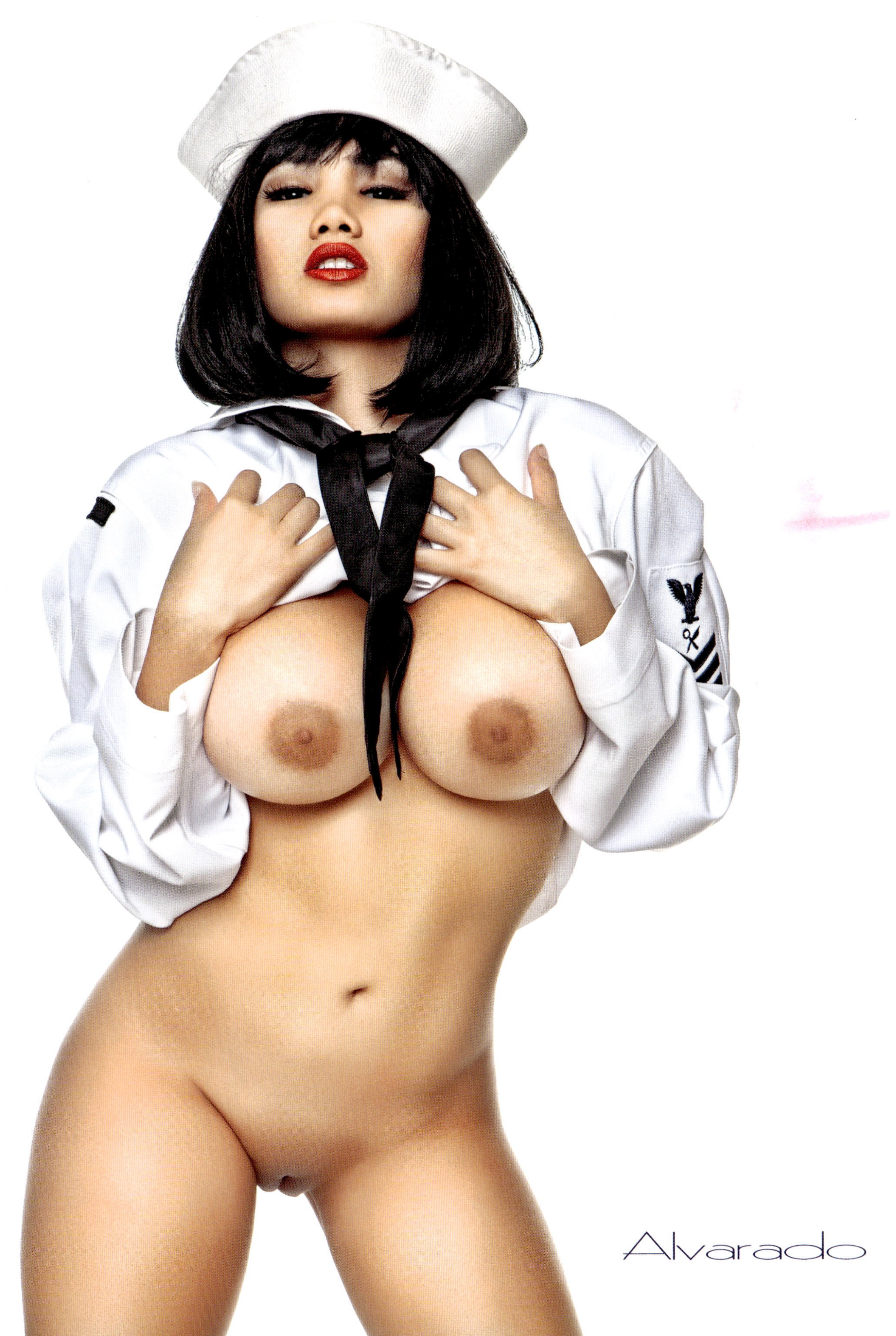
Alvarado

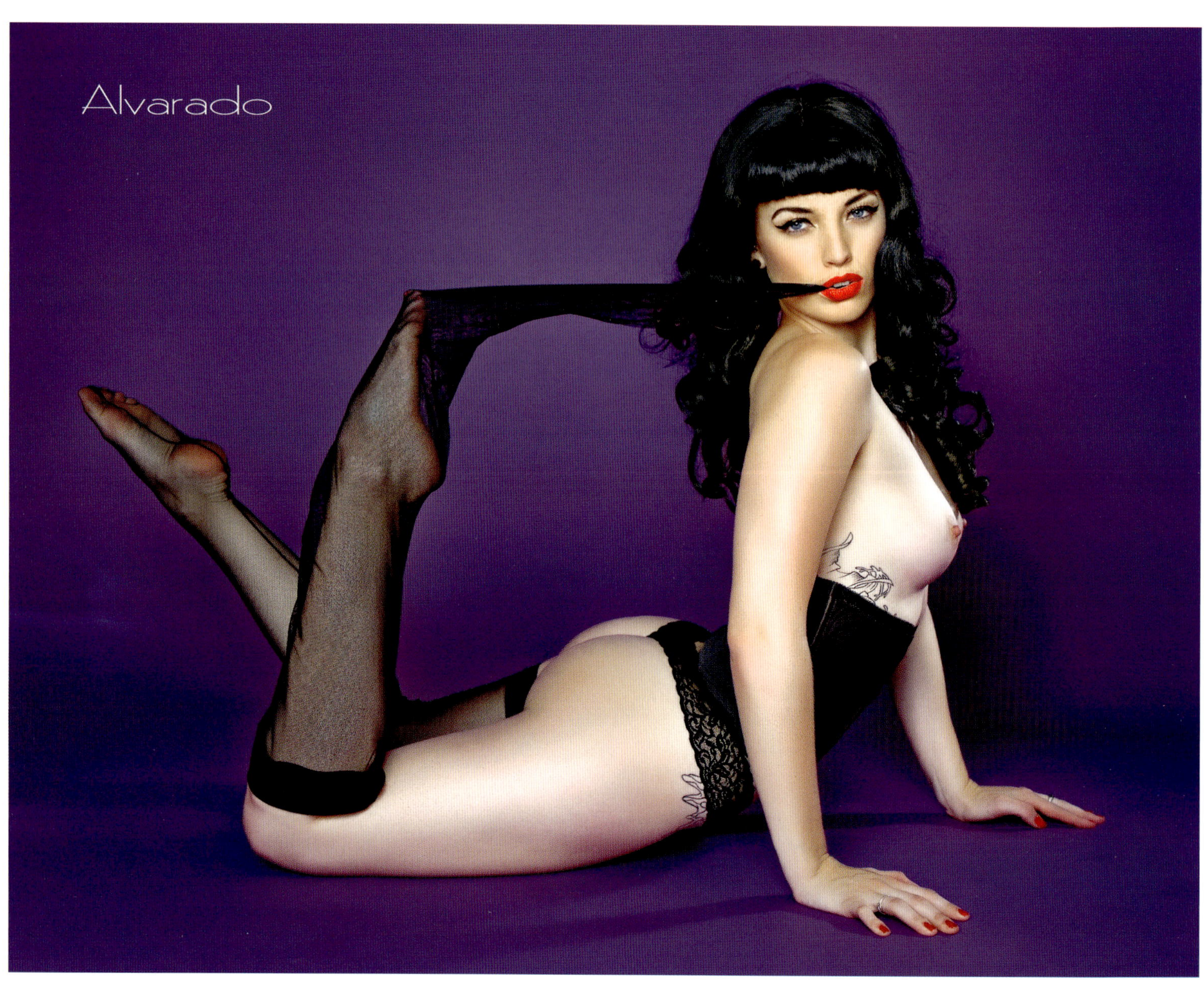
Alvarado

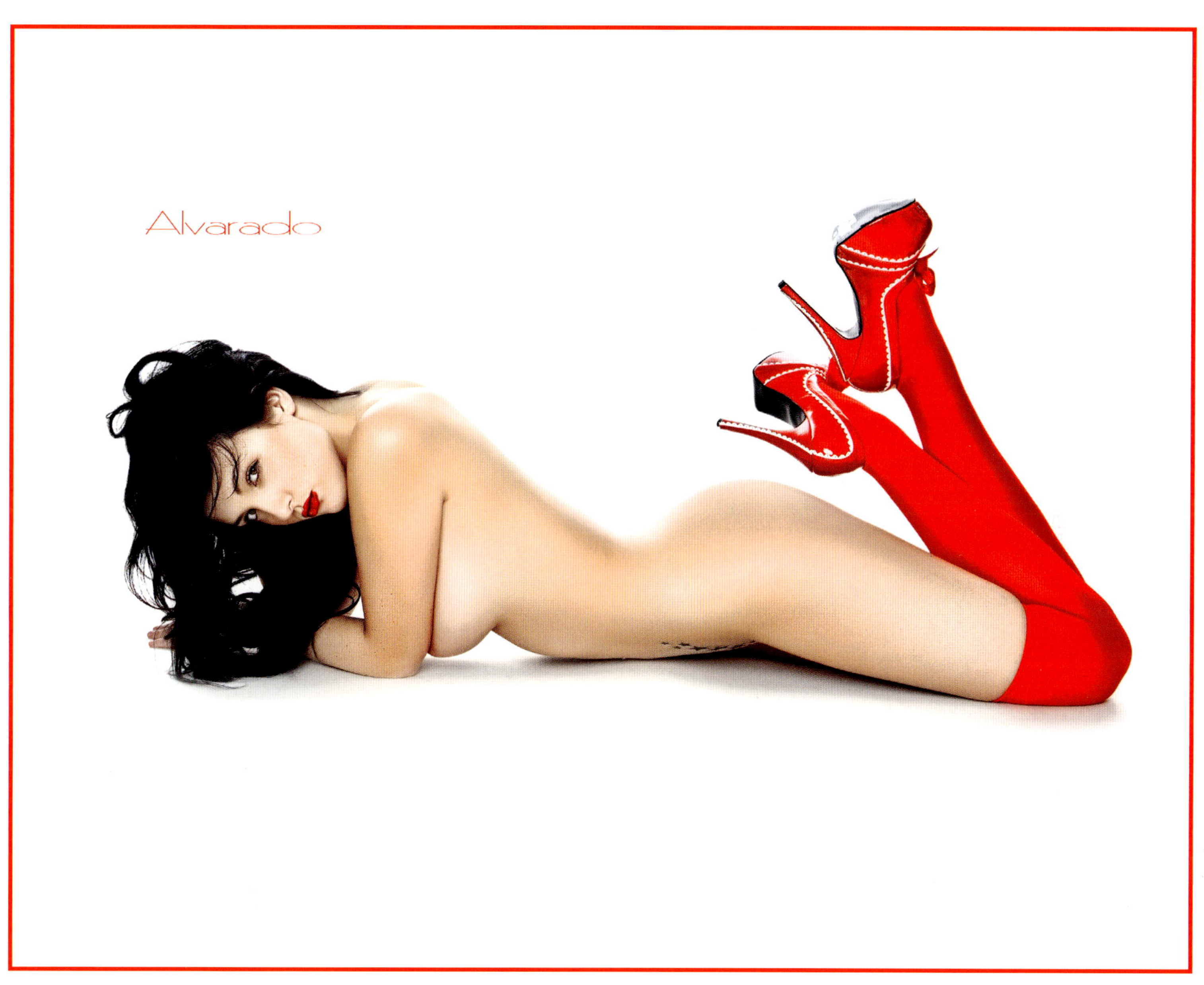
Alvarado

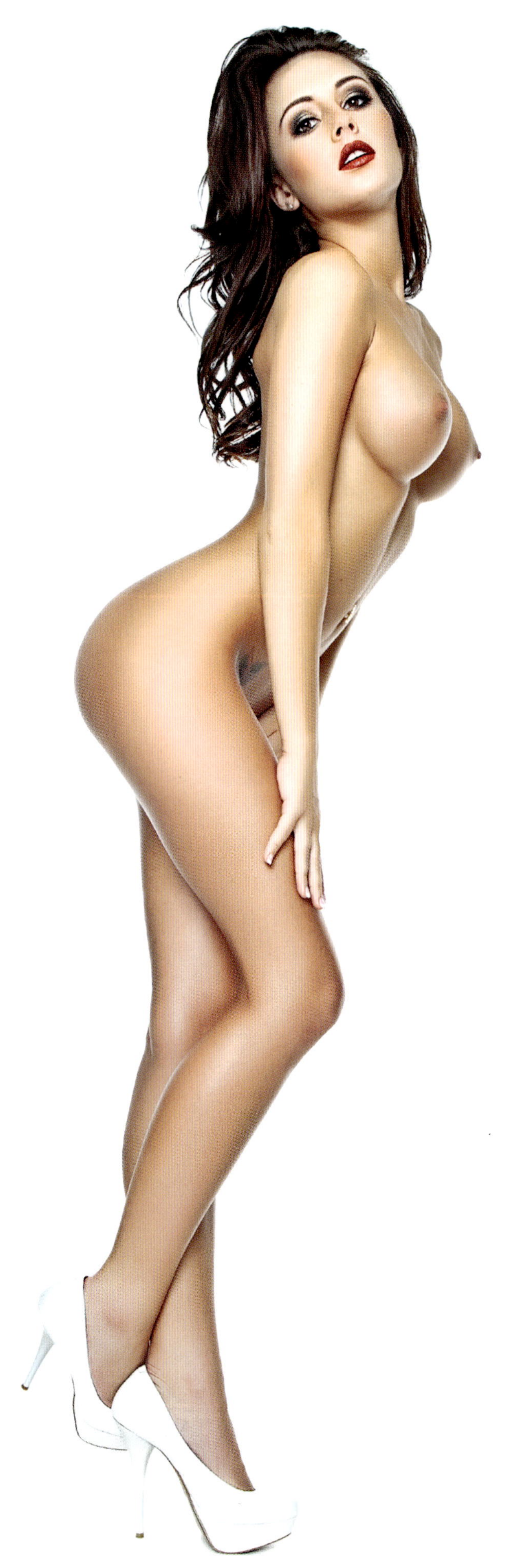

Alvarado

Alvarado

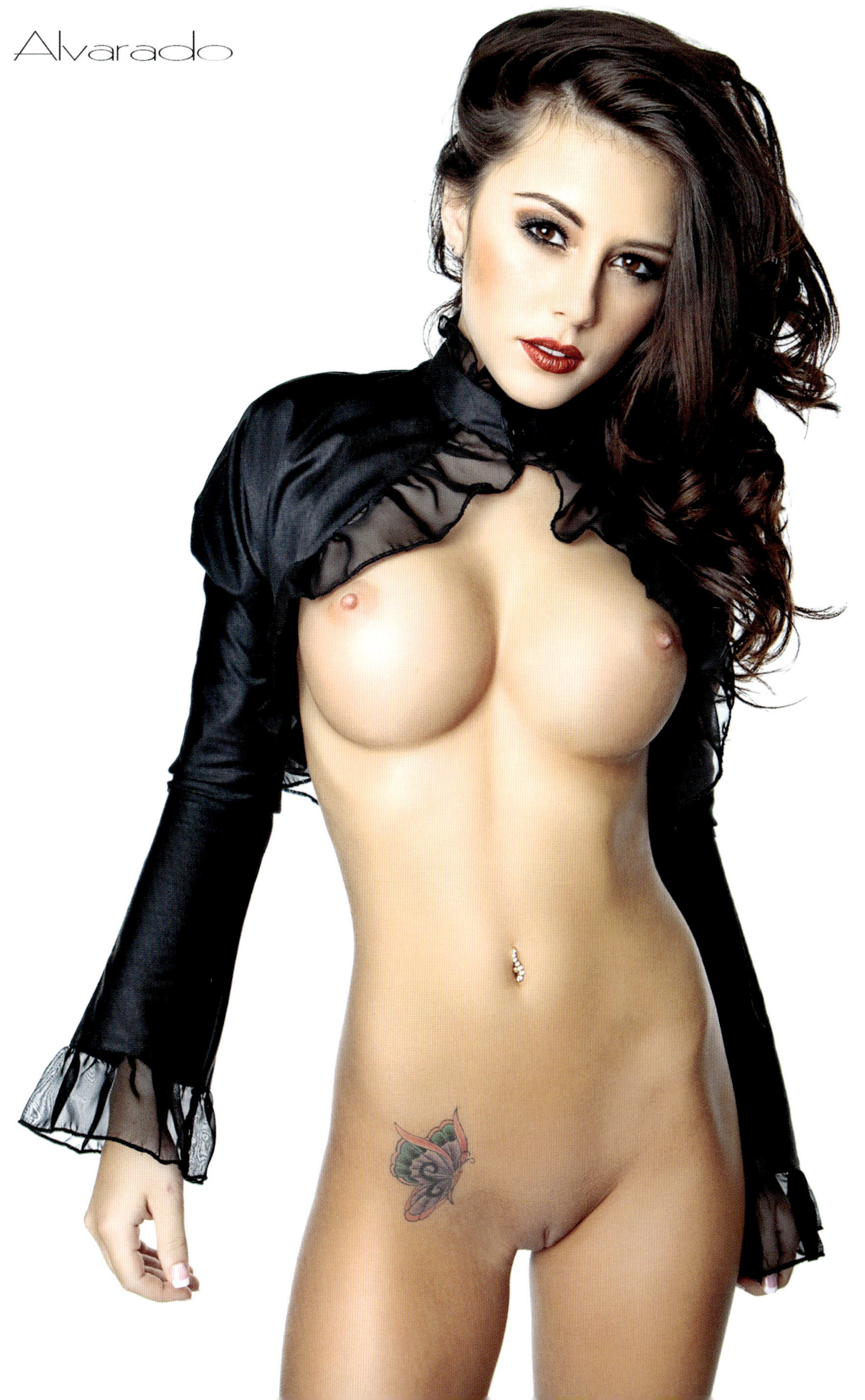

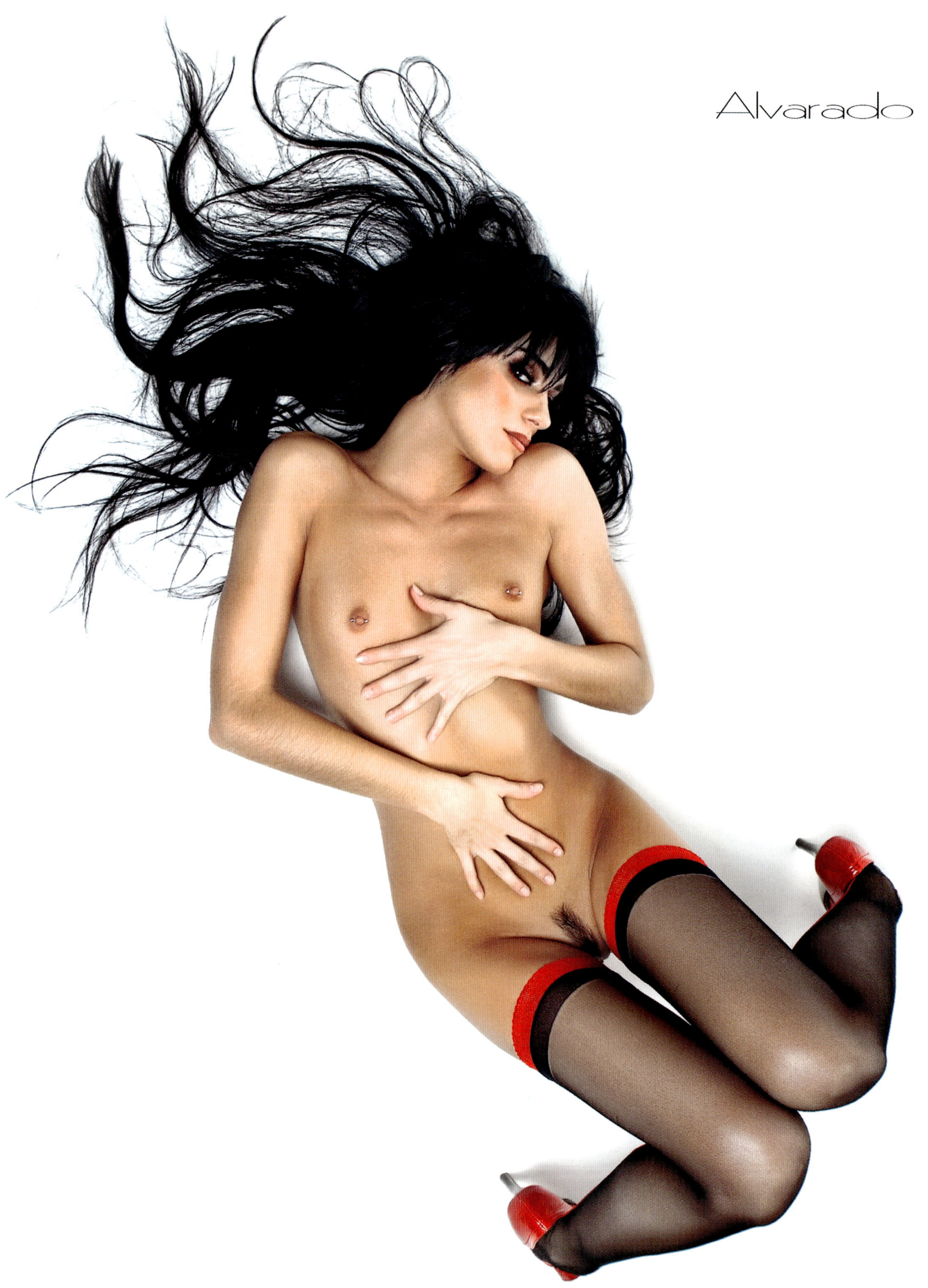

Alvarado

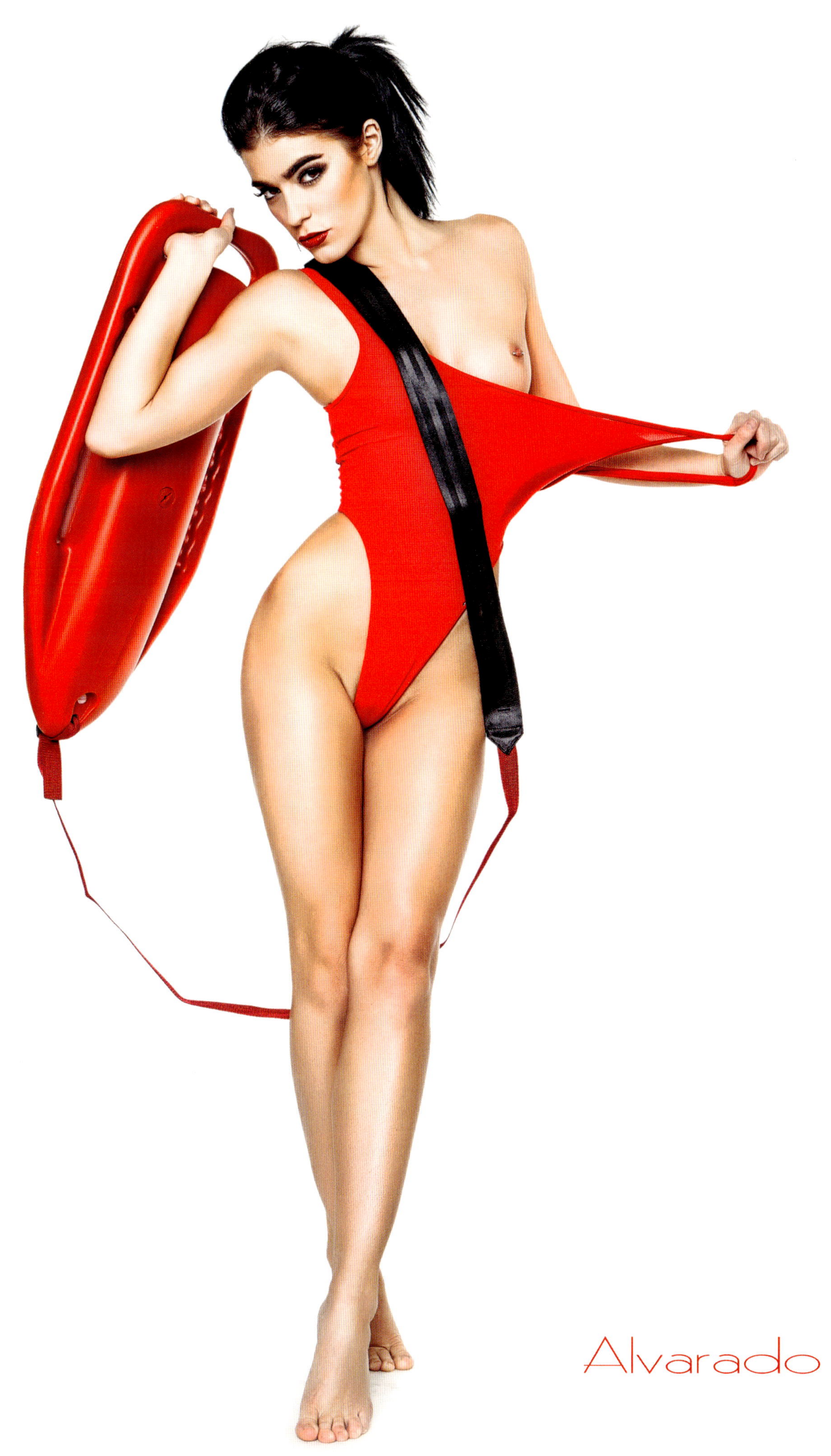
Alvarado

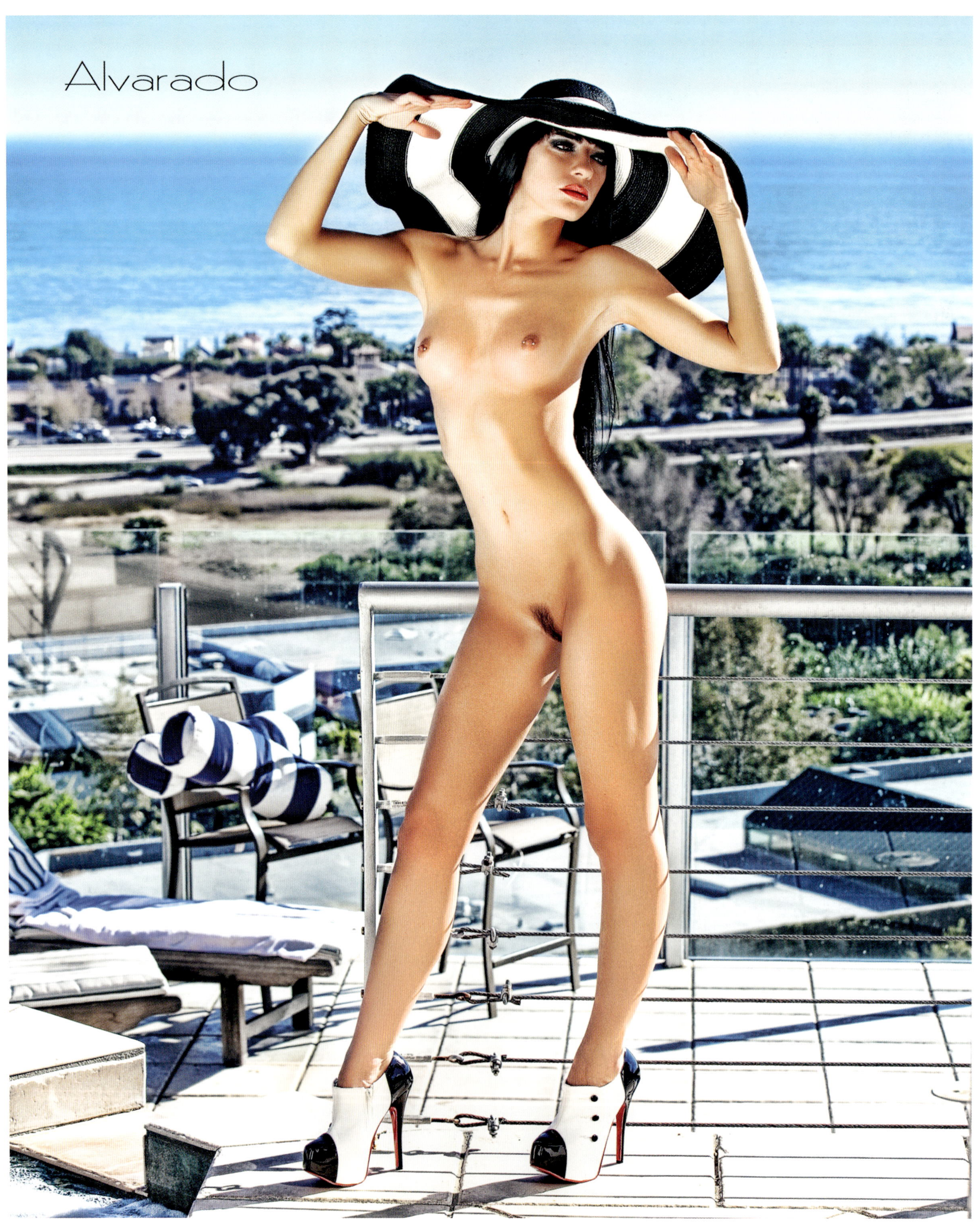
Alvarado

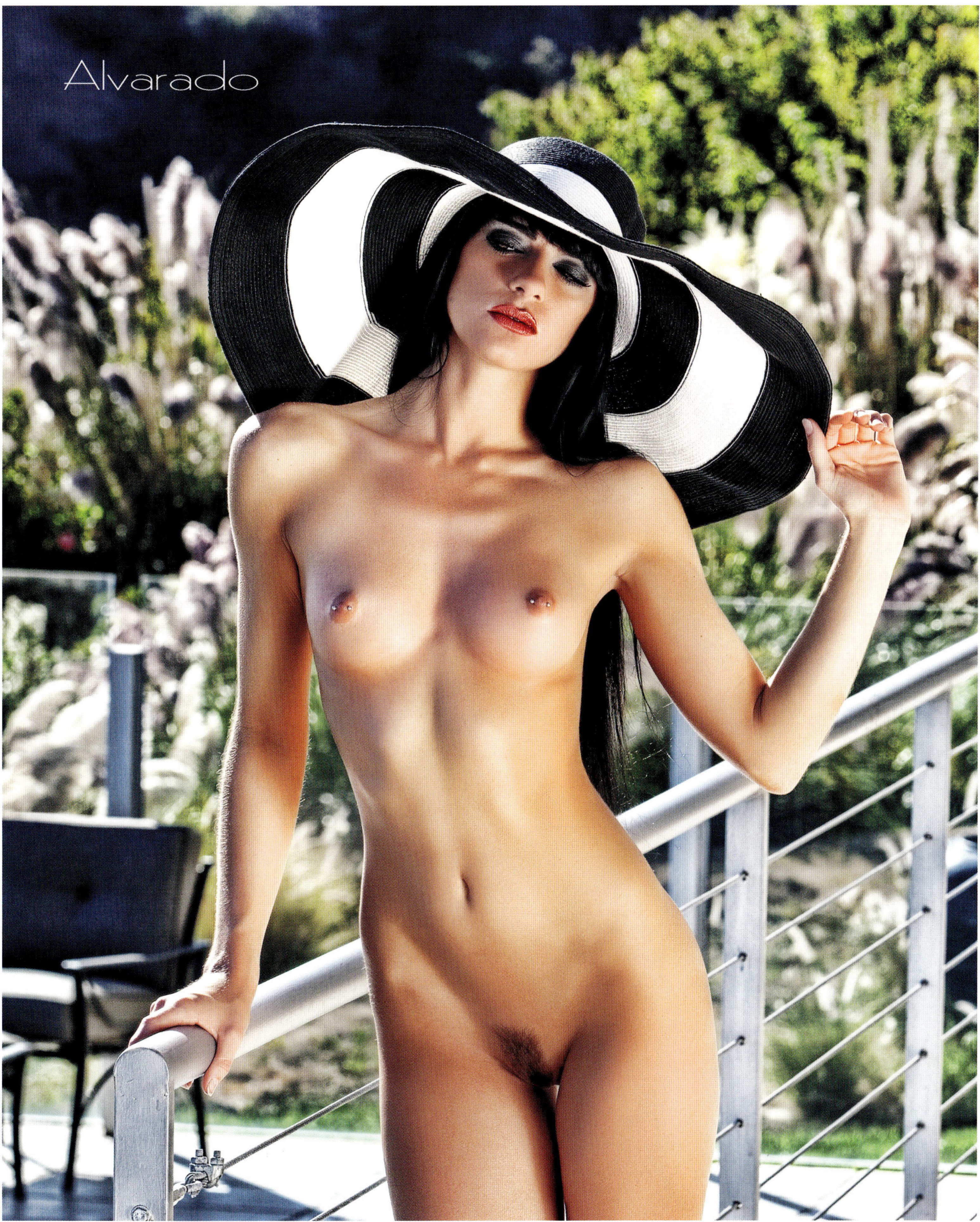
Alvarado

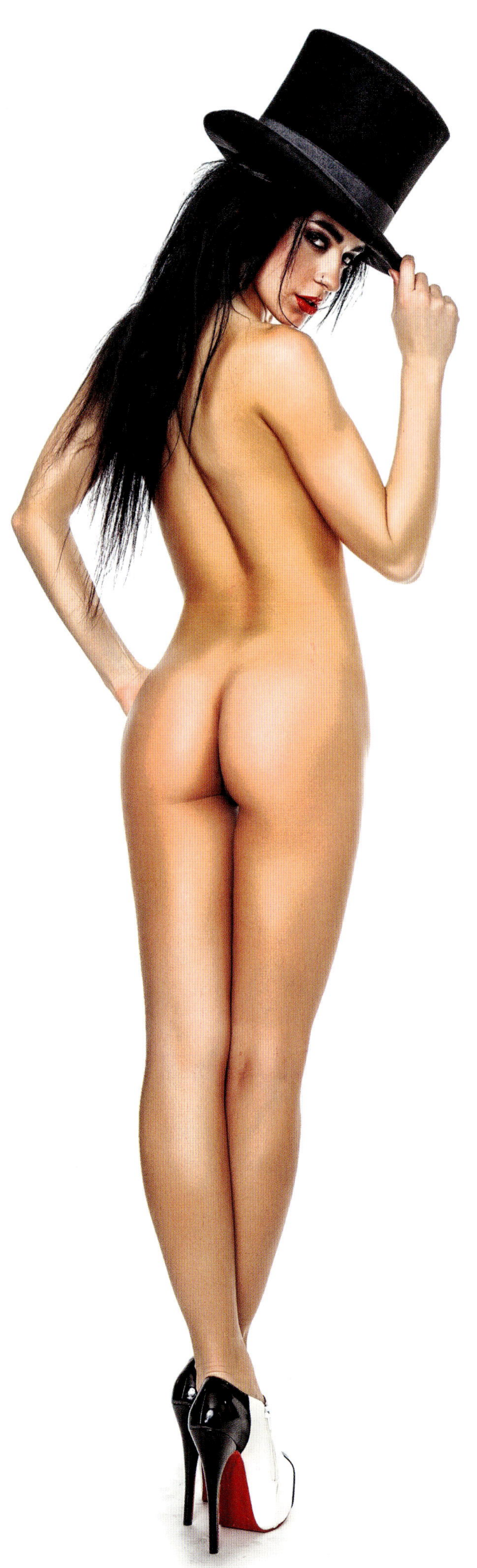

Alvarado

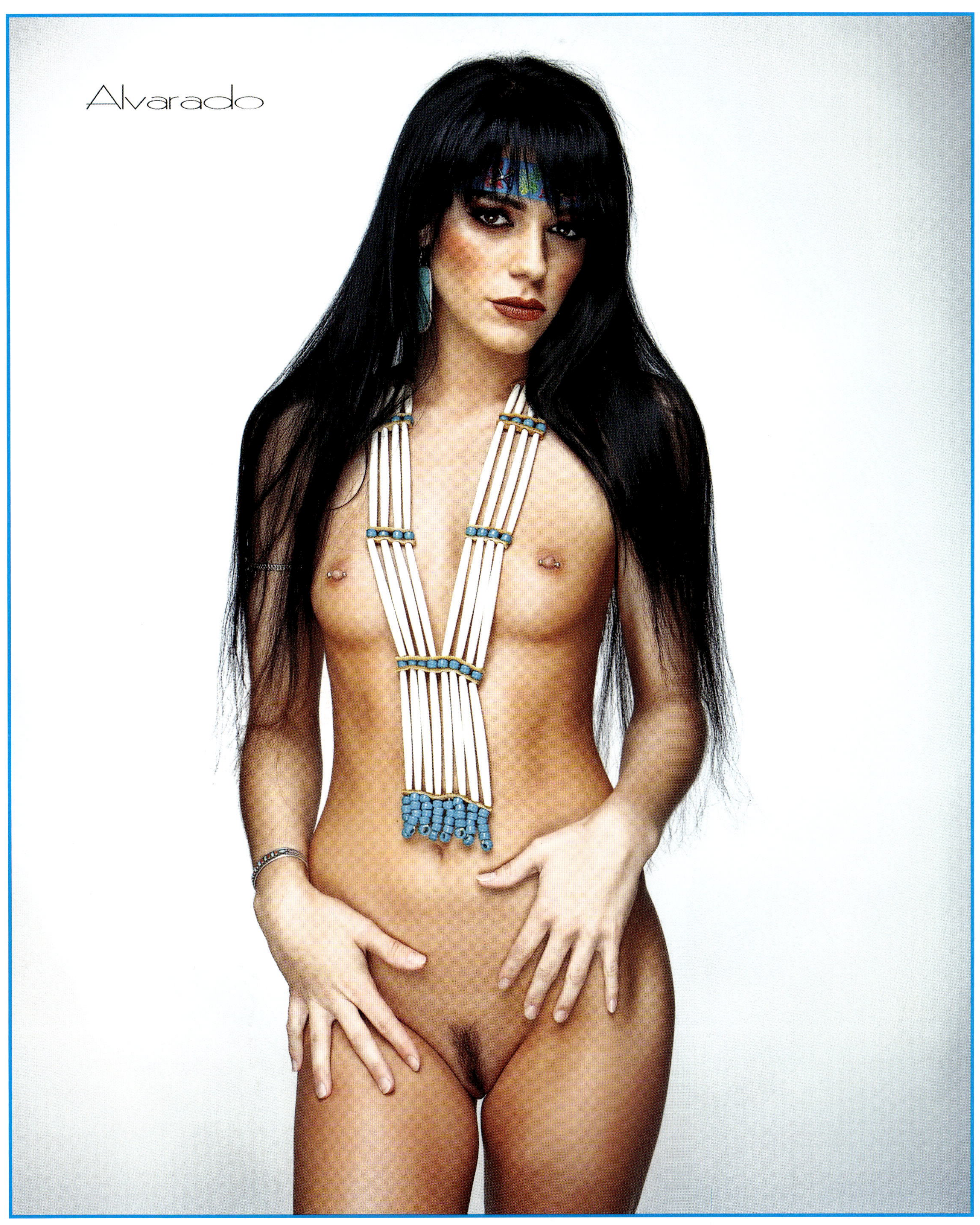
Alvarado

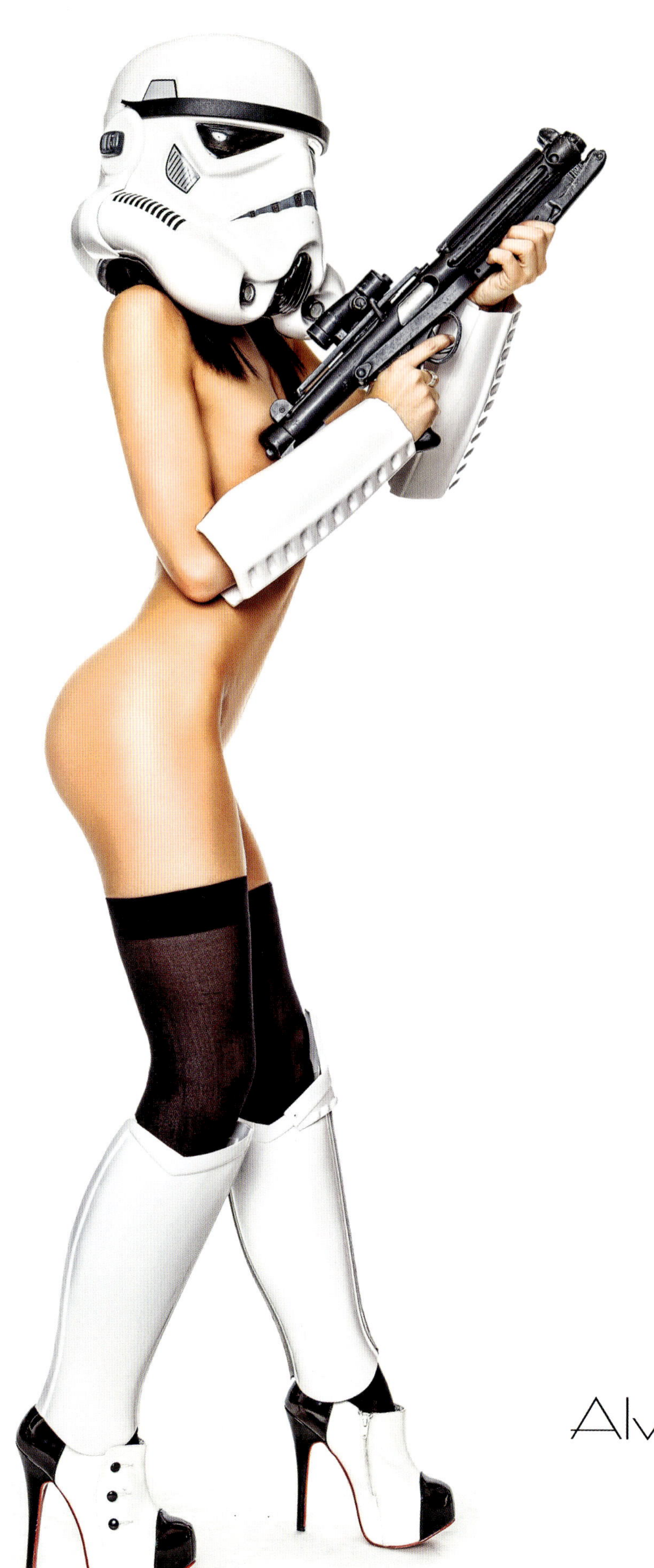

Alvarado

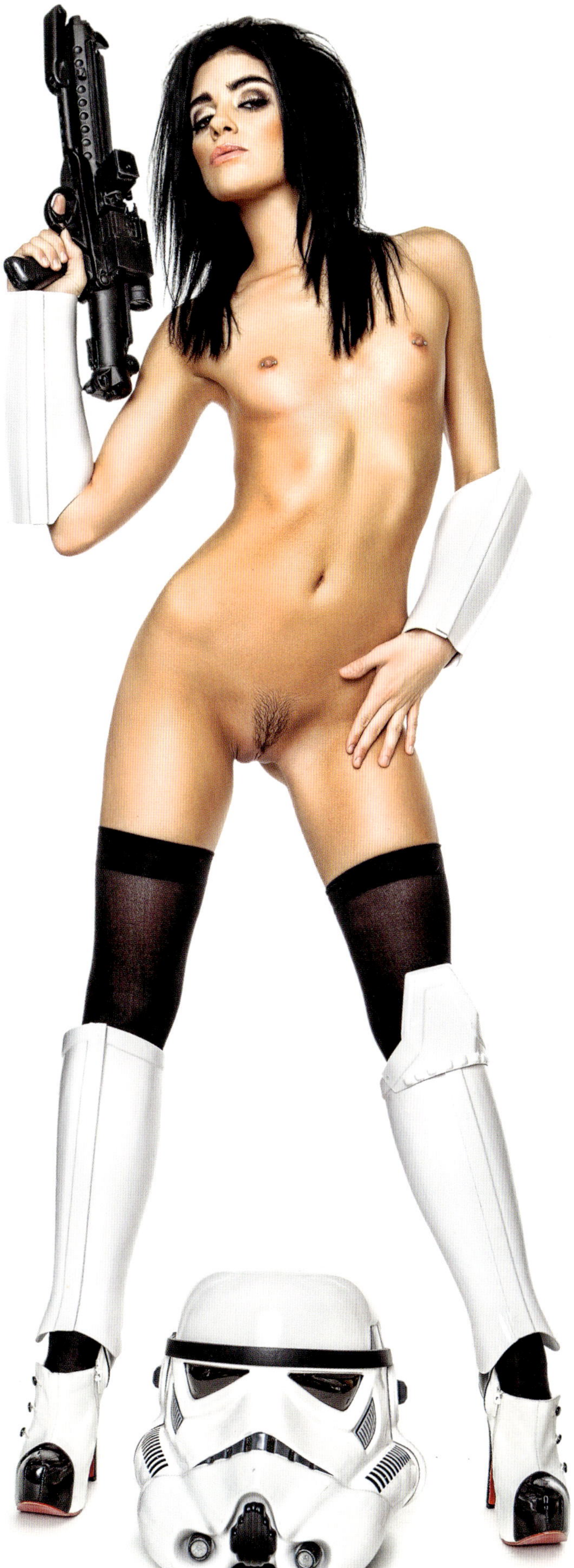

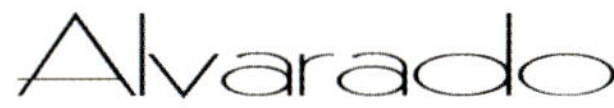
Alvarado

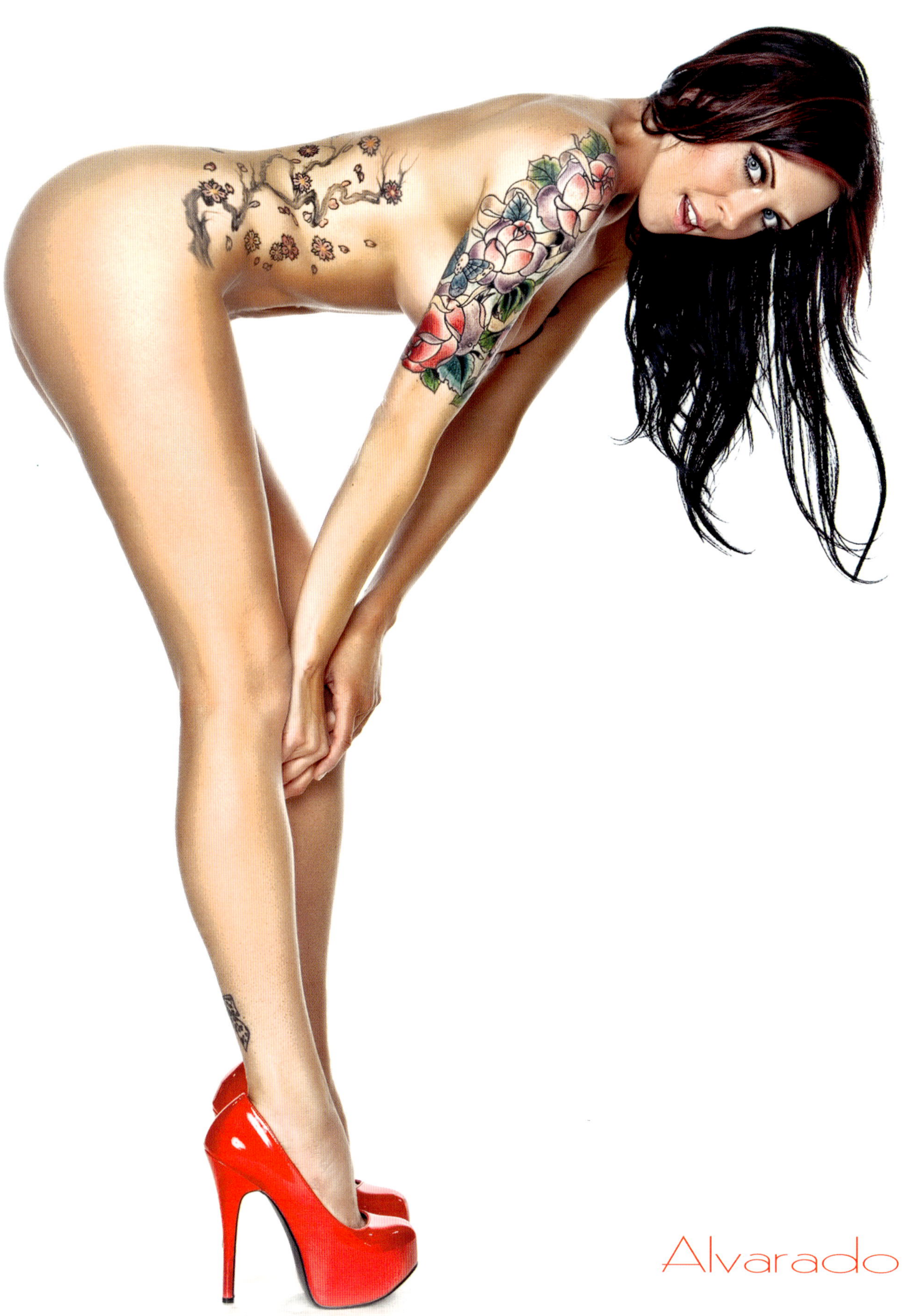

Alvarado

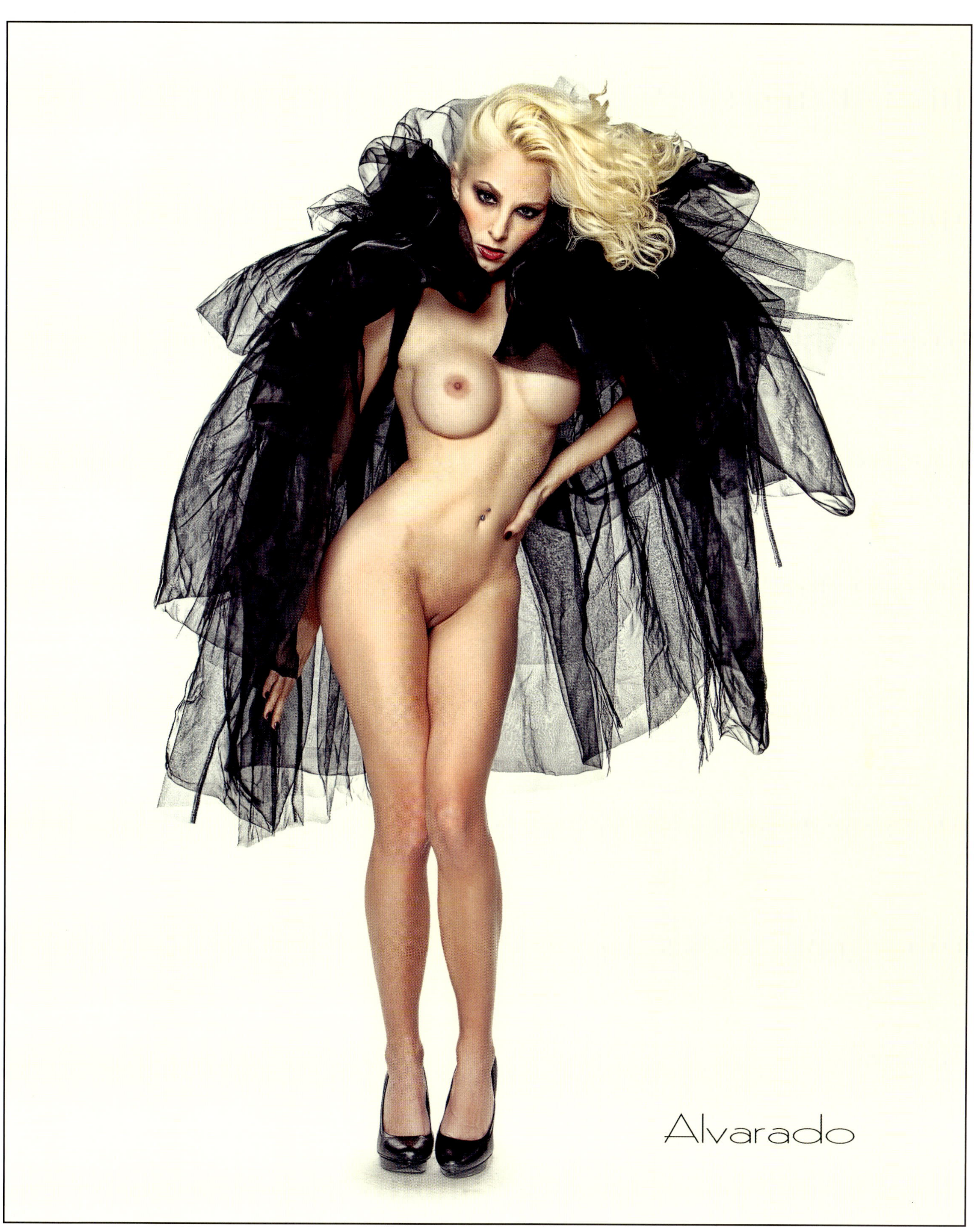
Alvarado

Alvarado

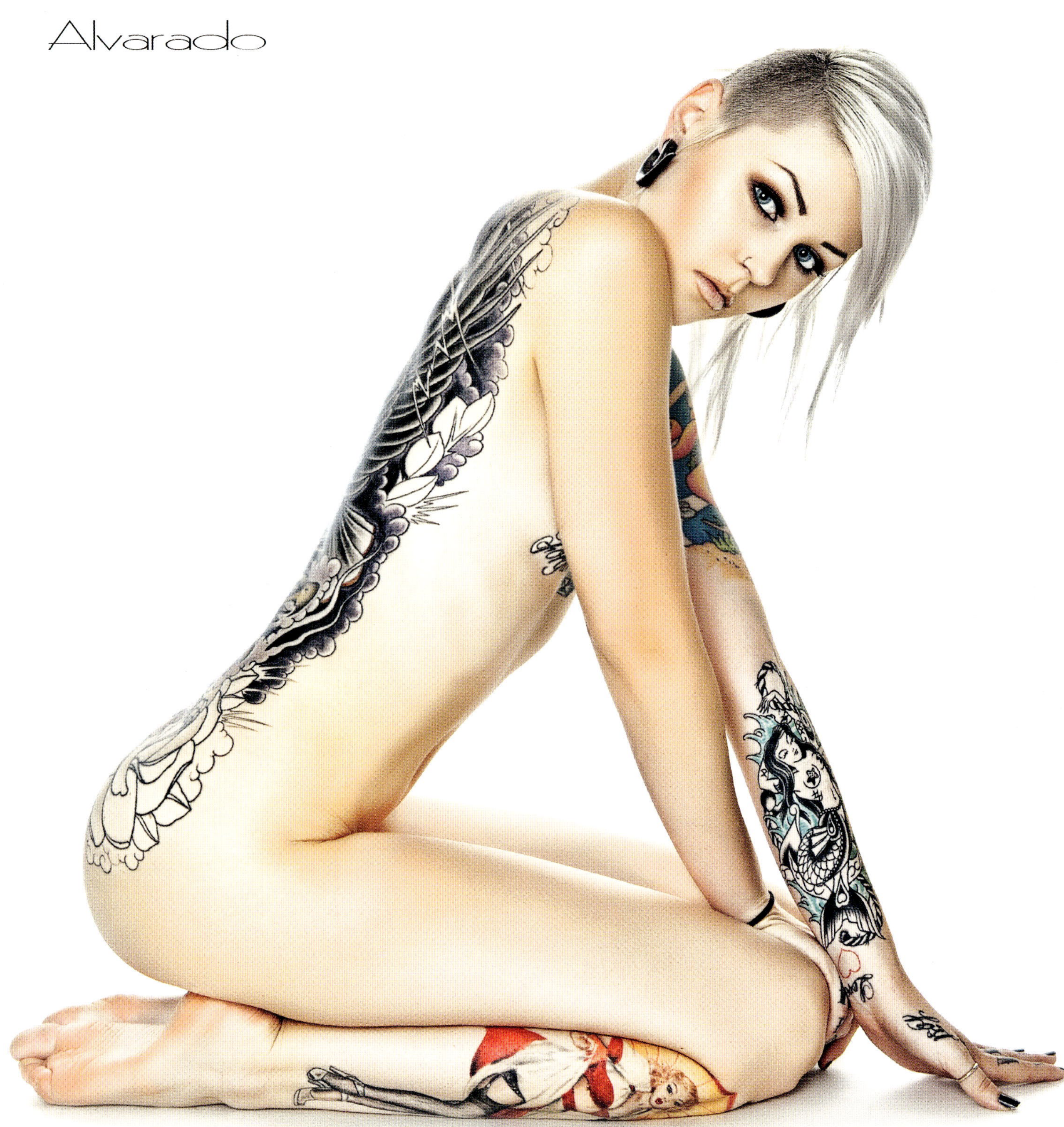

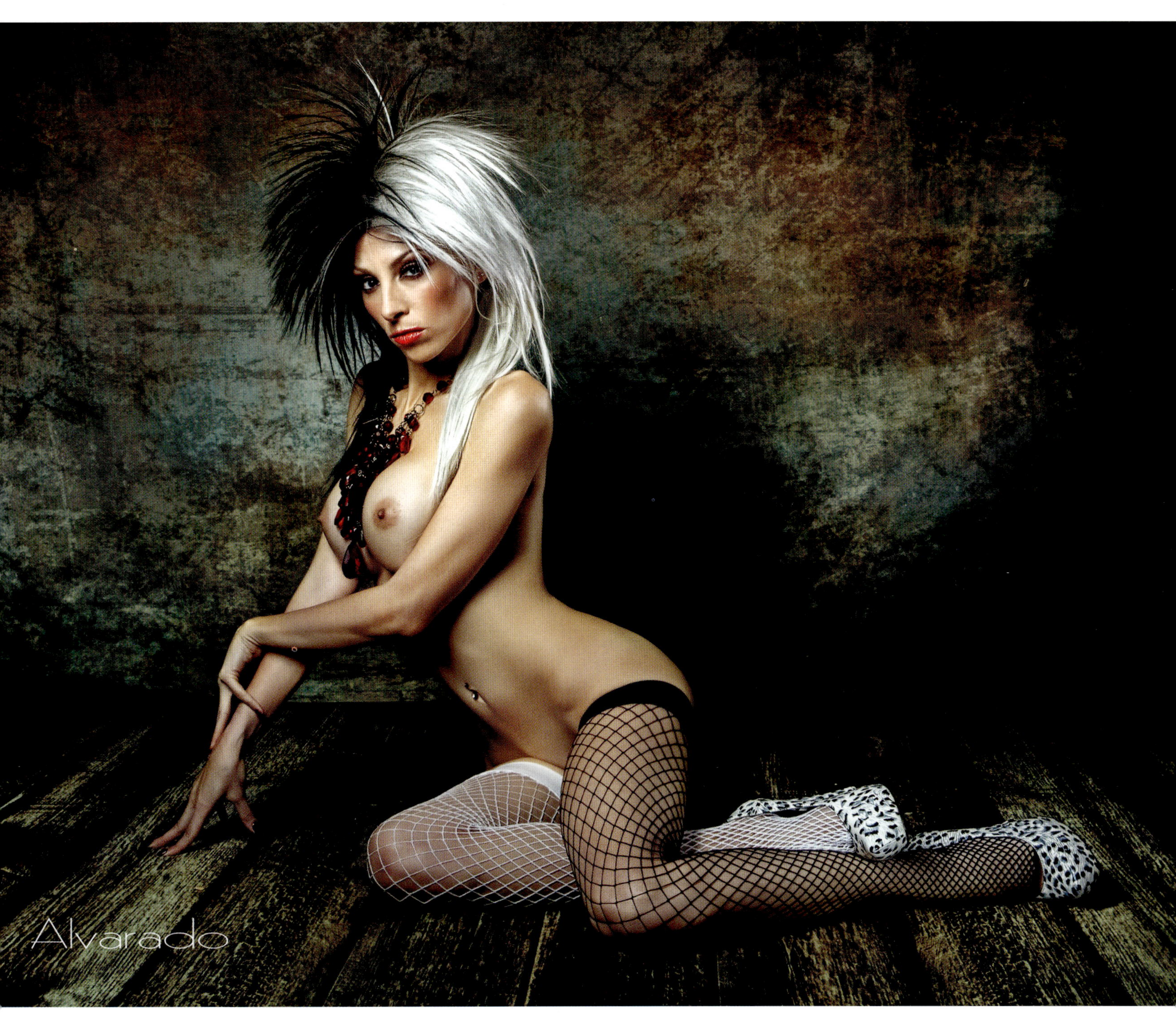
Alvarado

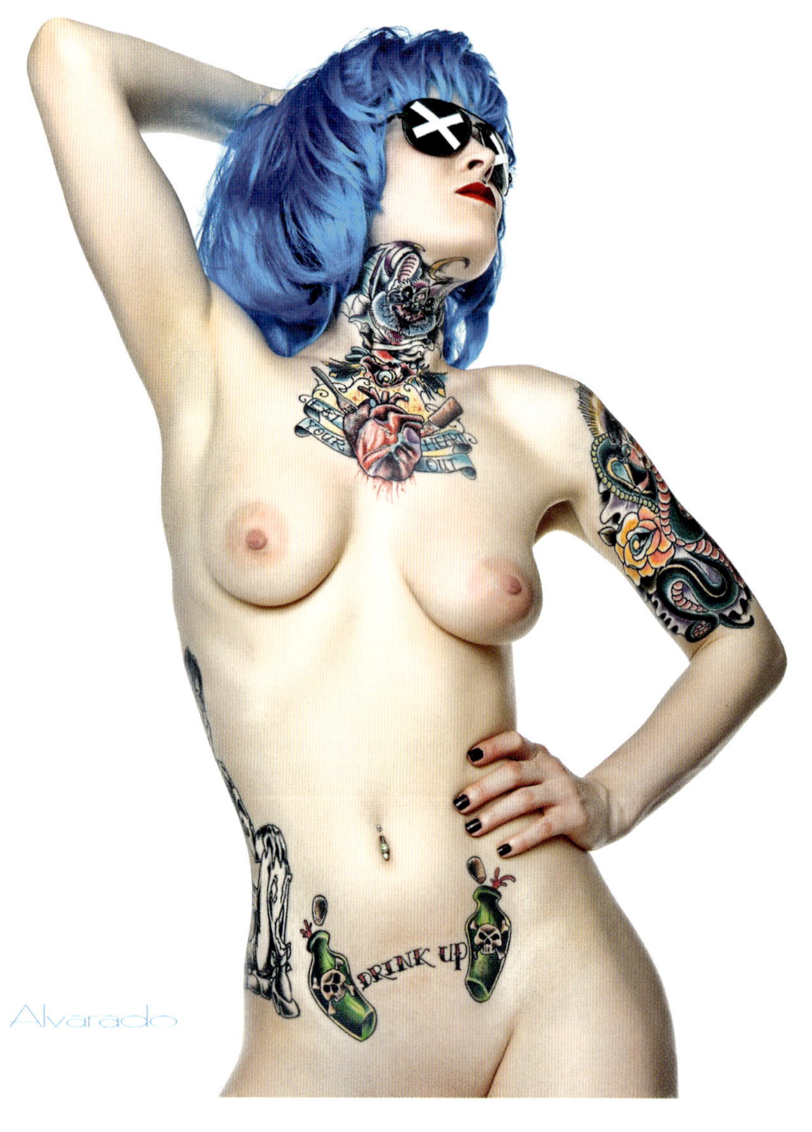

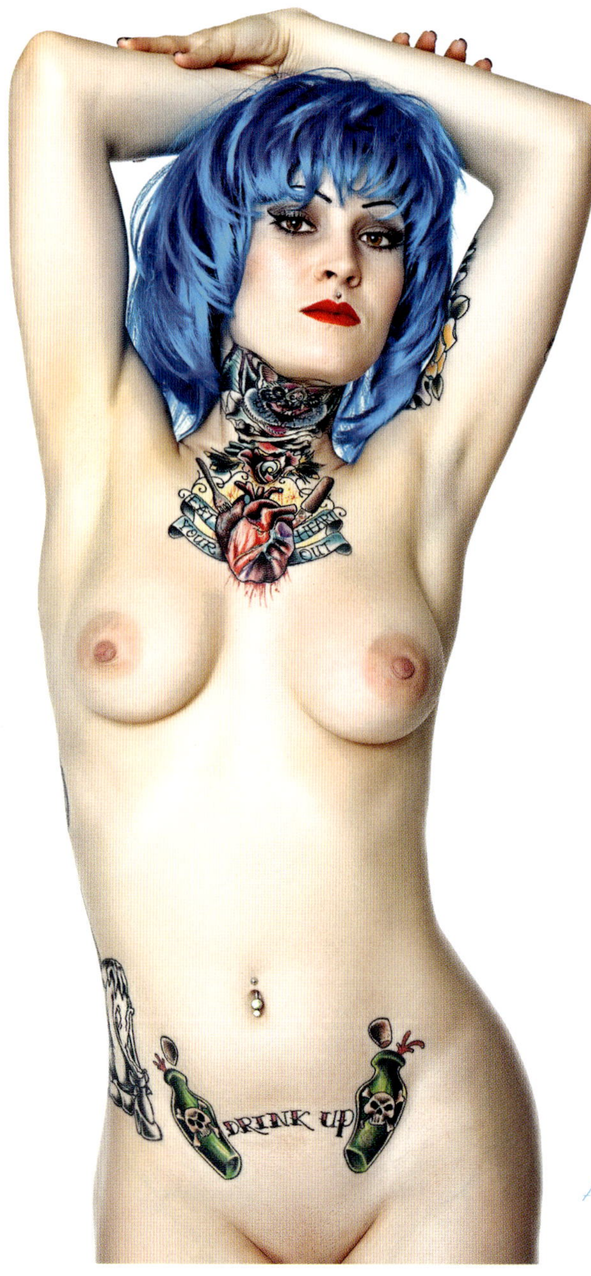

Alvarado

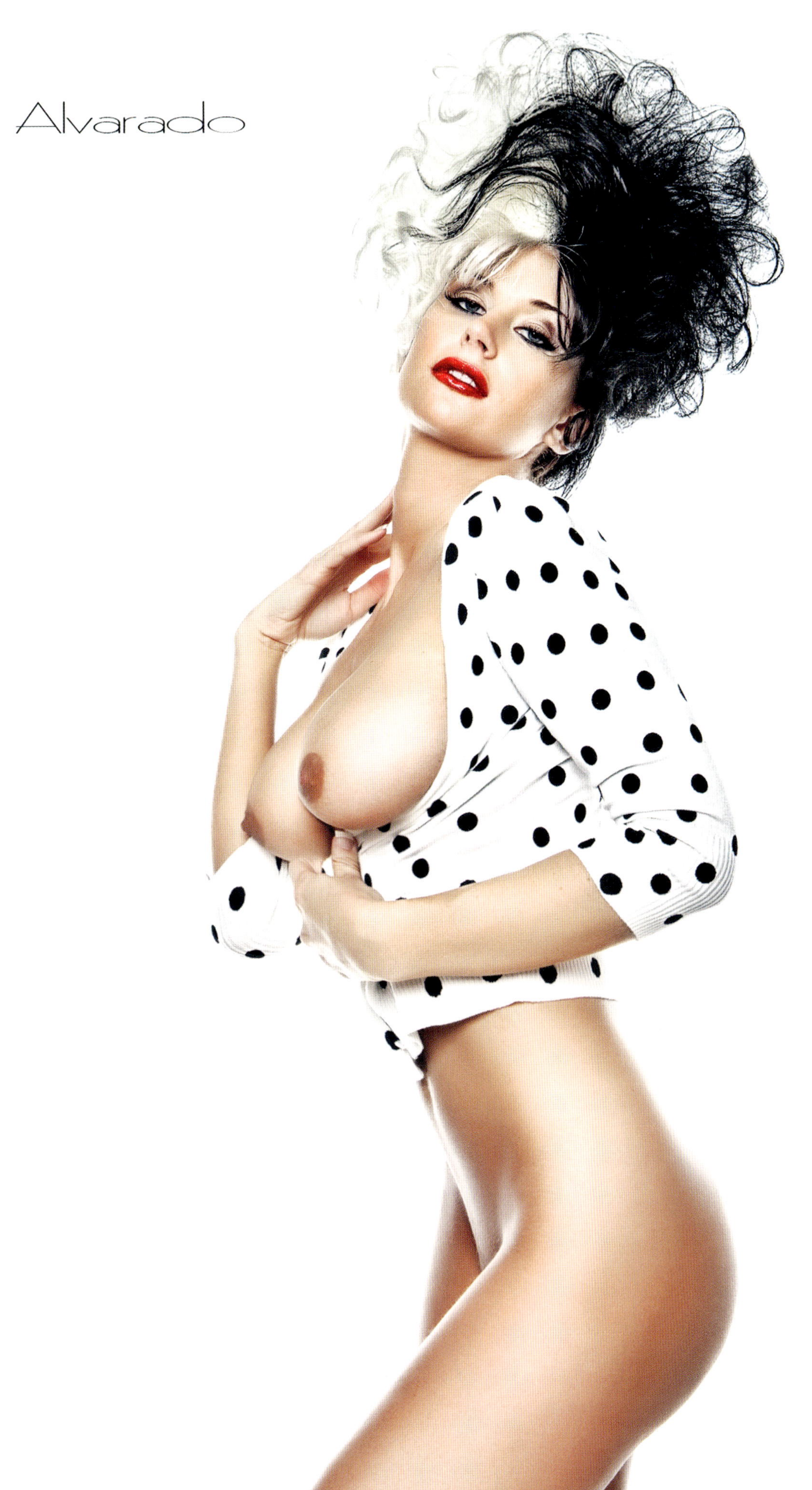
Alvarado

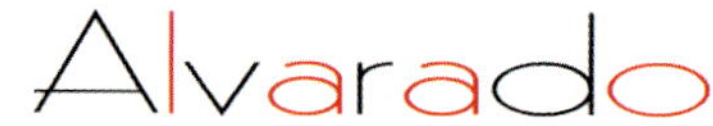
Alvarado

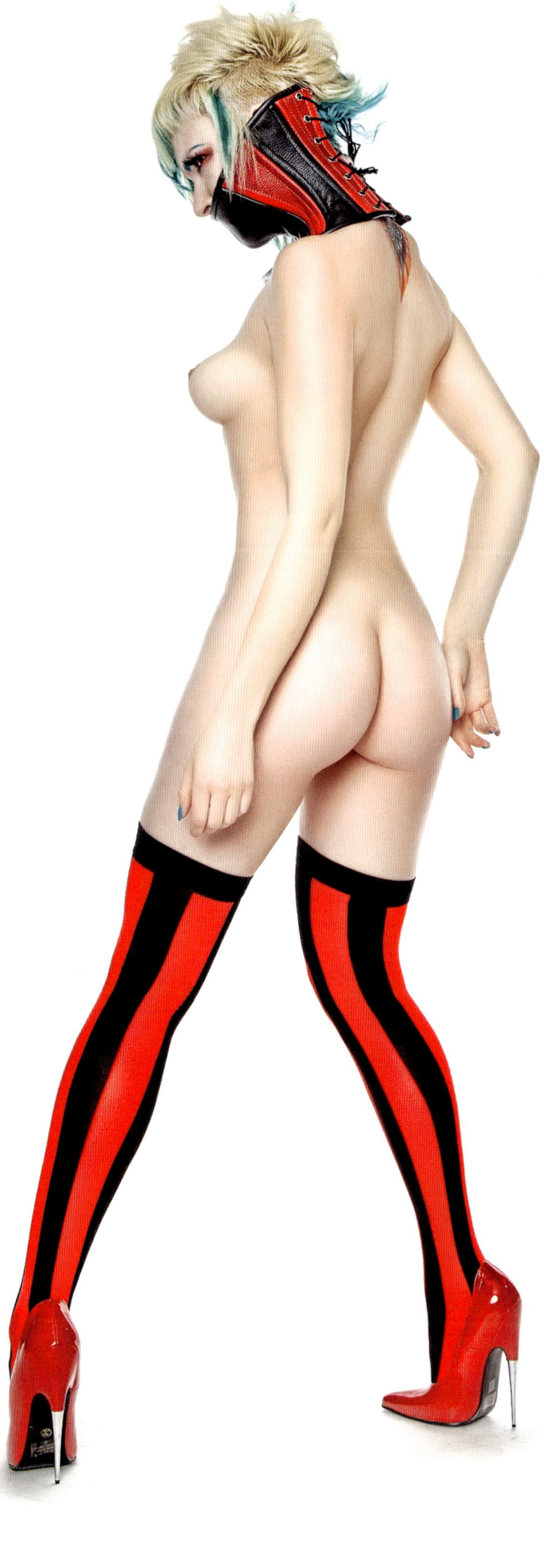

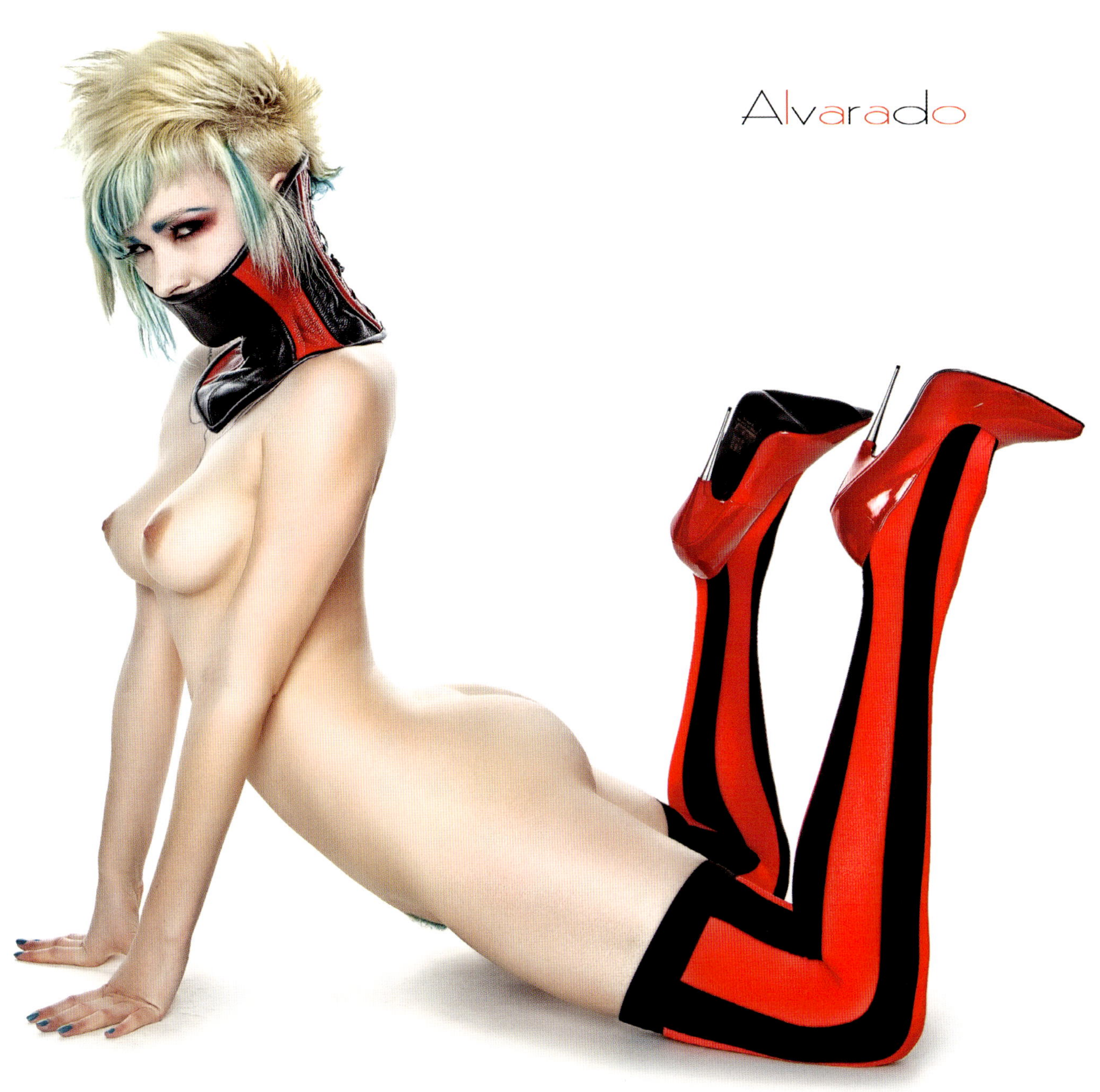

Alvarado

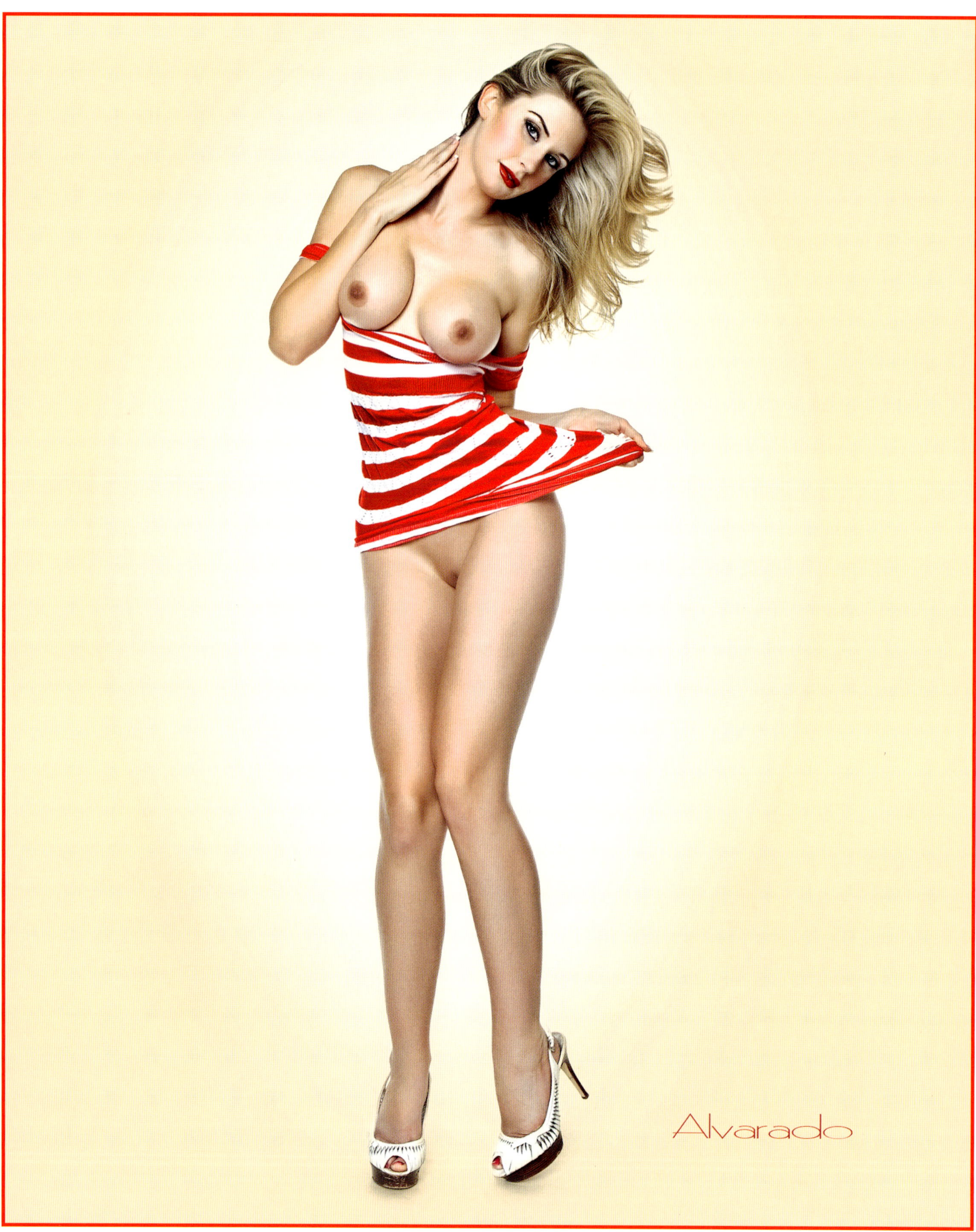
Alvarado

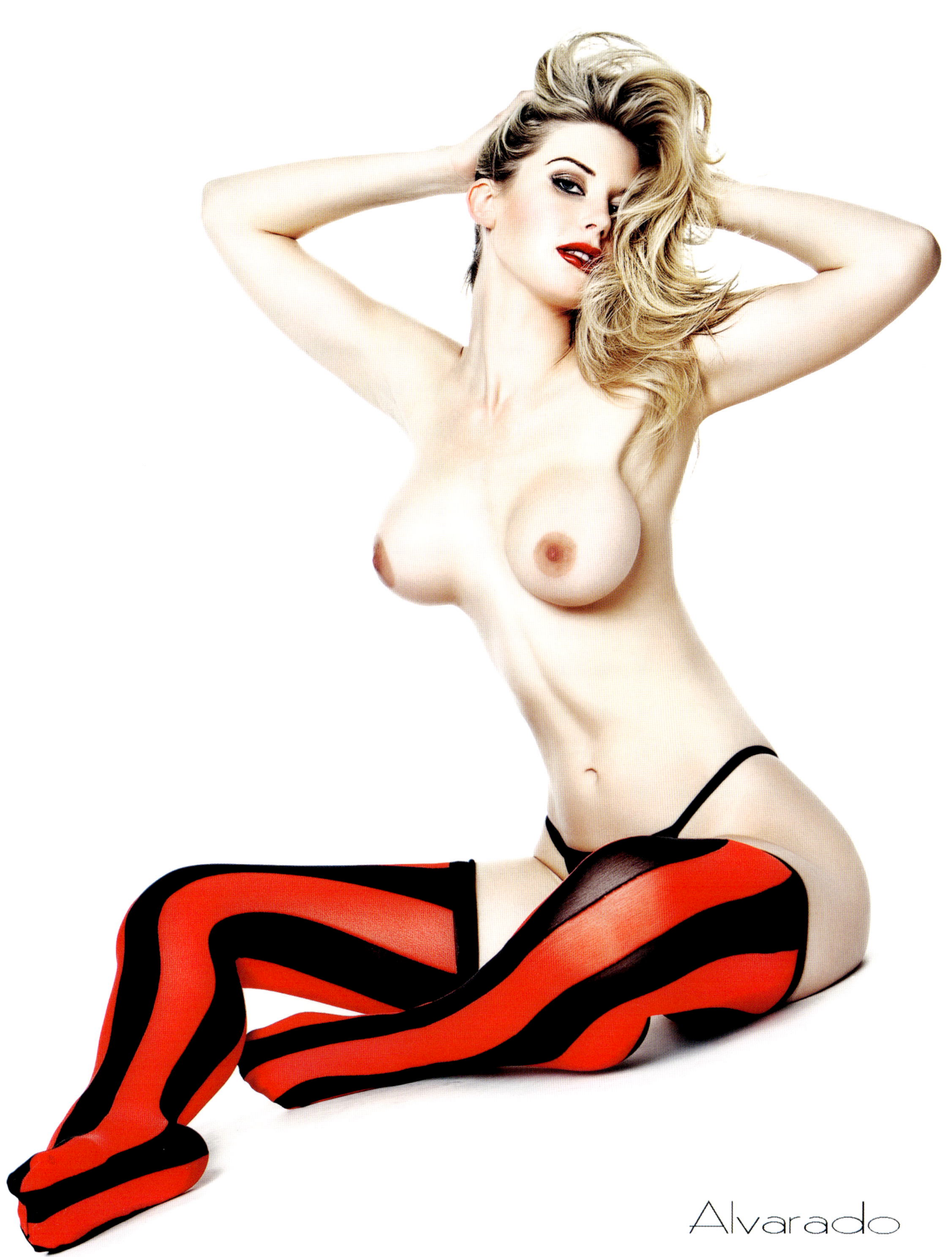
Alvarado

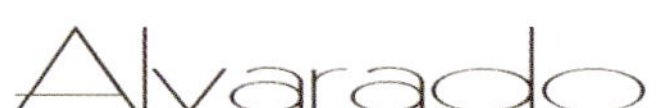
Alvarado

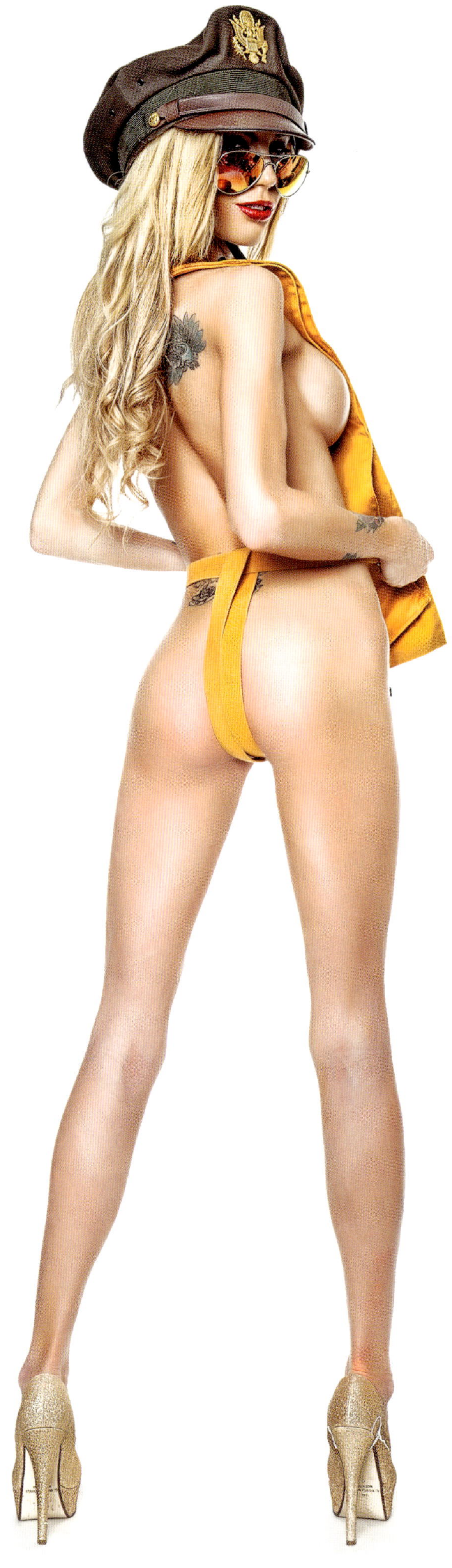

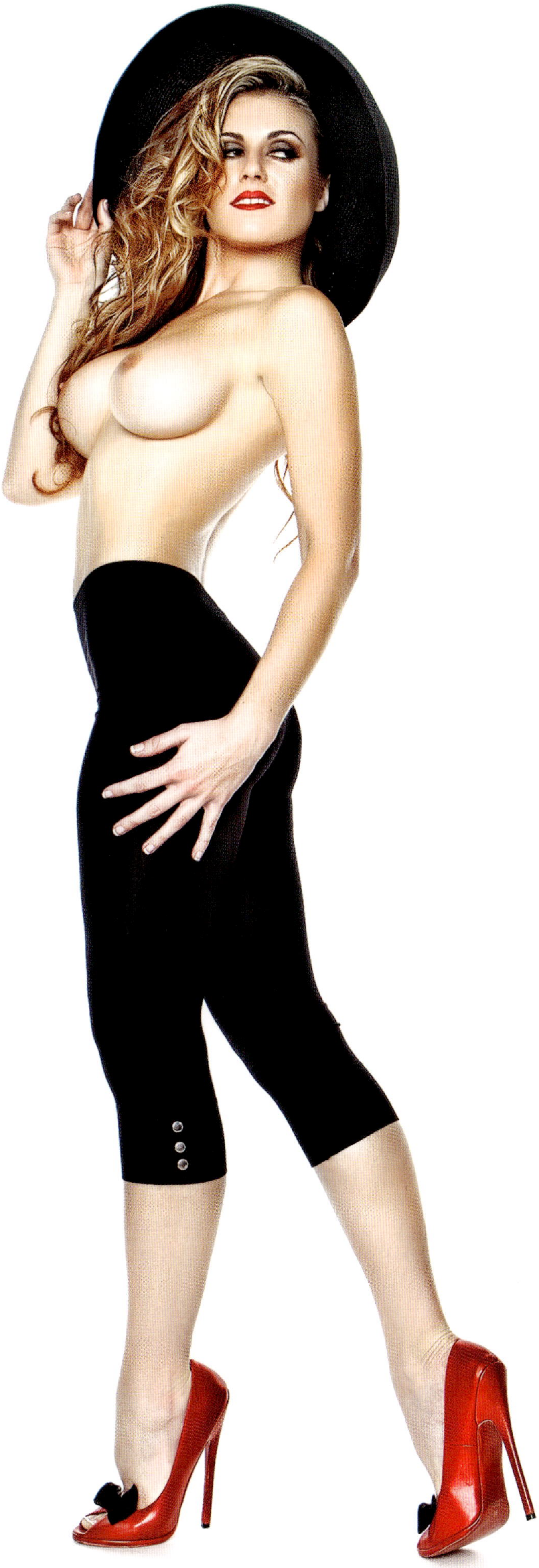

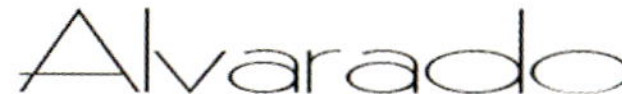

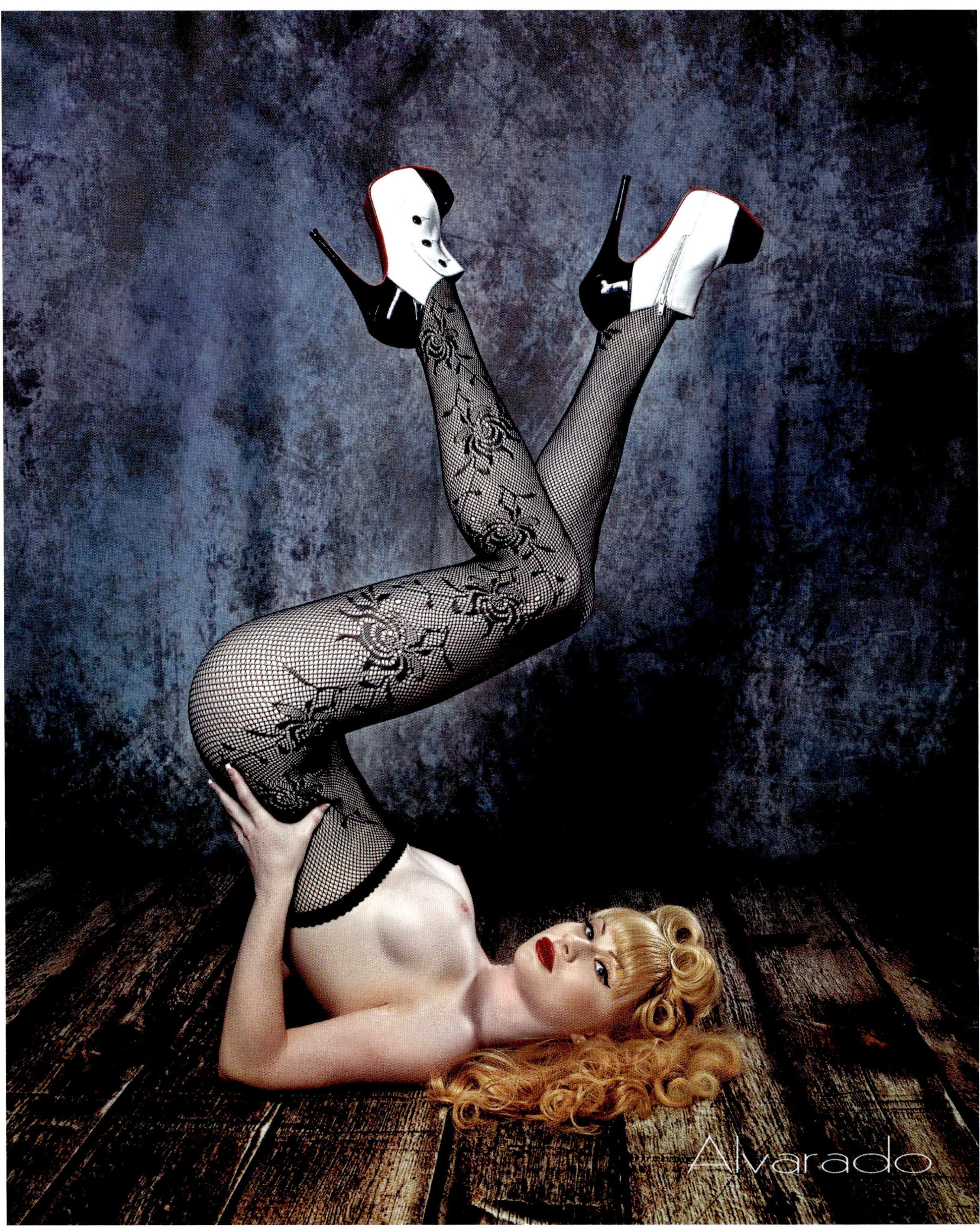
Alvarado

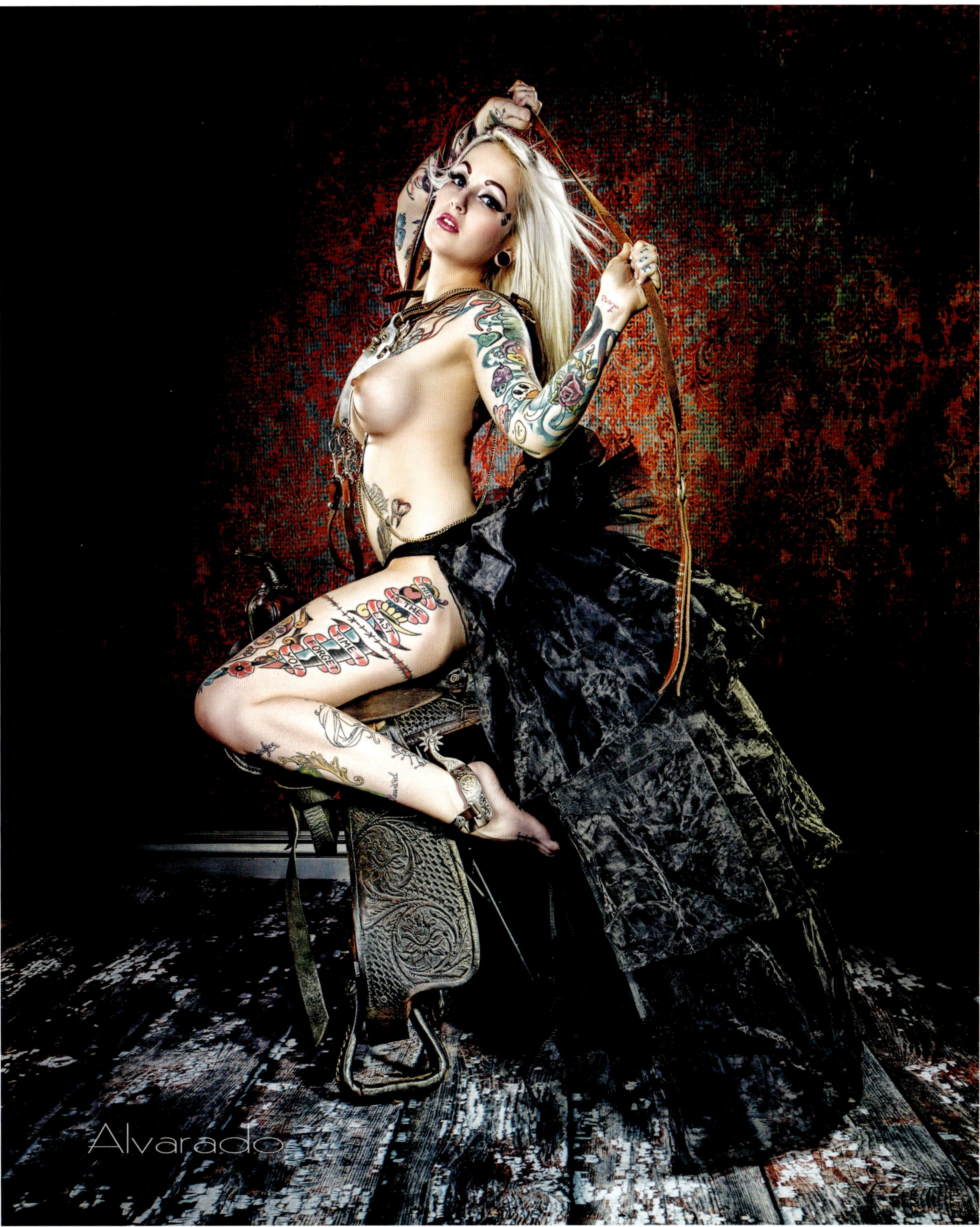
Alvarado

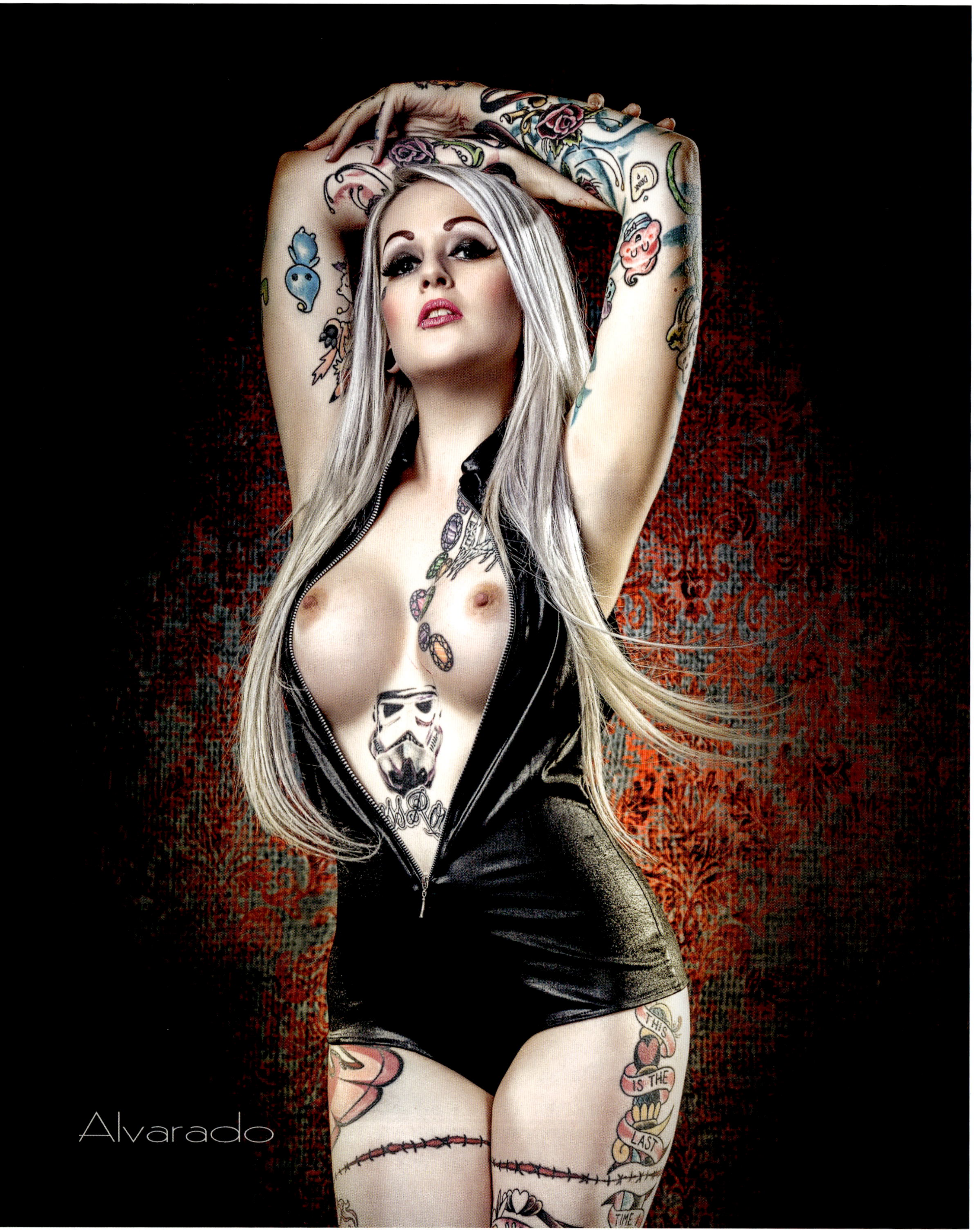
THIS
IS THE
LAST
TIME
Alvarado

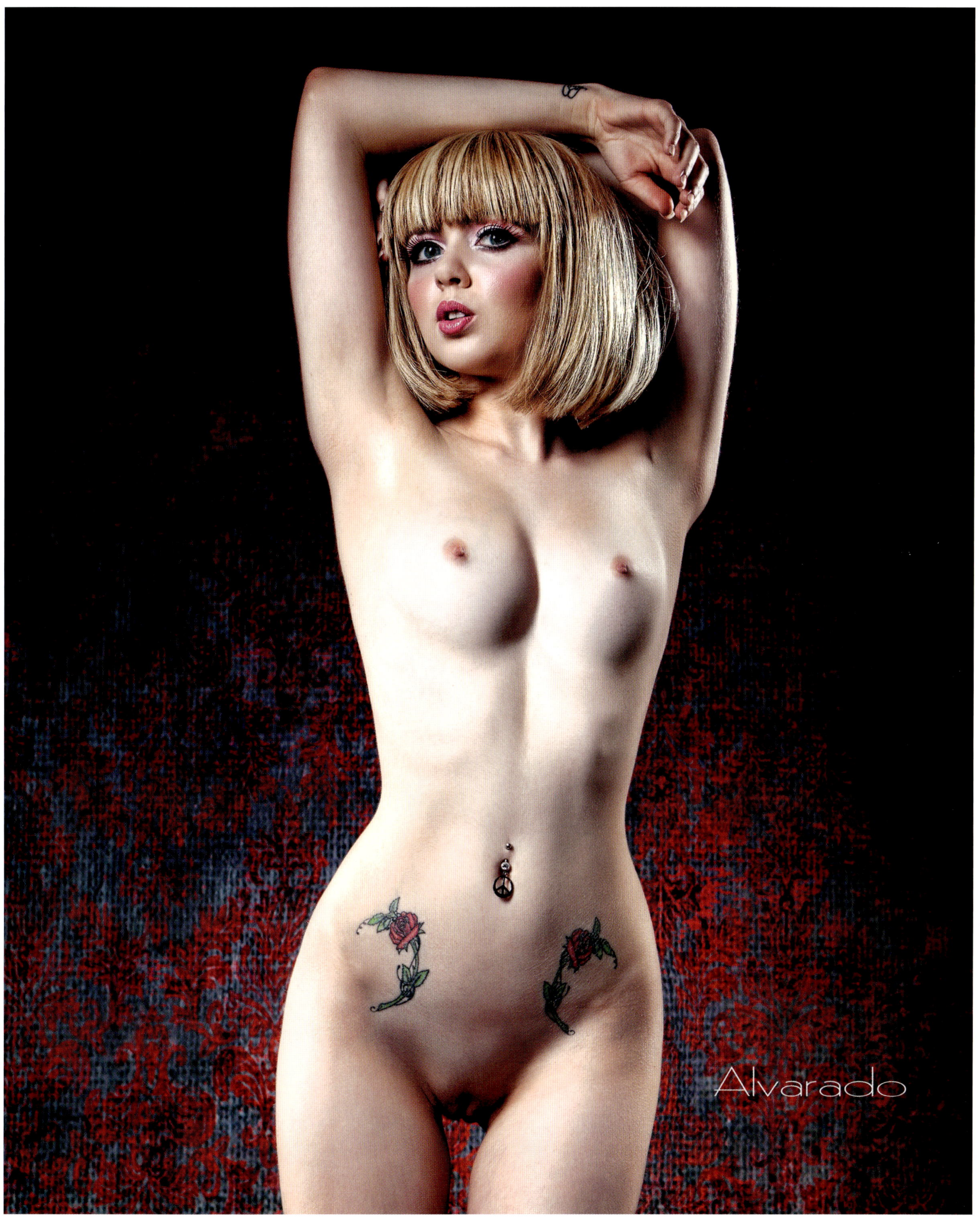
Alvarado

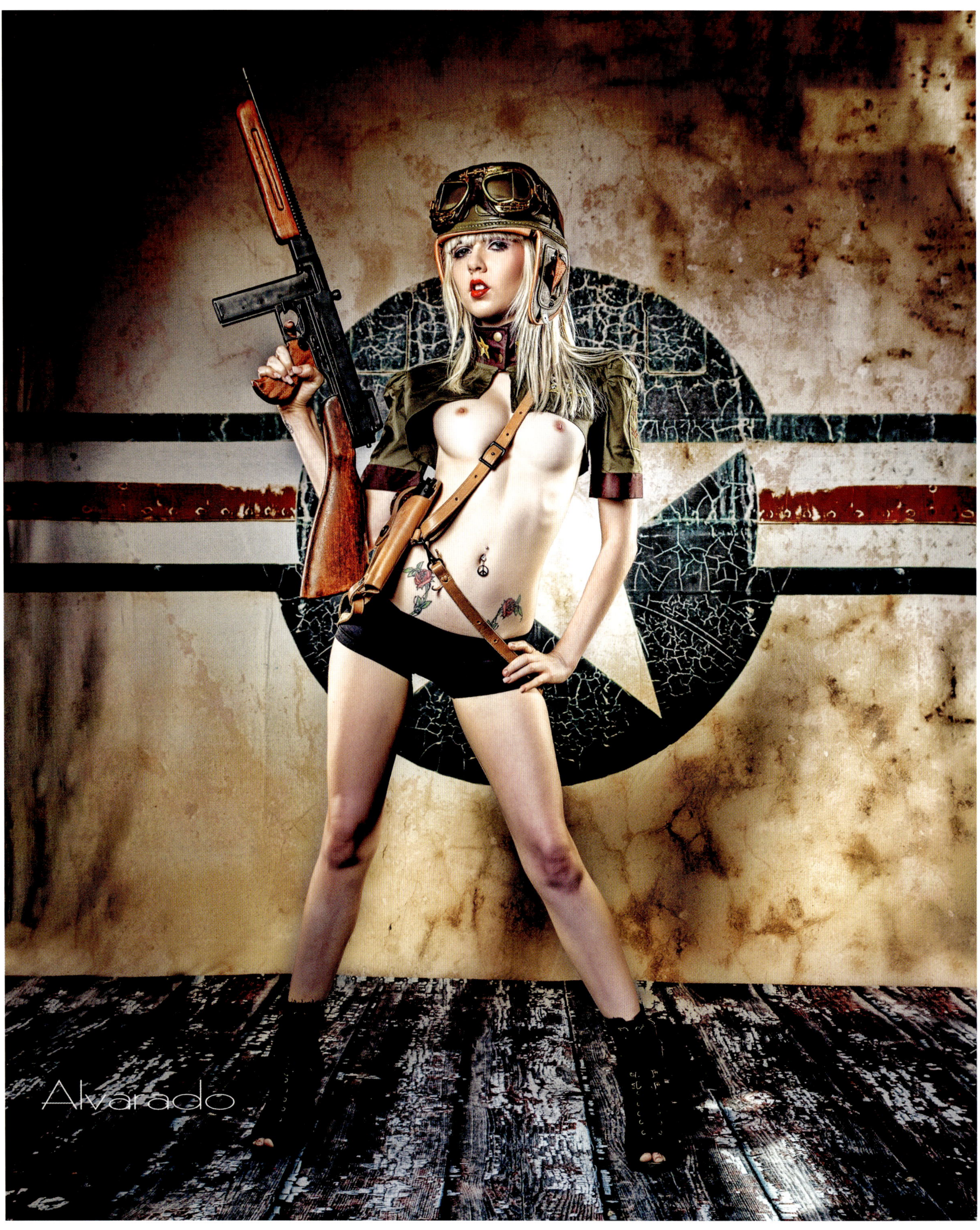
Alvarado

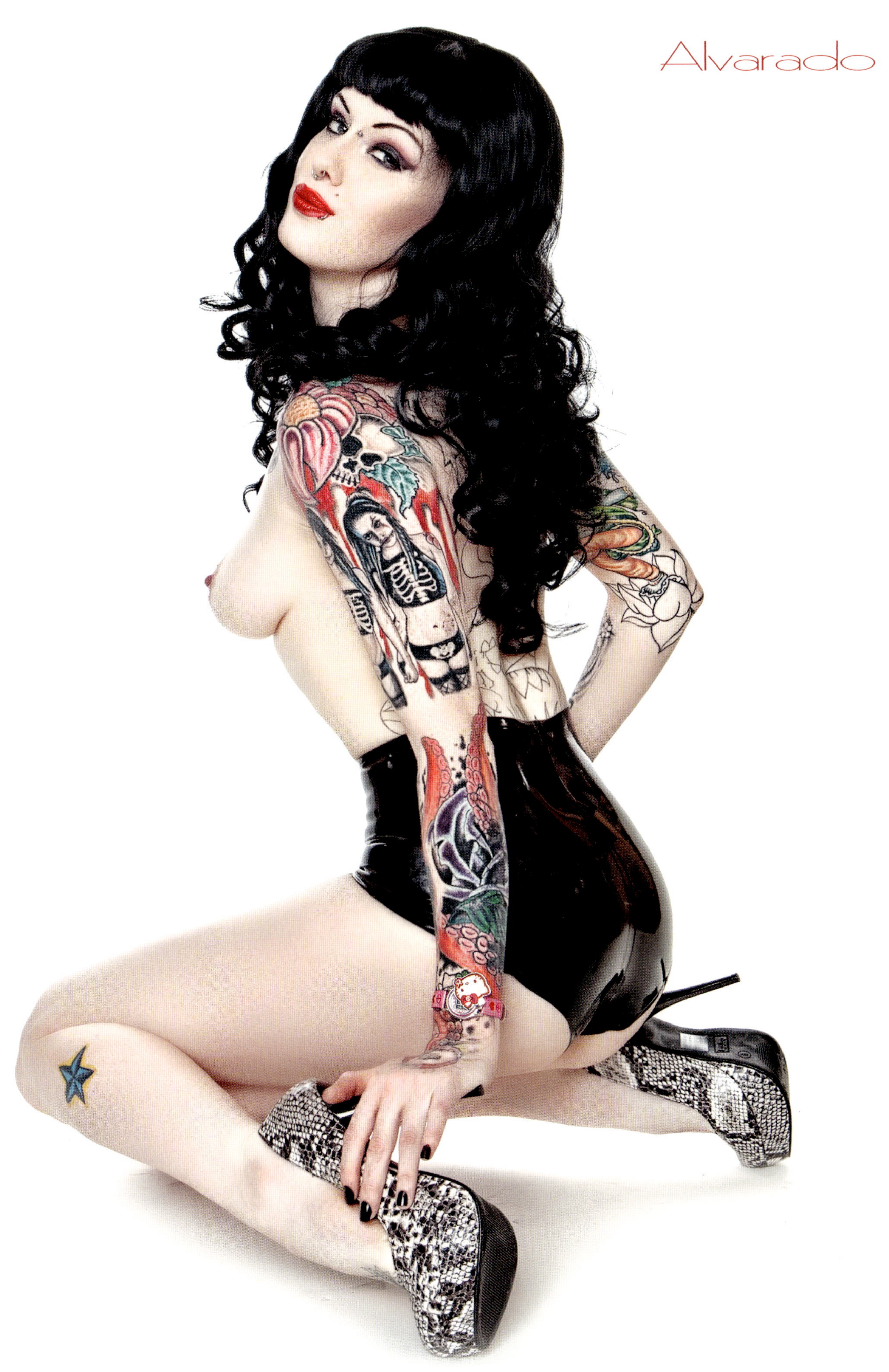

Alvarado

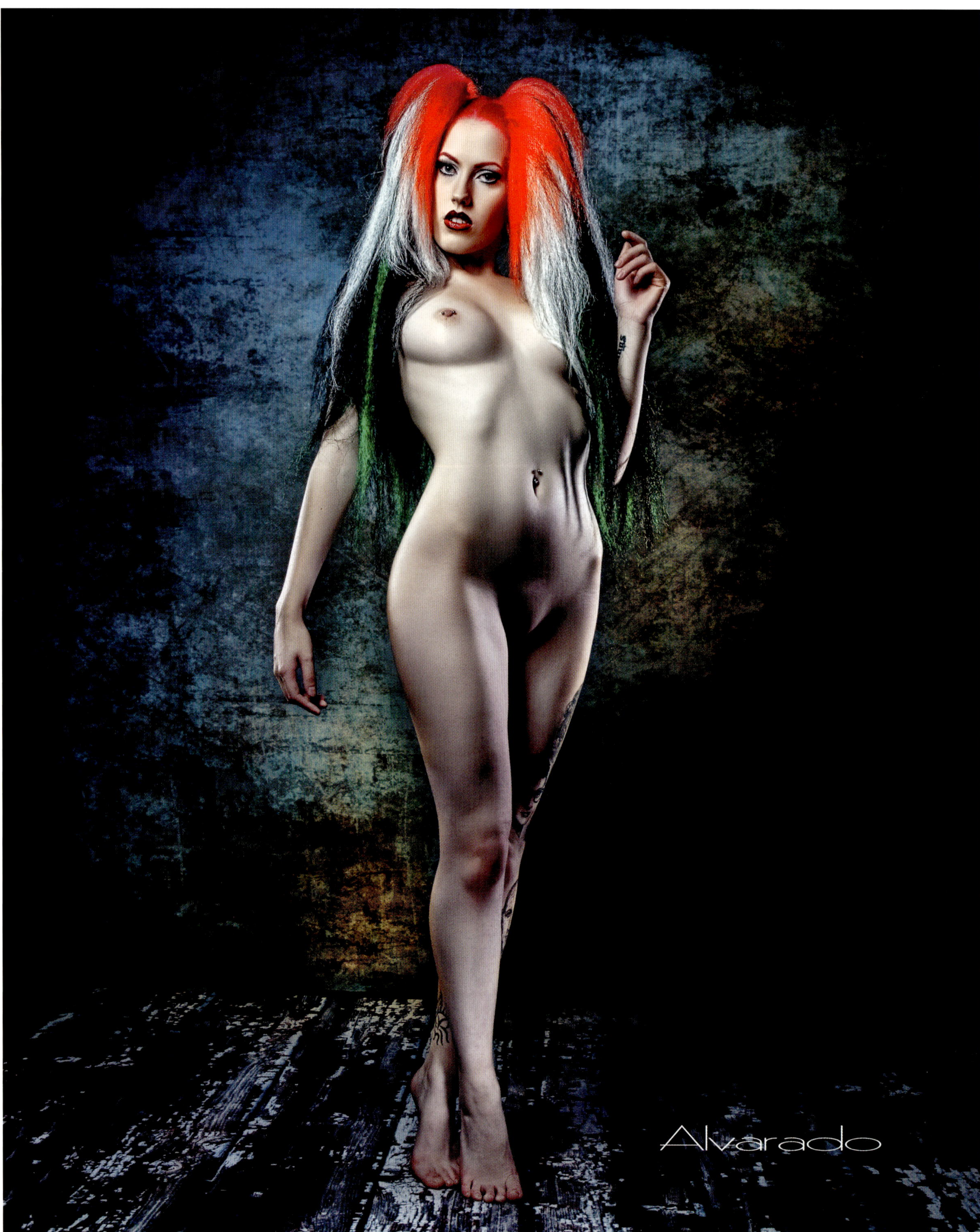
Alvarado

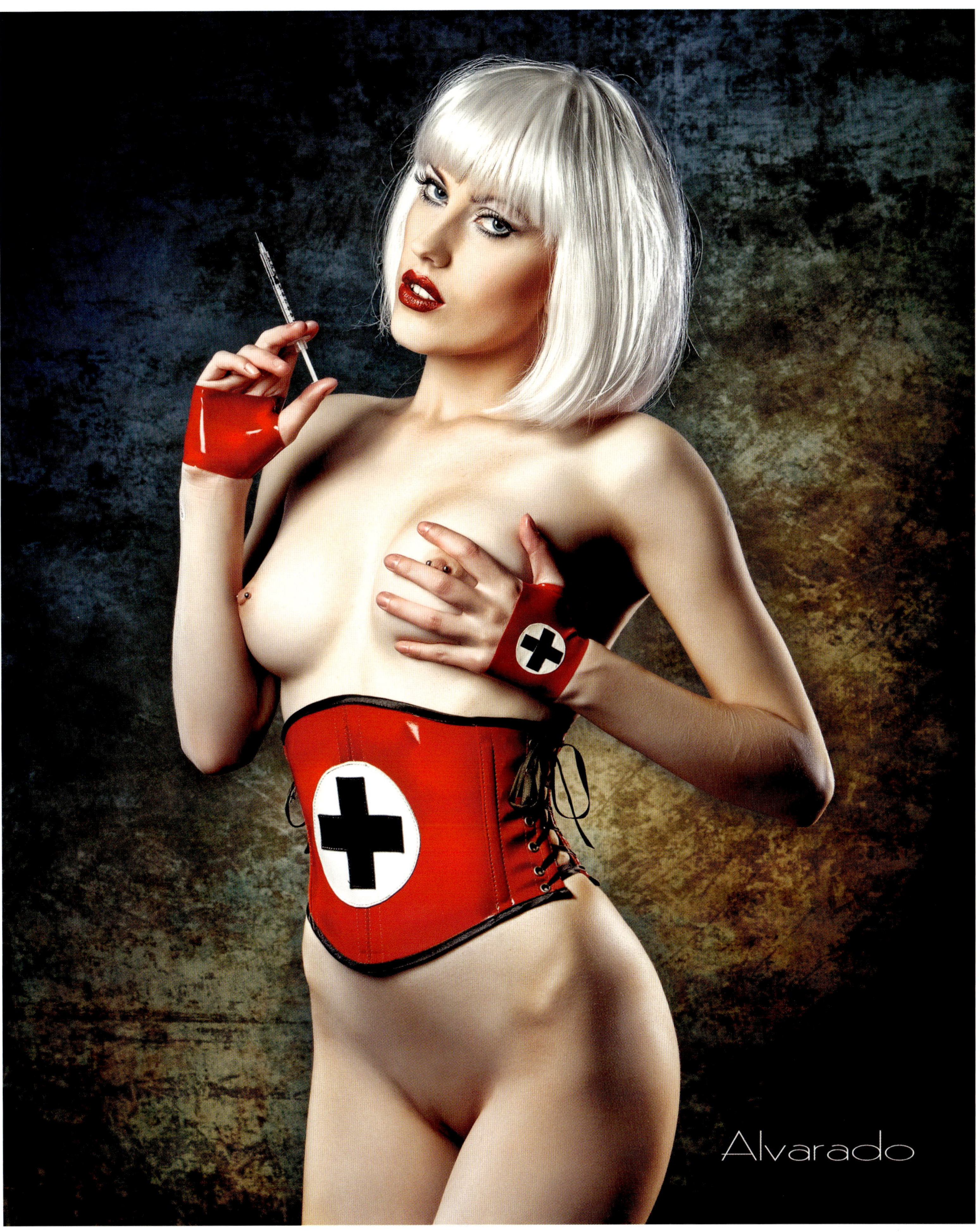
Alvarado

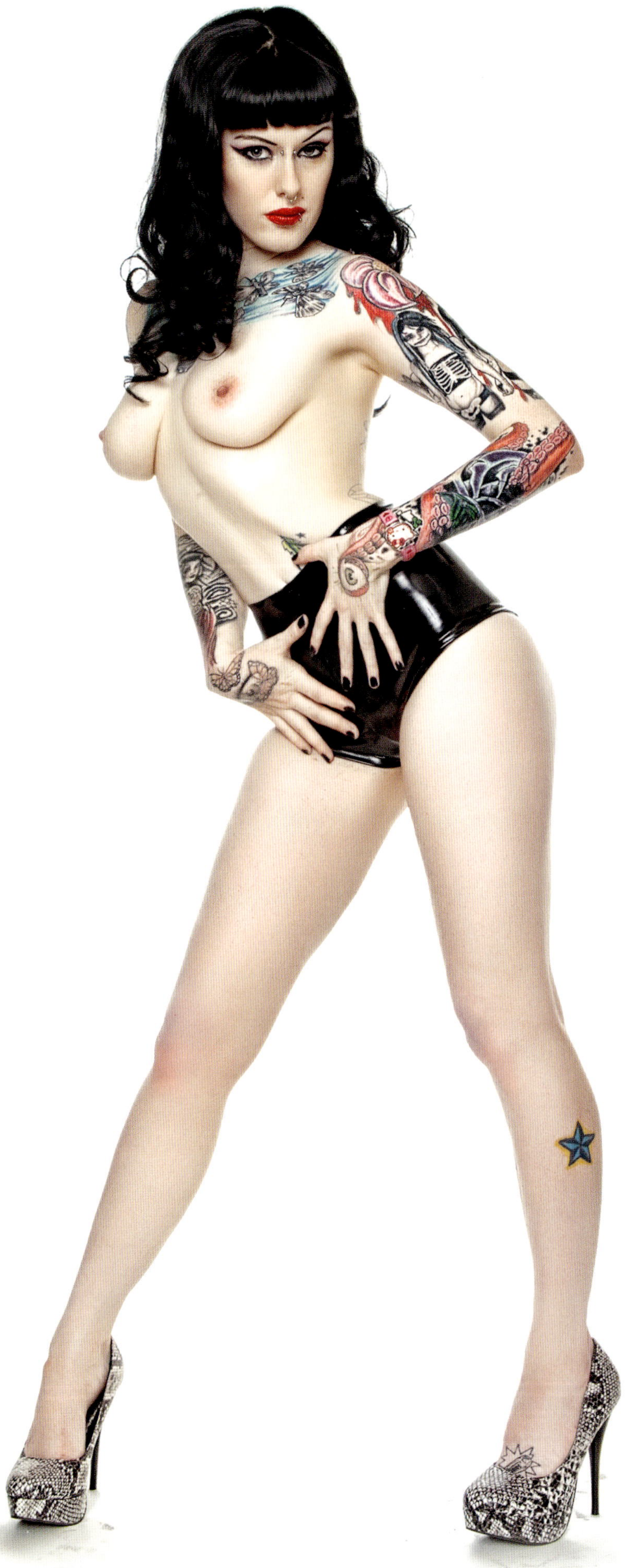

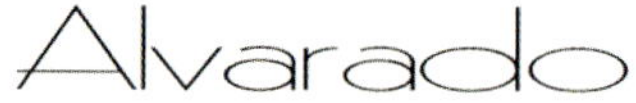
Alvarado

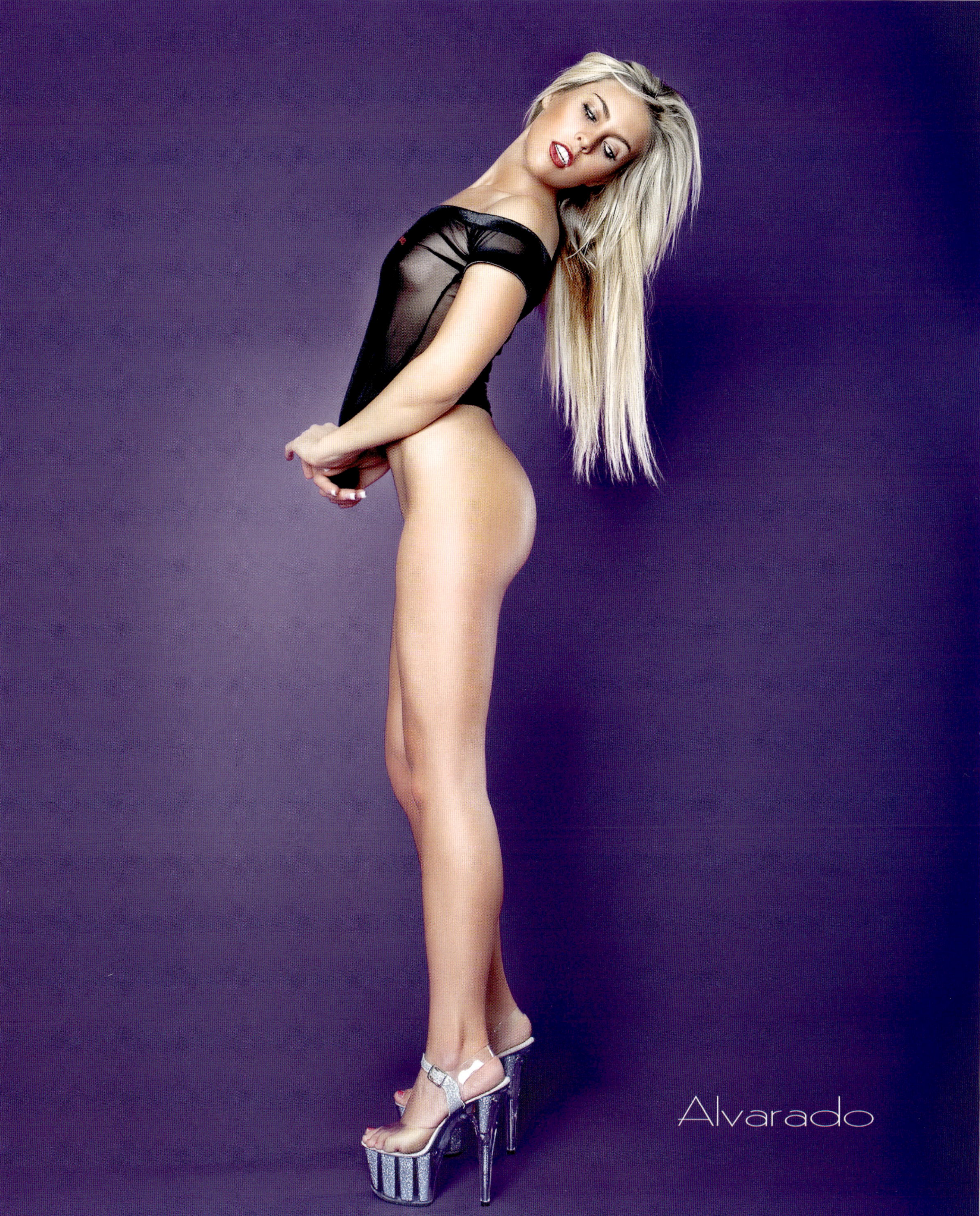
Alvarado

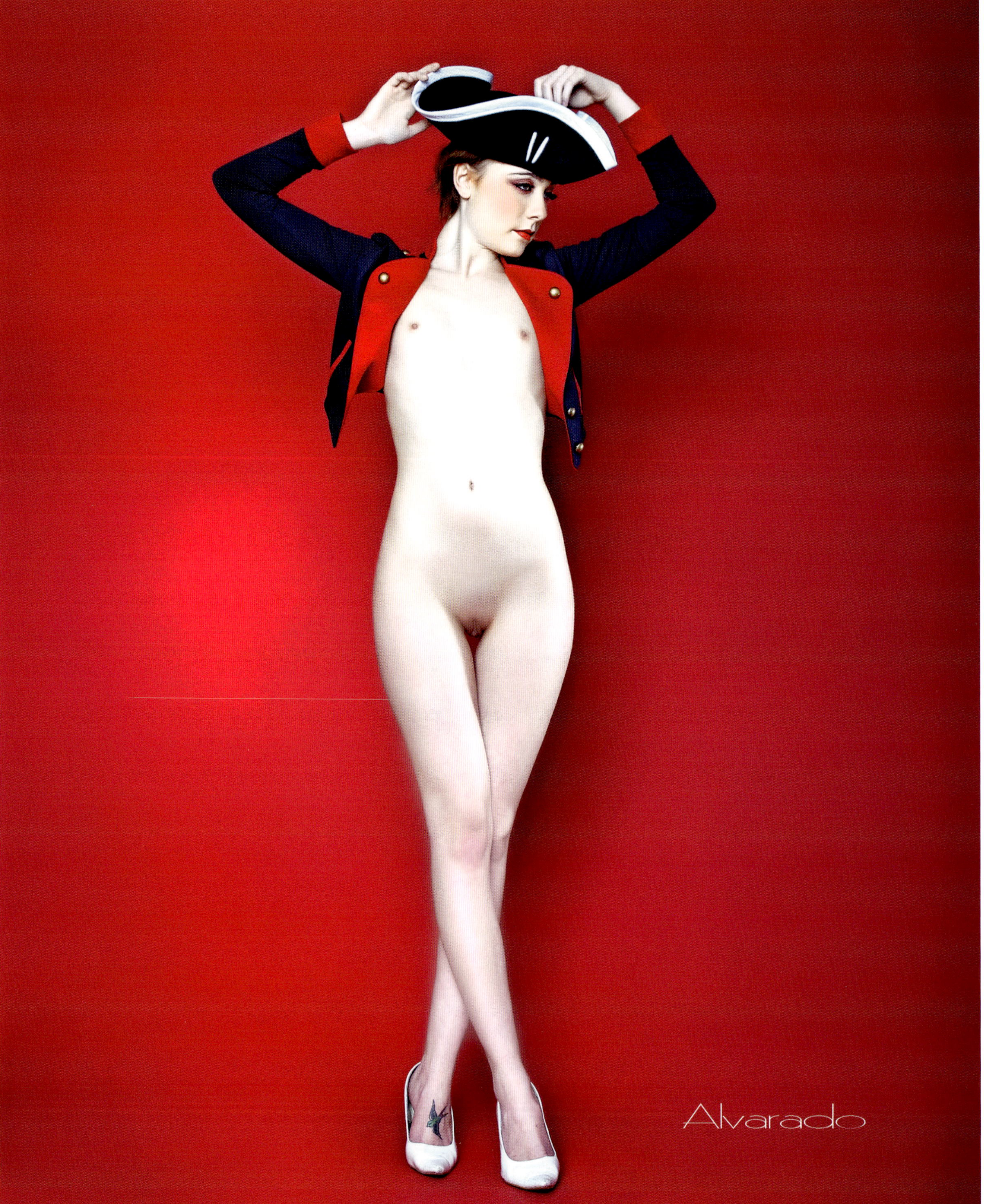
Alvarado

Alvarado

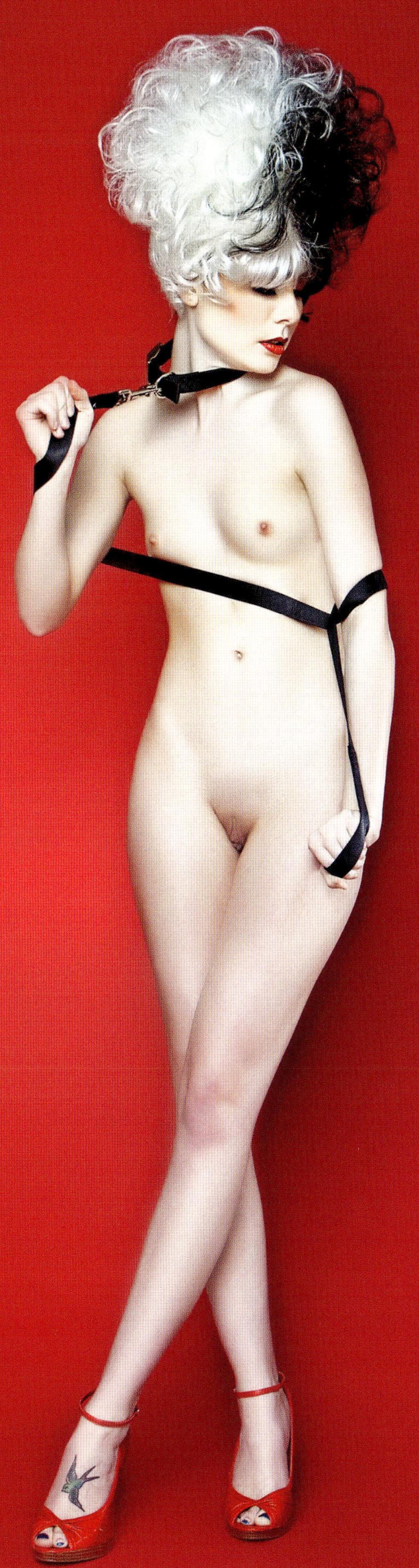

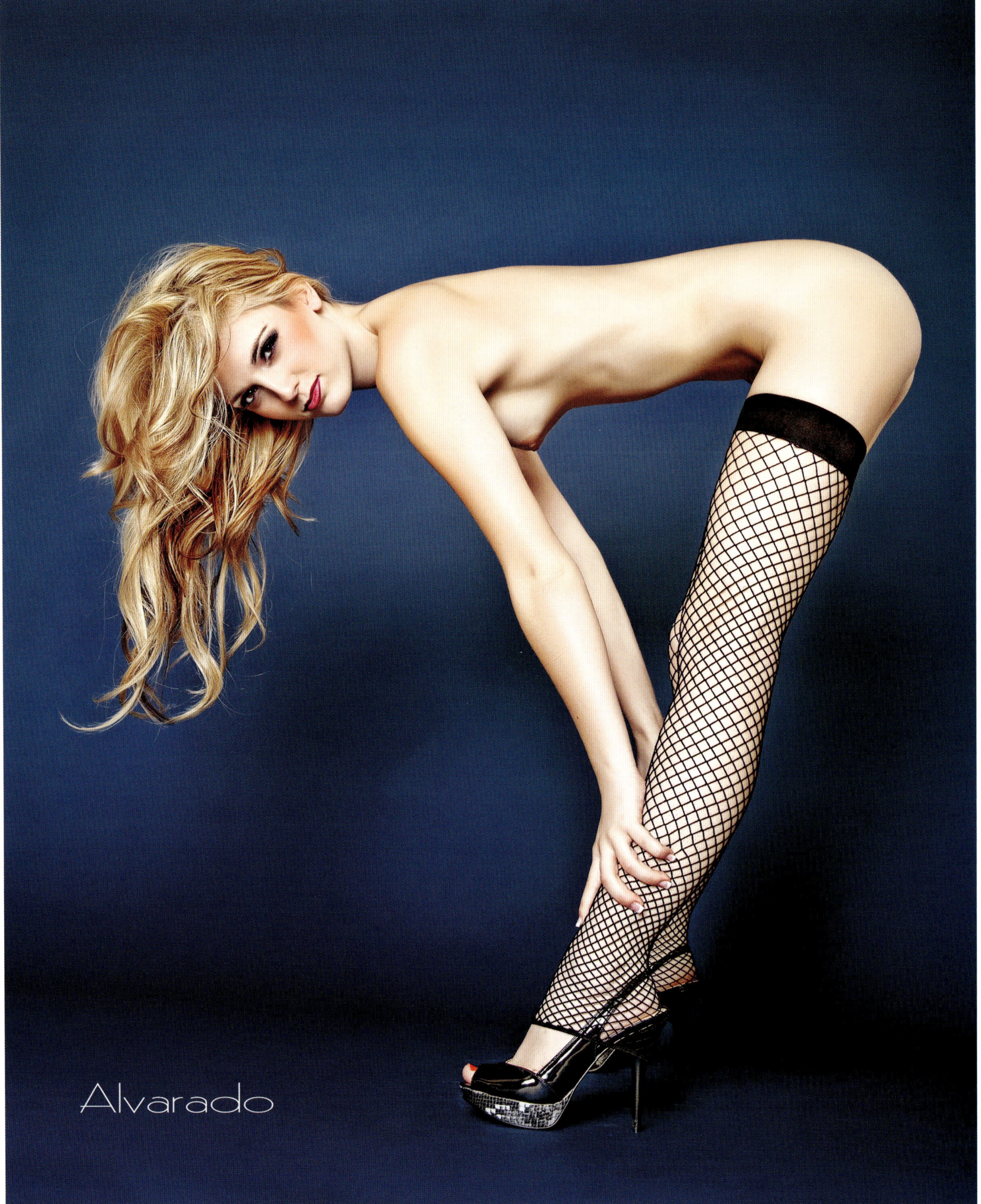
Alvarado

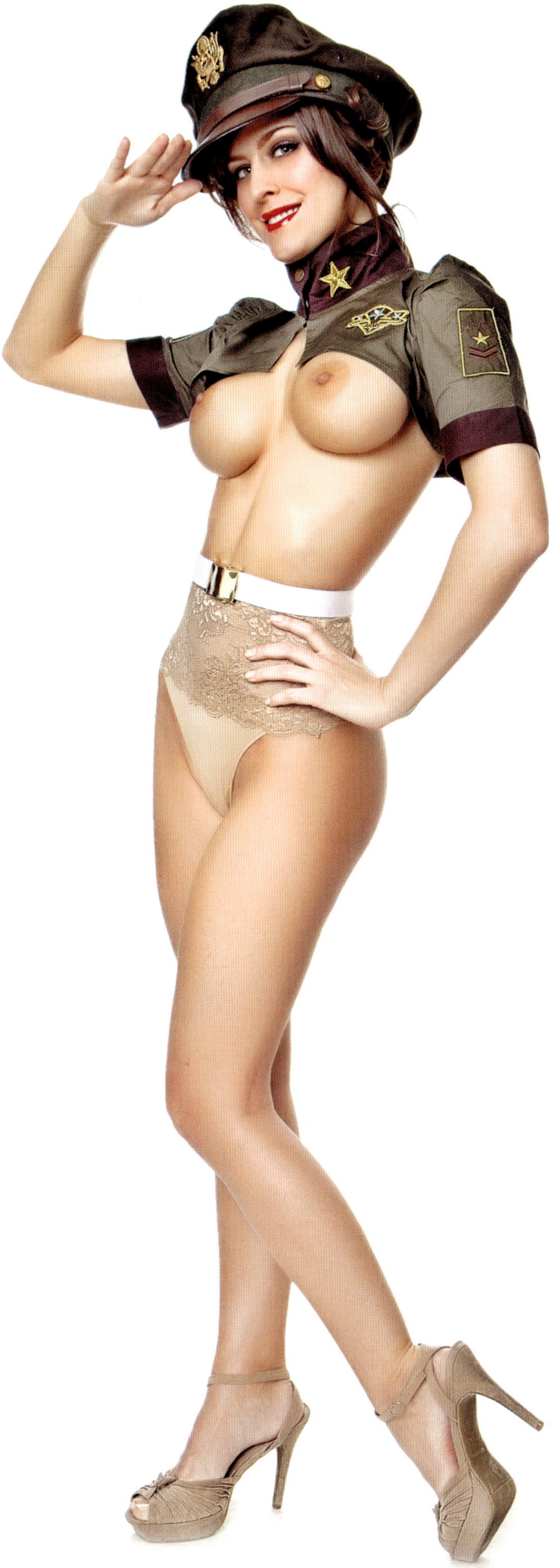

Alvarado

Alvarado

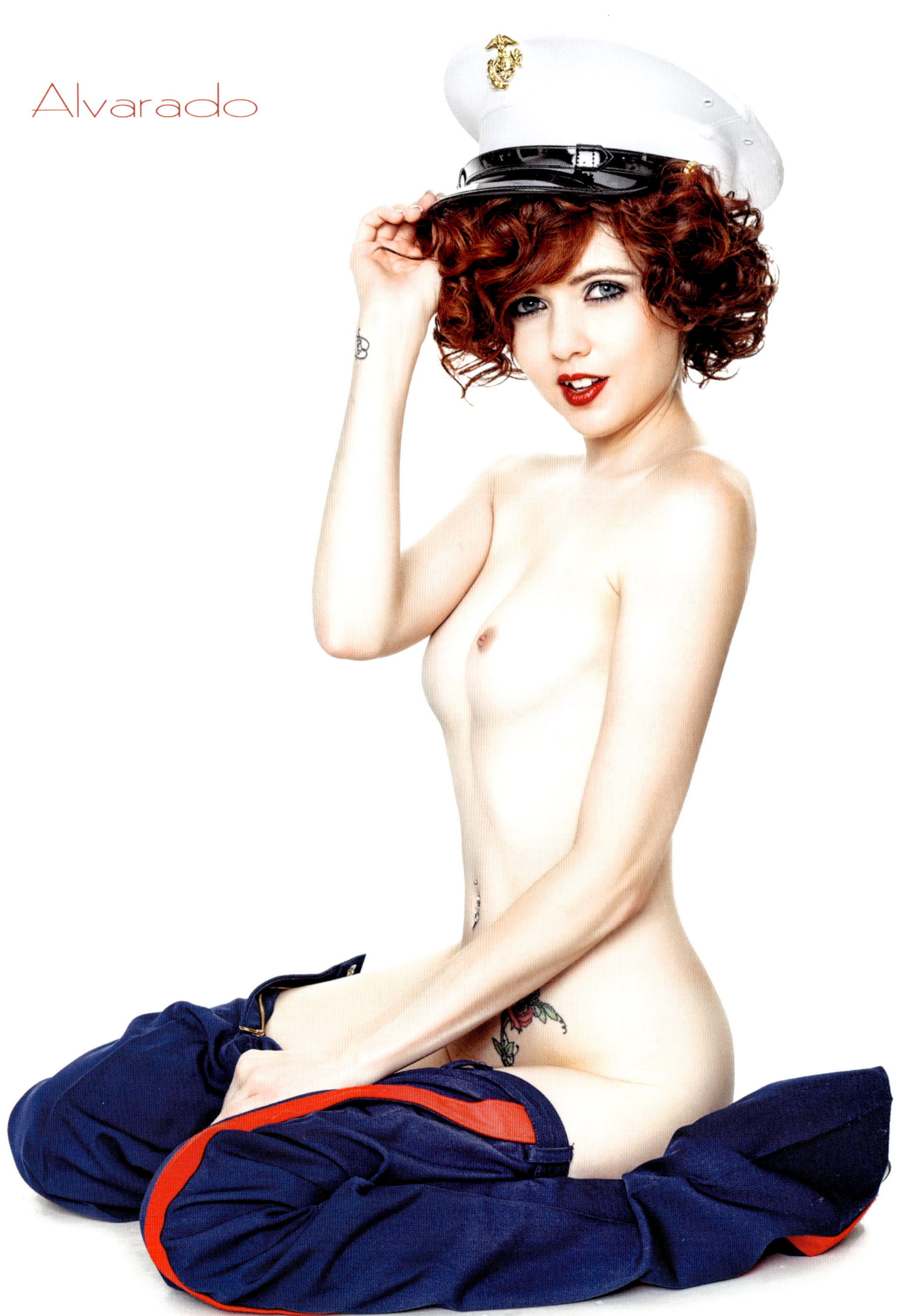

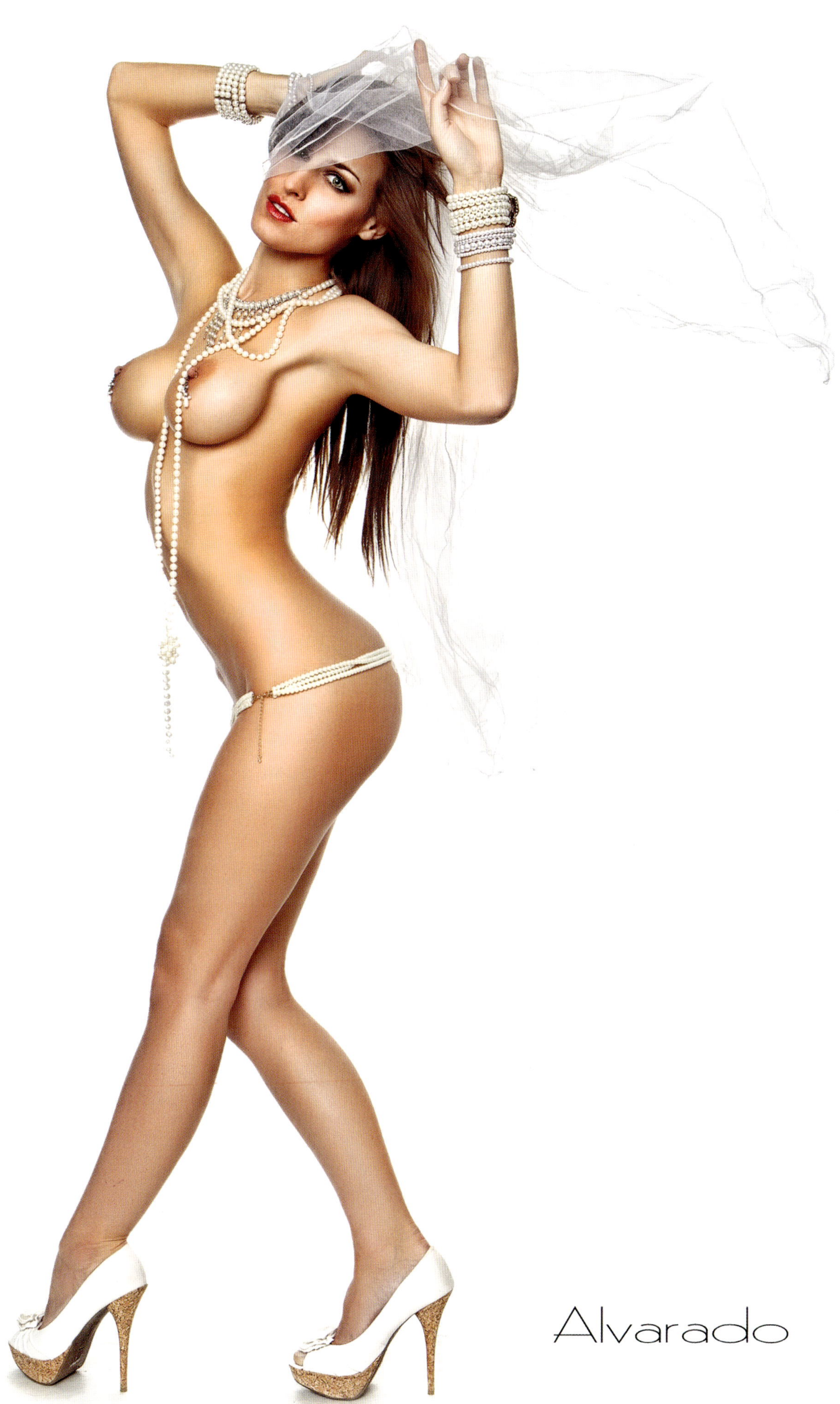

Alvarado

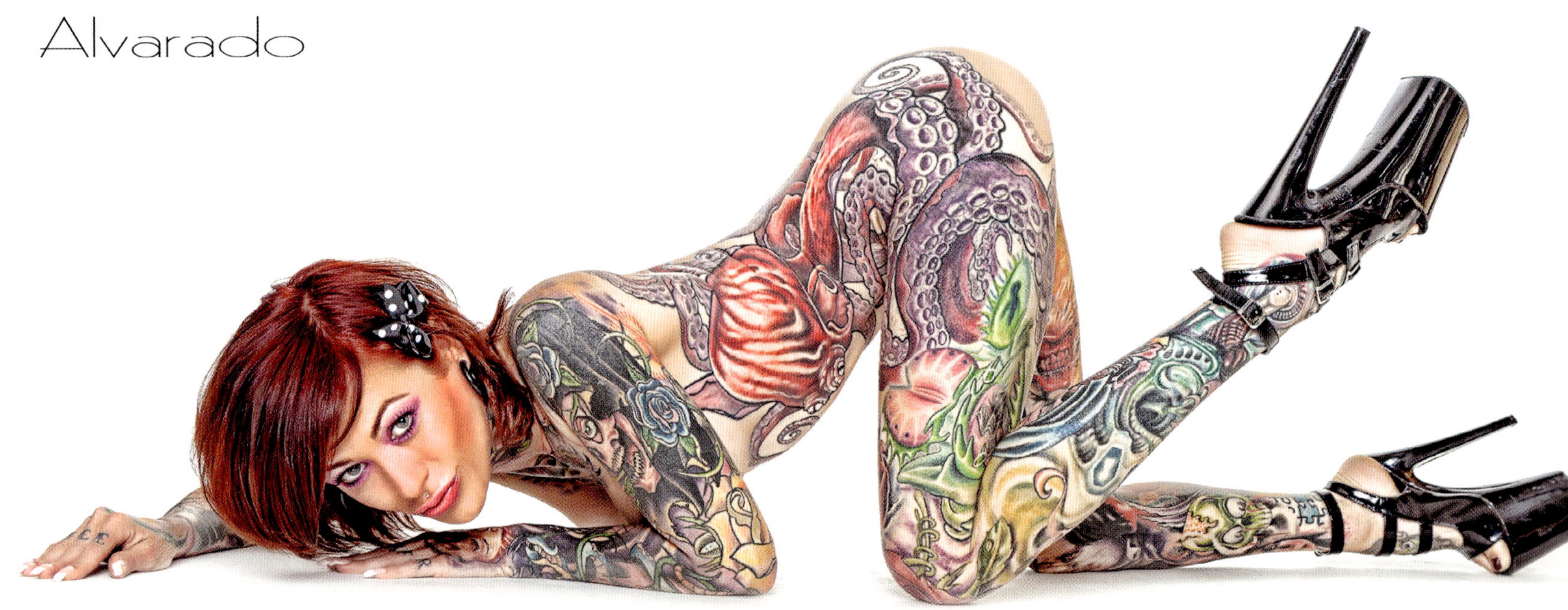

Alvarado

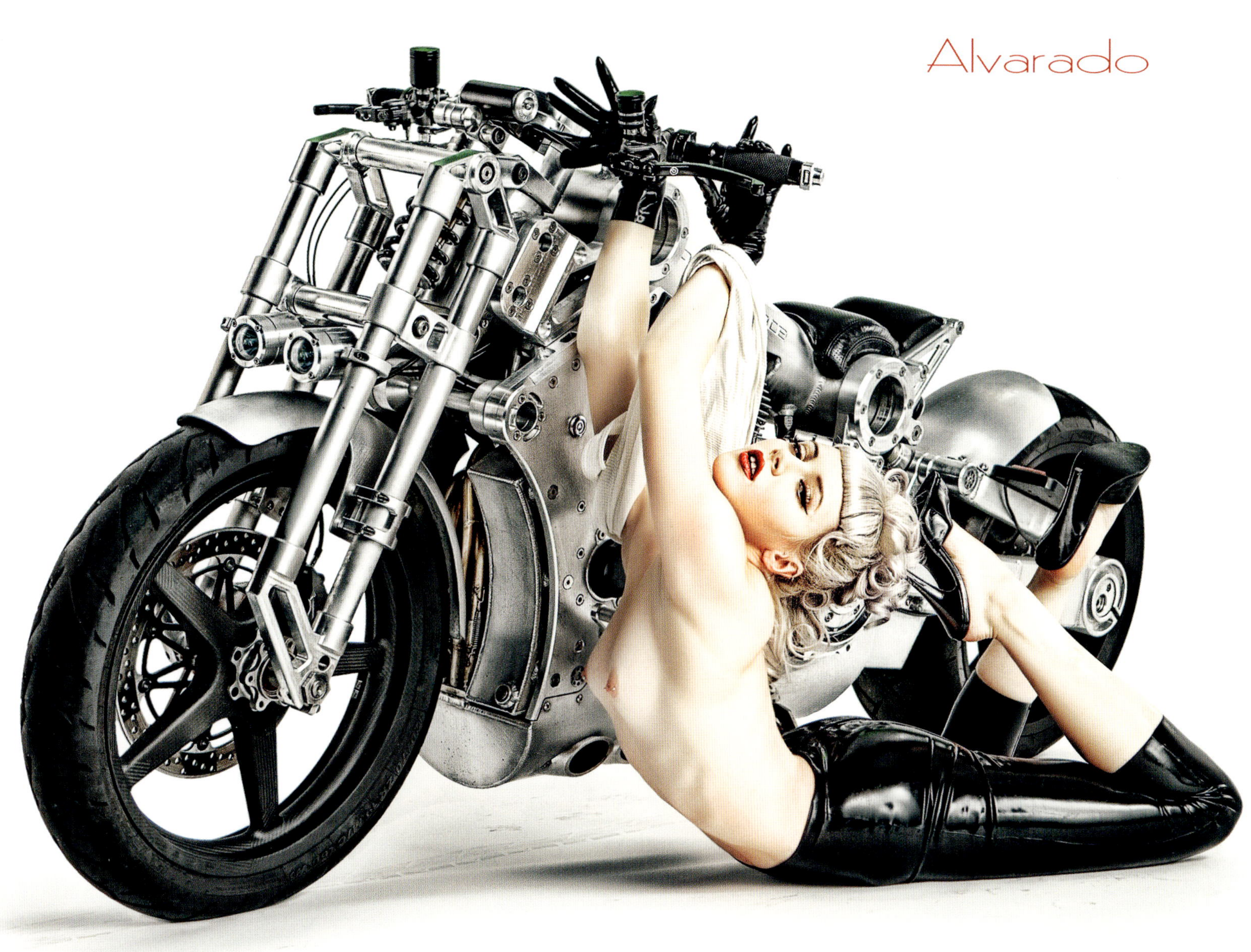

Alvarado

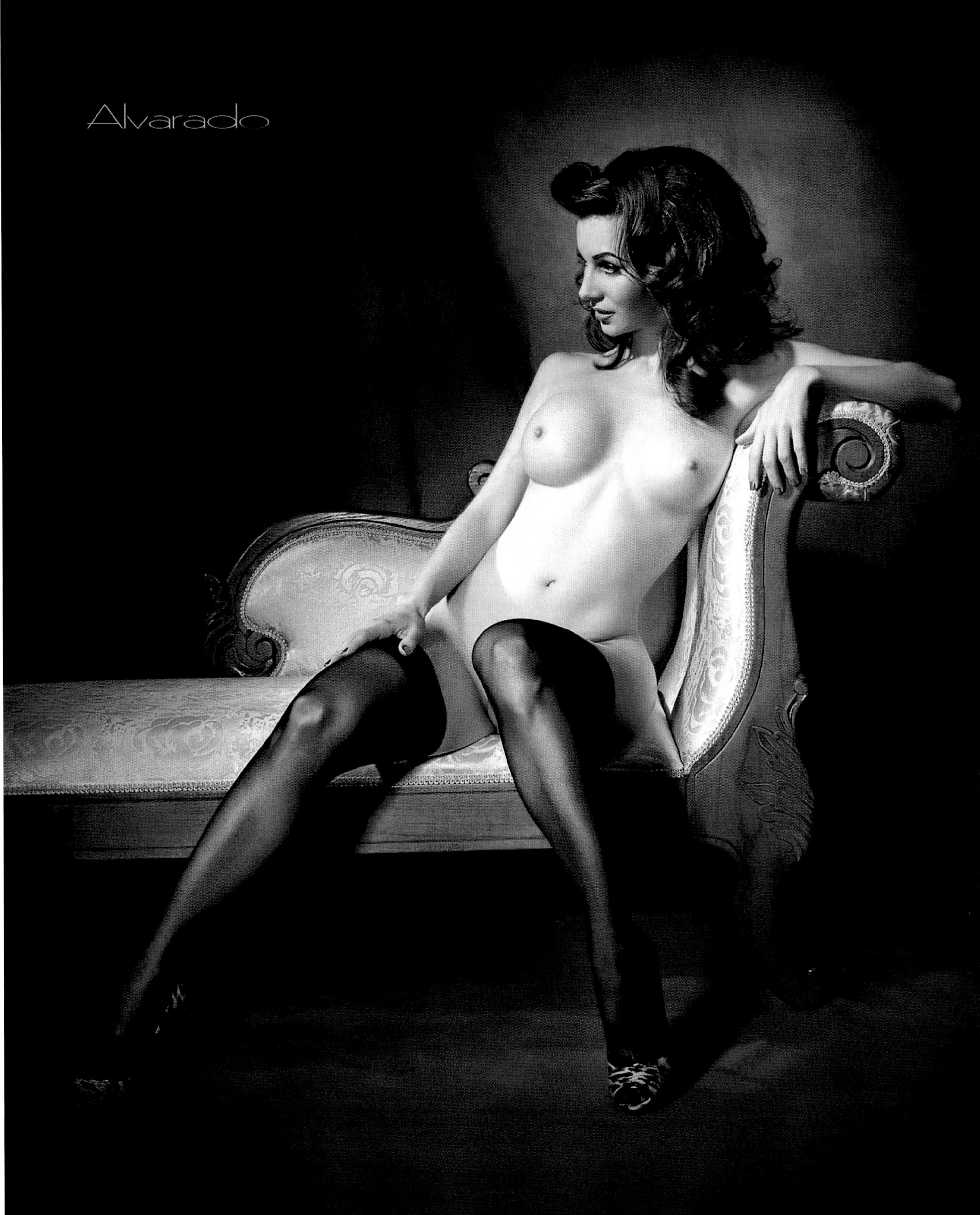
Alvarado

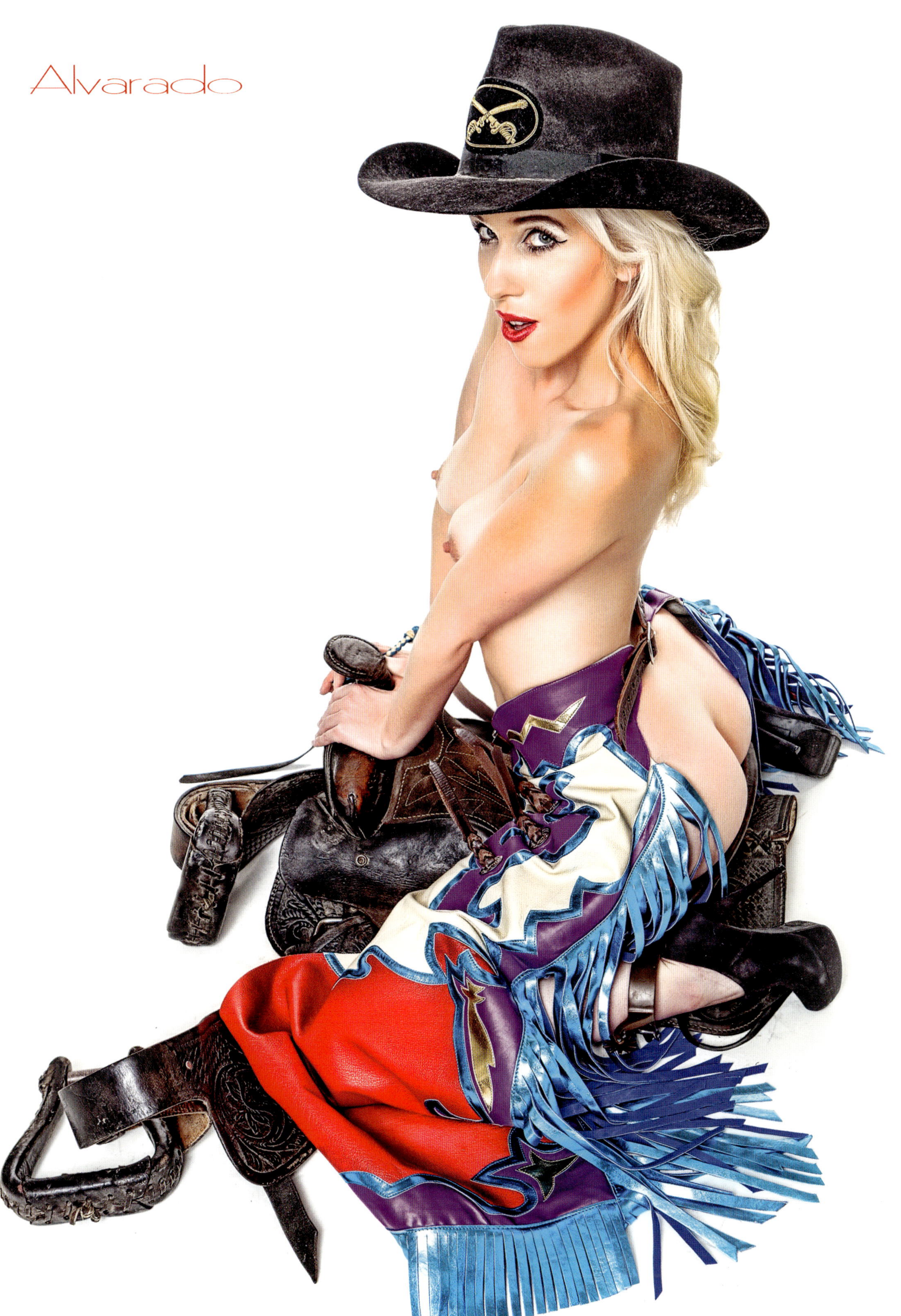
Alvarado

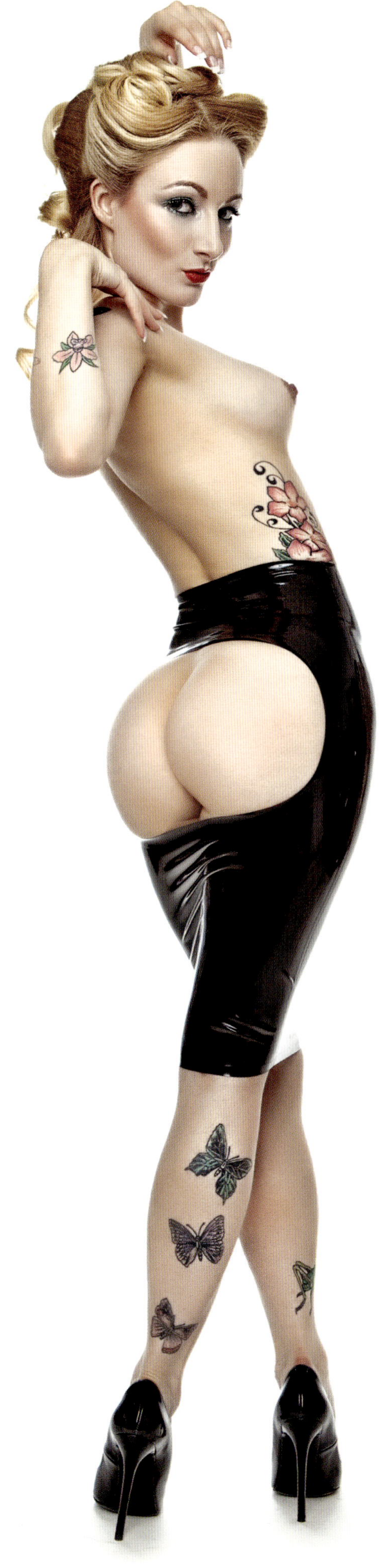

Alvarado

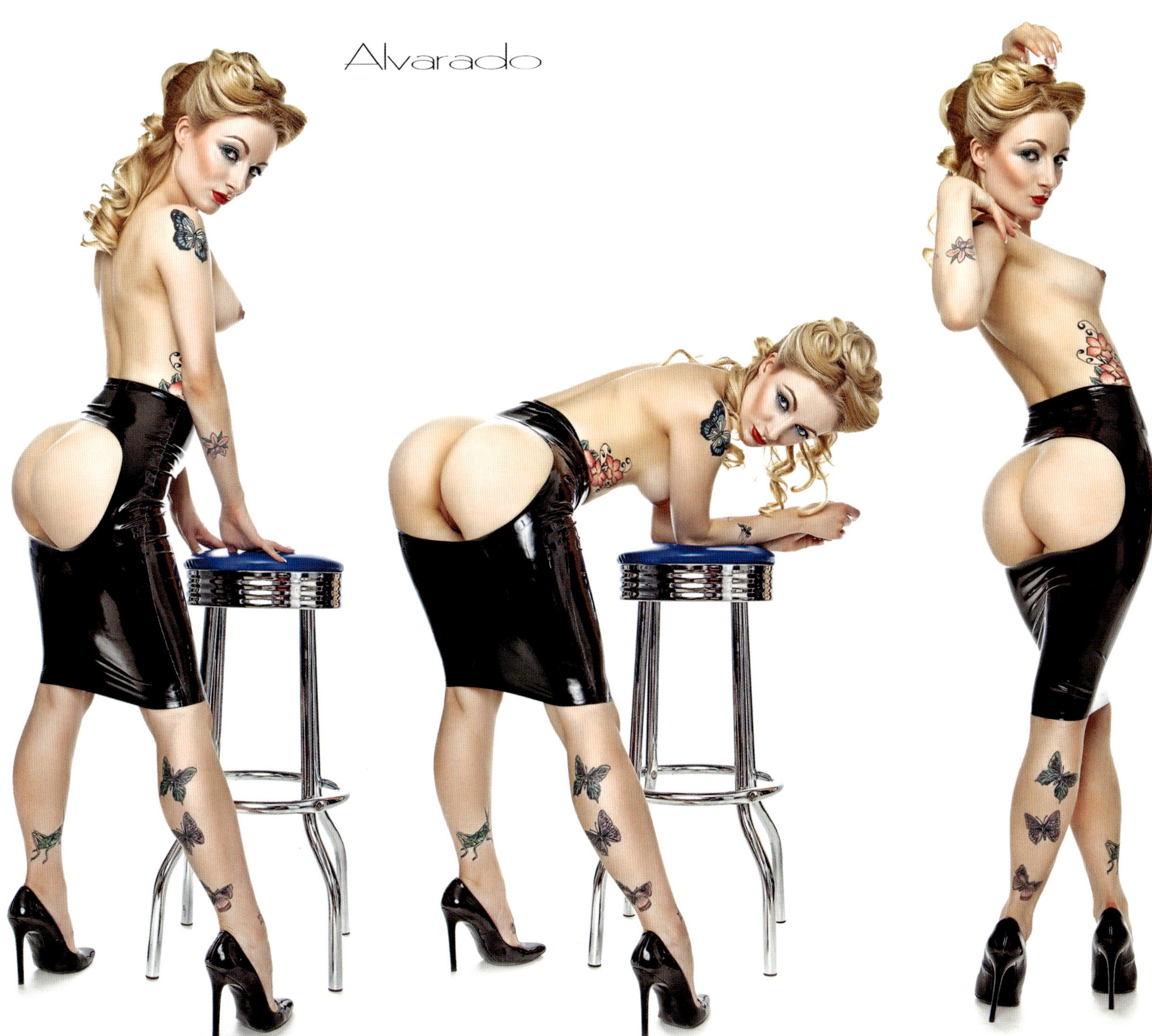

Alvarado

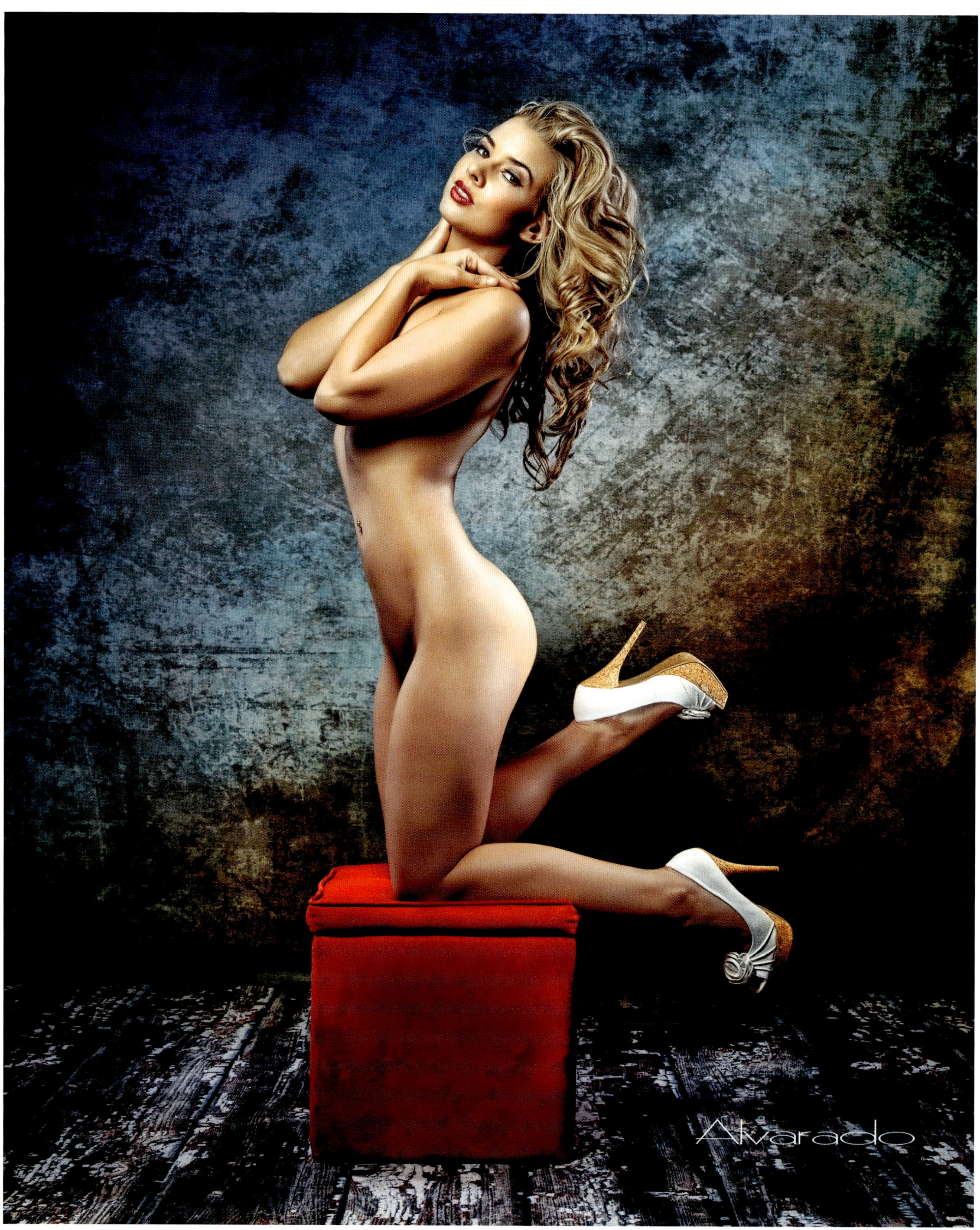
Alvarado

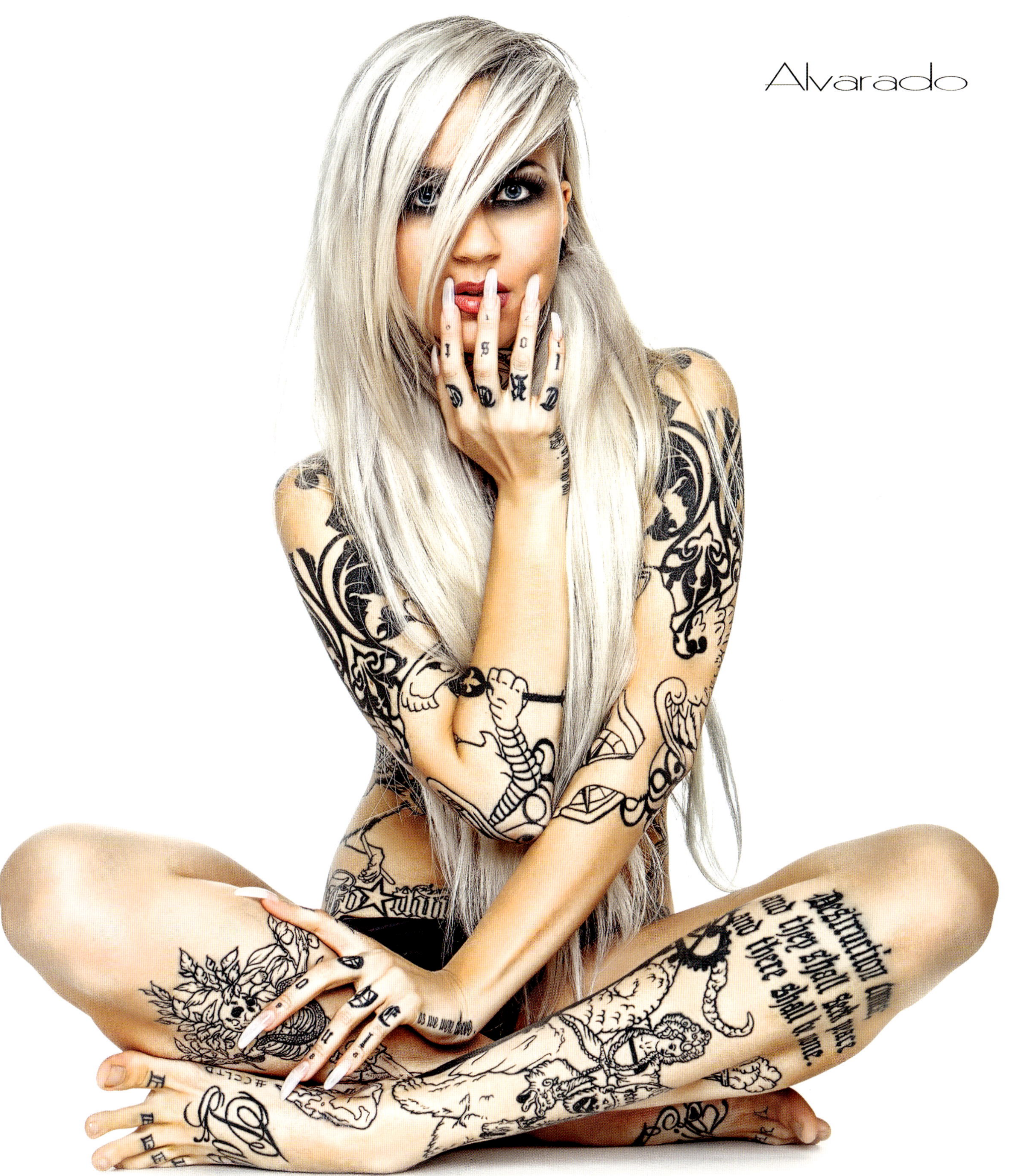

Alvarado

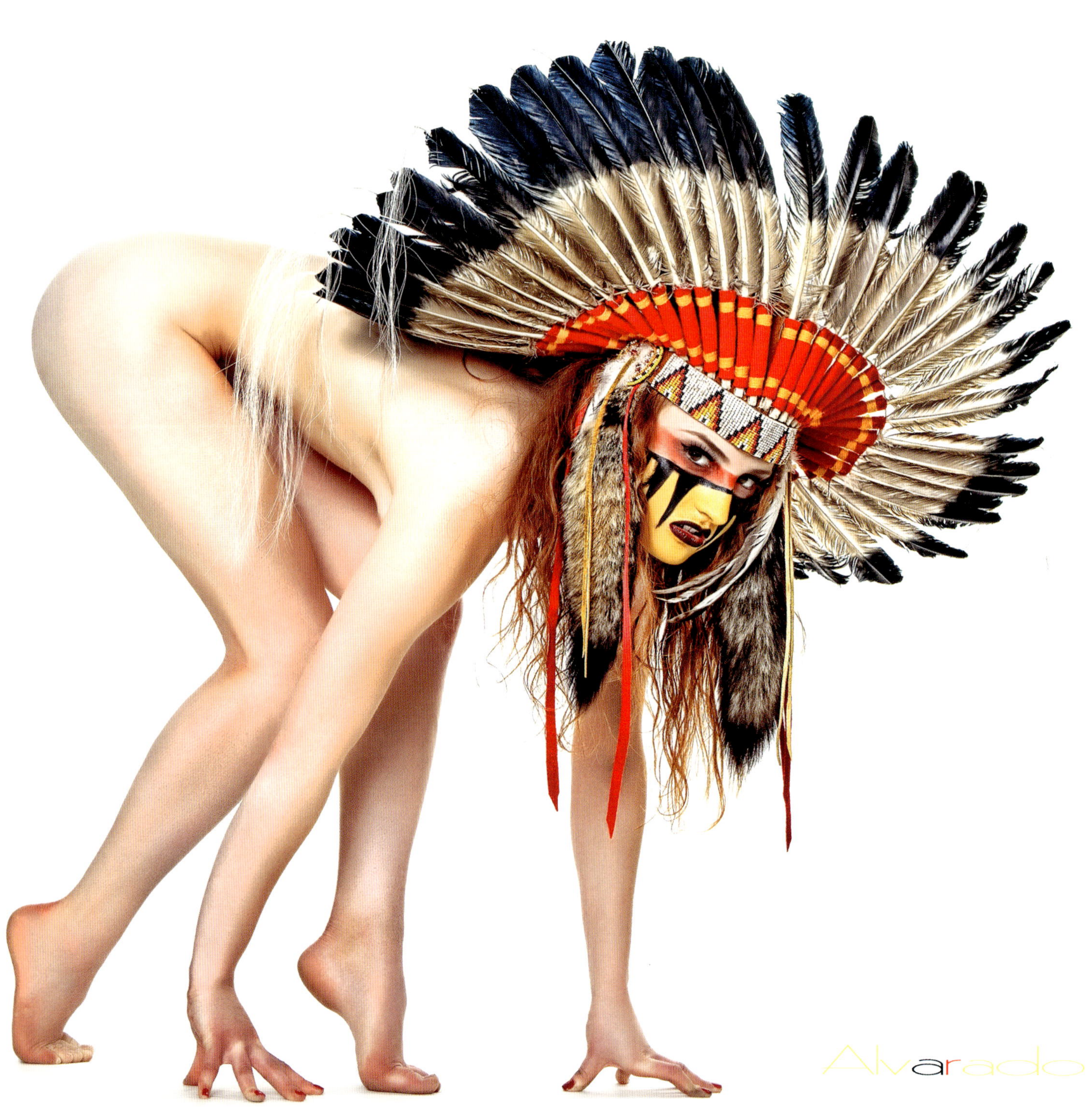
Alvarado

Alvarado

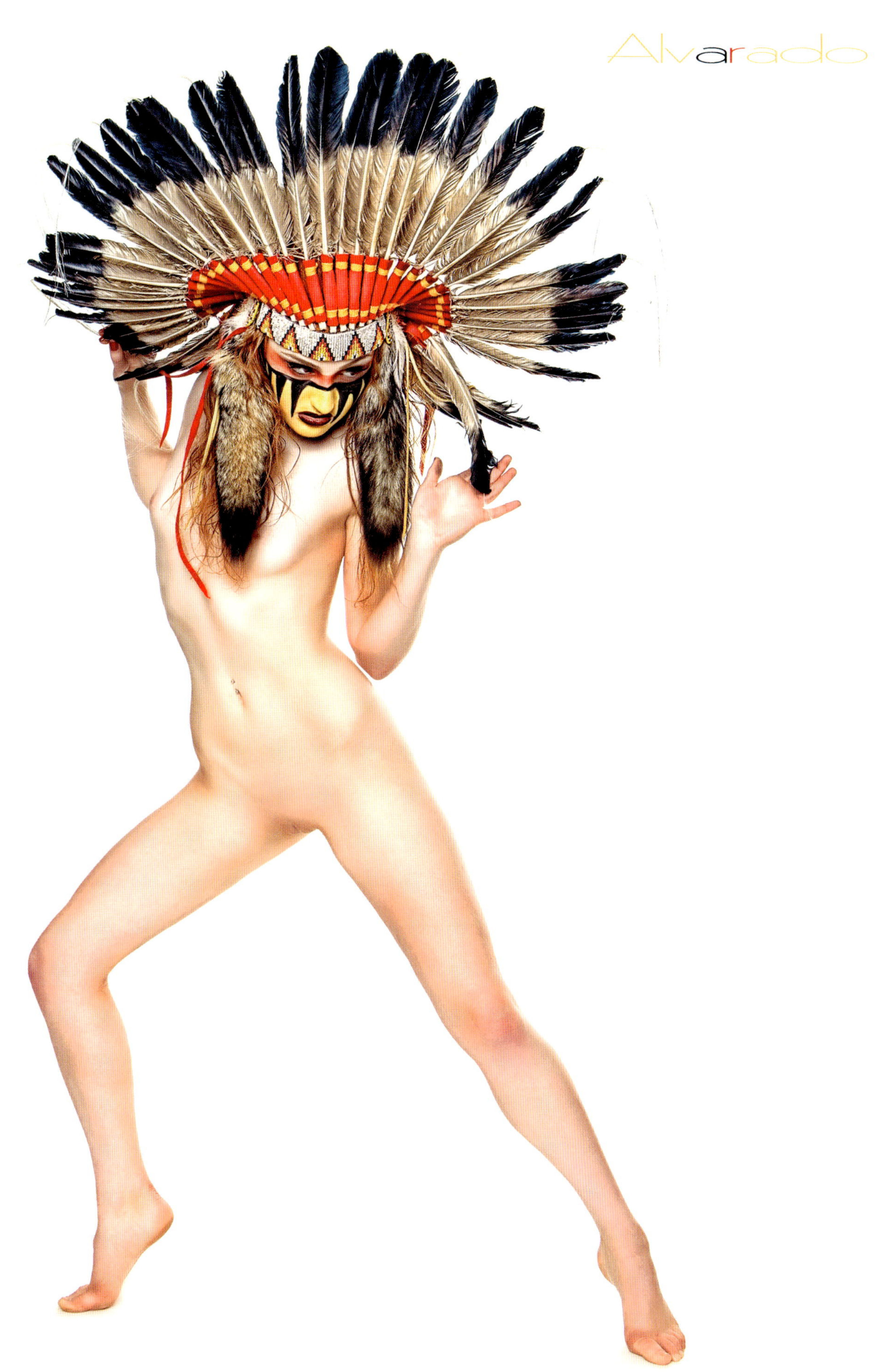

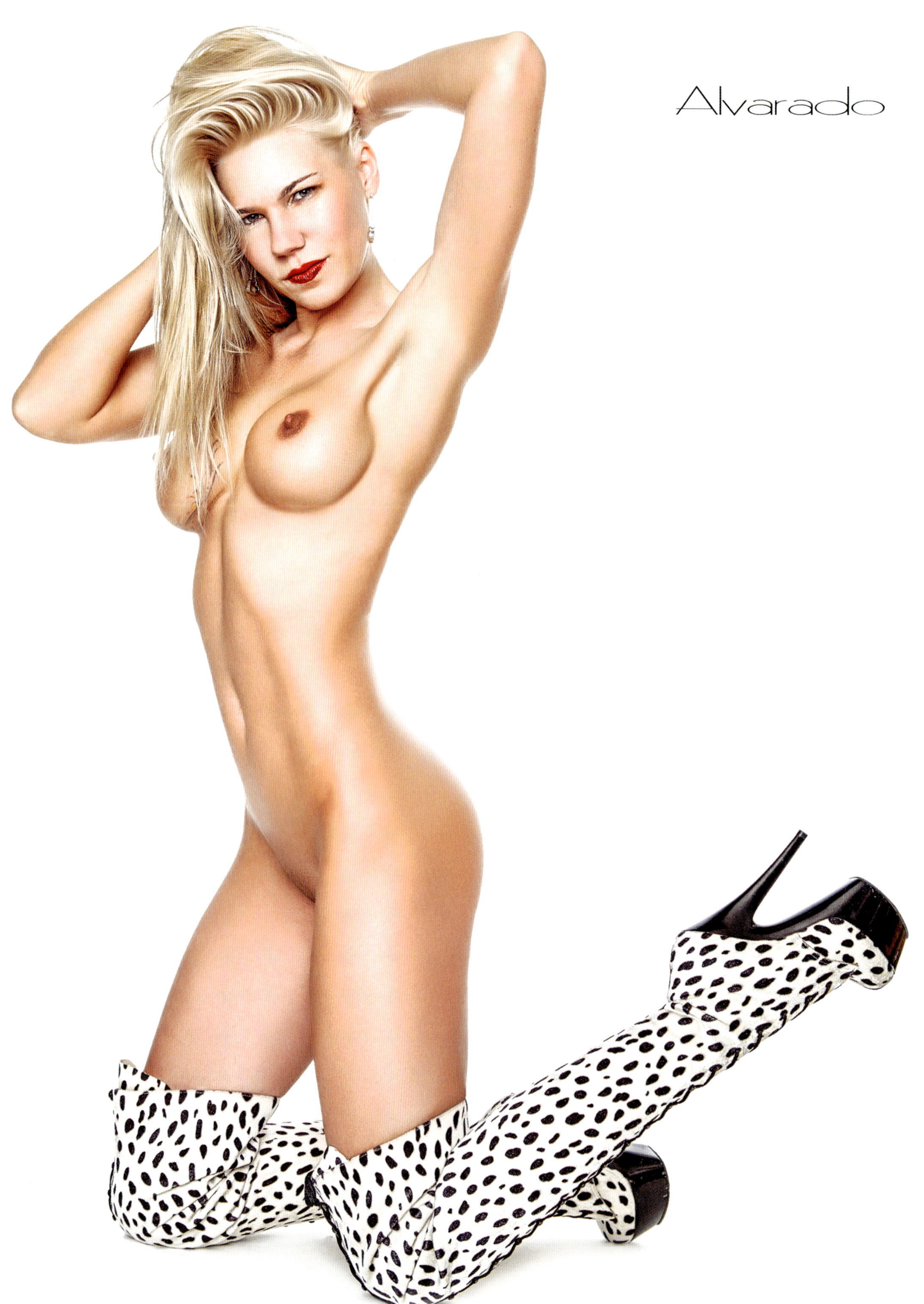
Alvarado

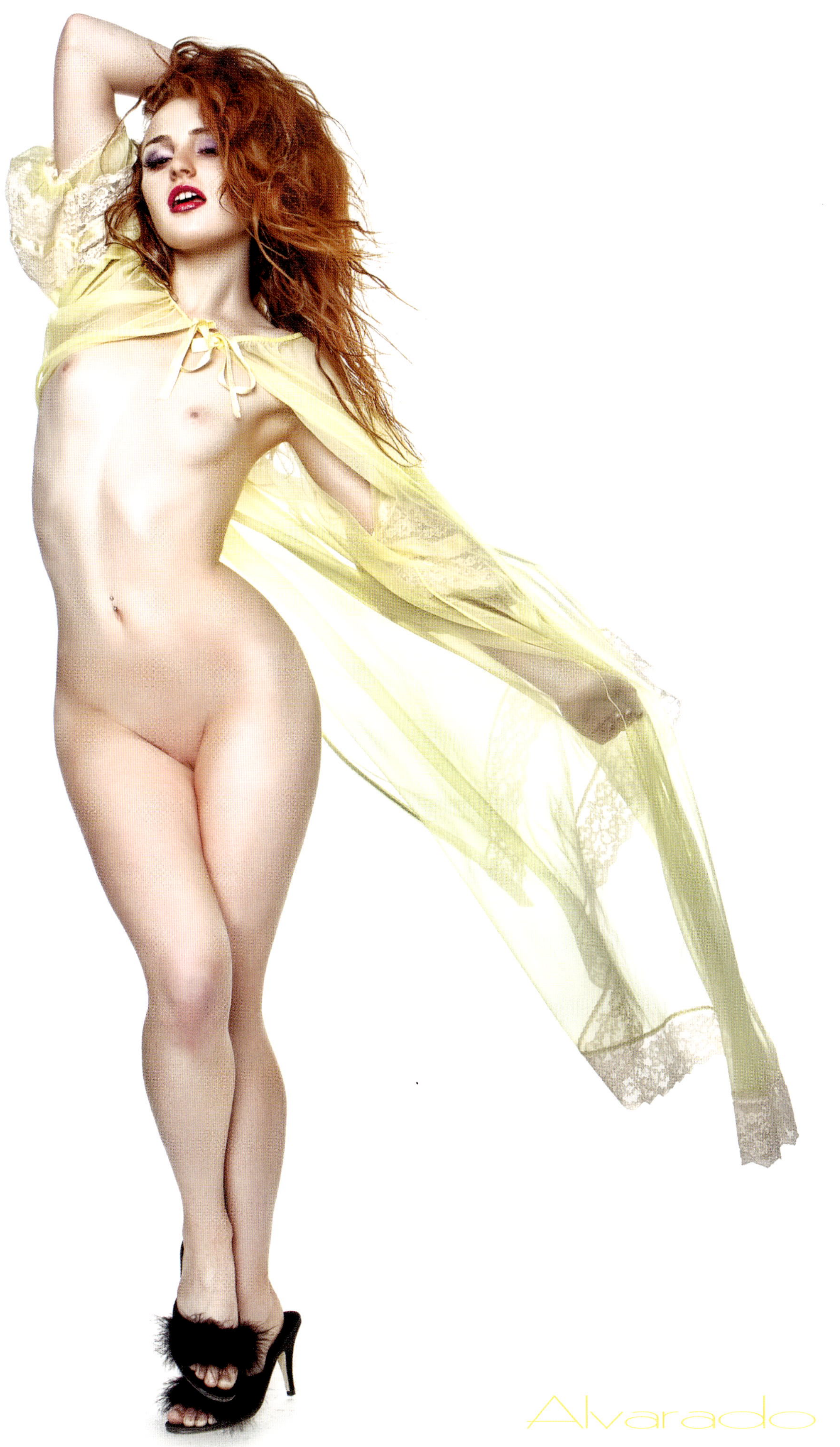
Alvarado

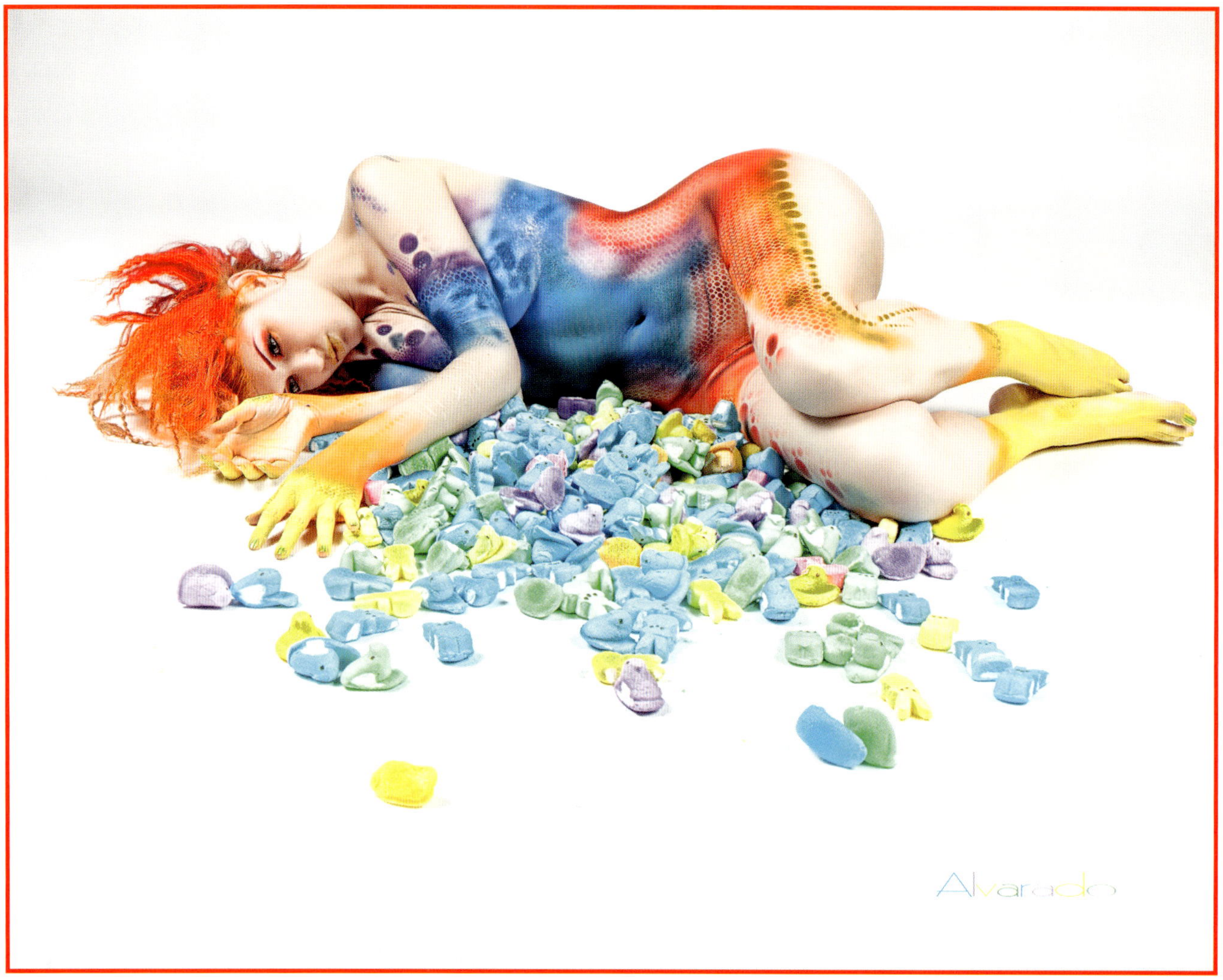

Alvarado

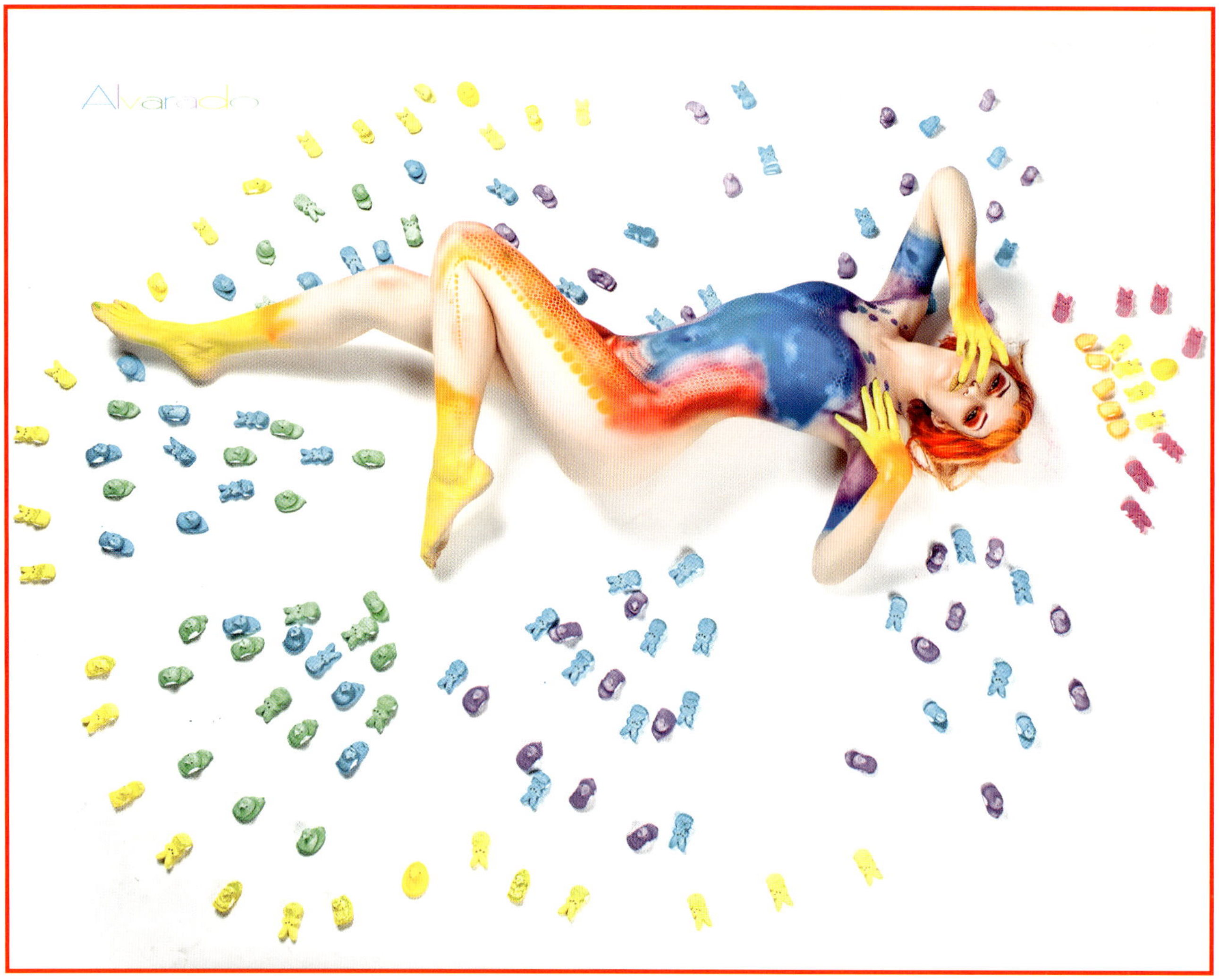

Alvarado

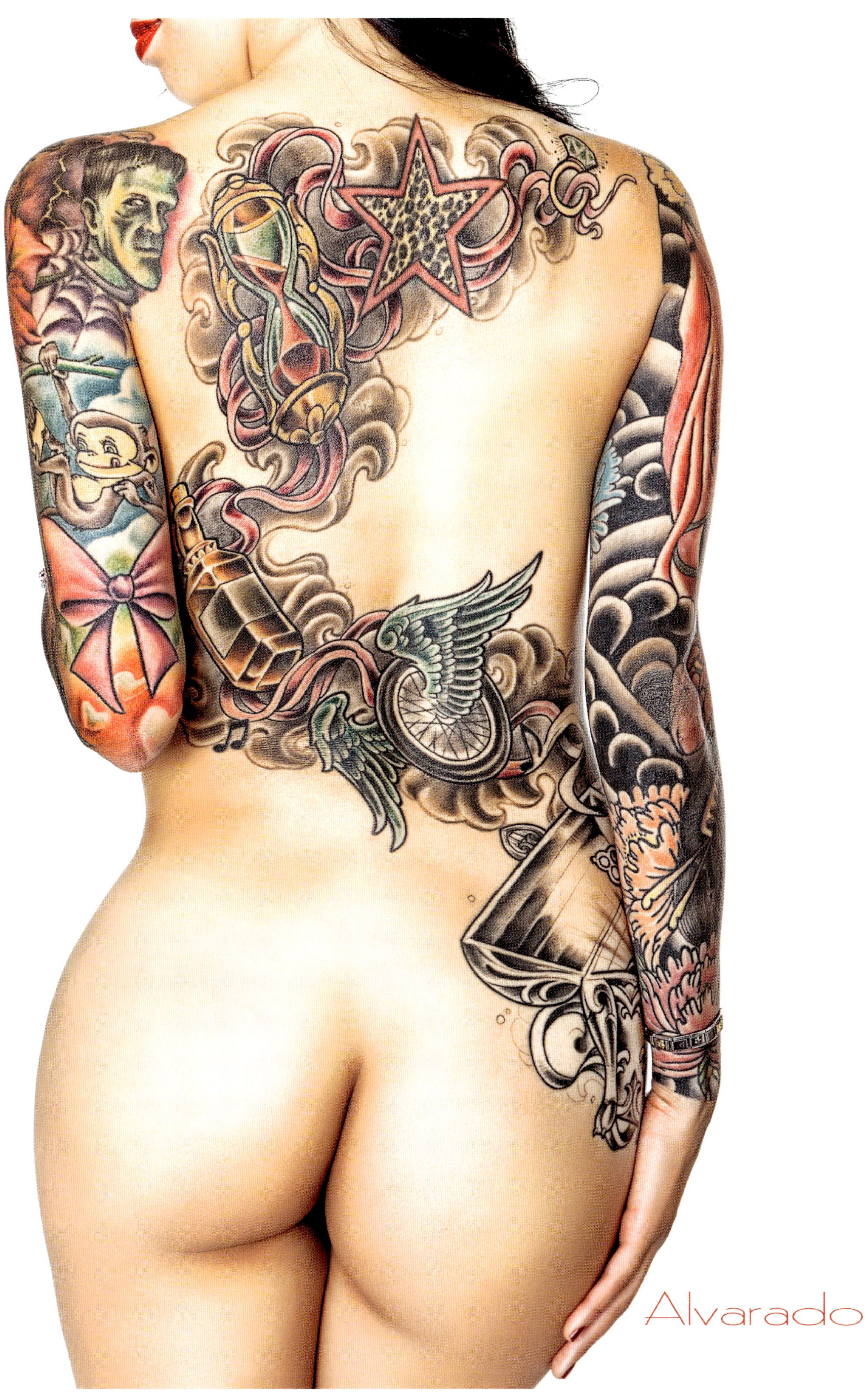

Alvarado

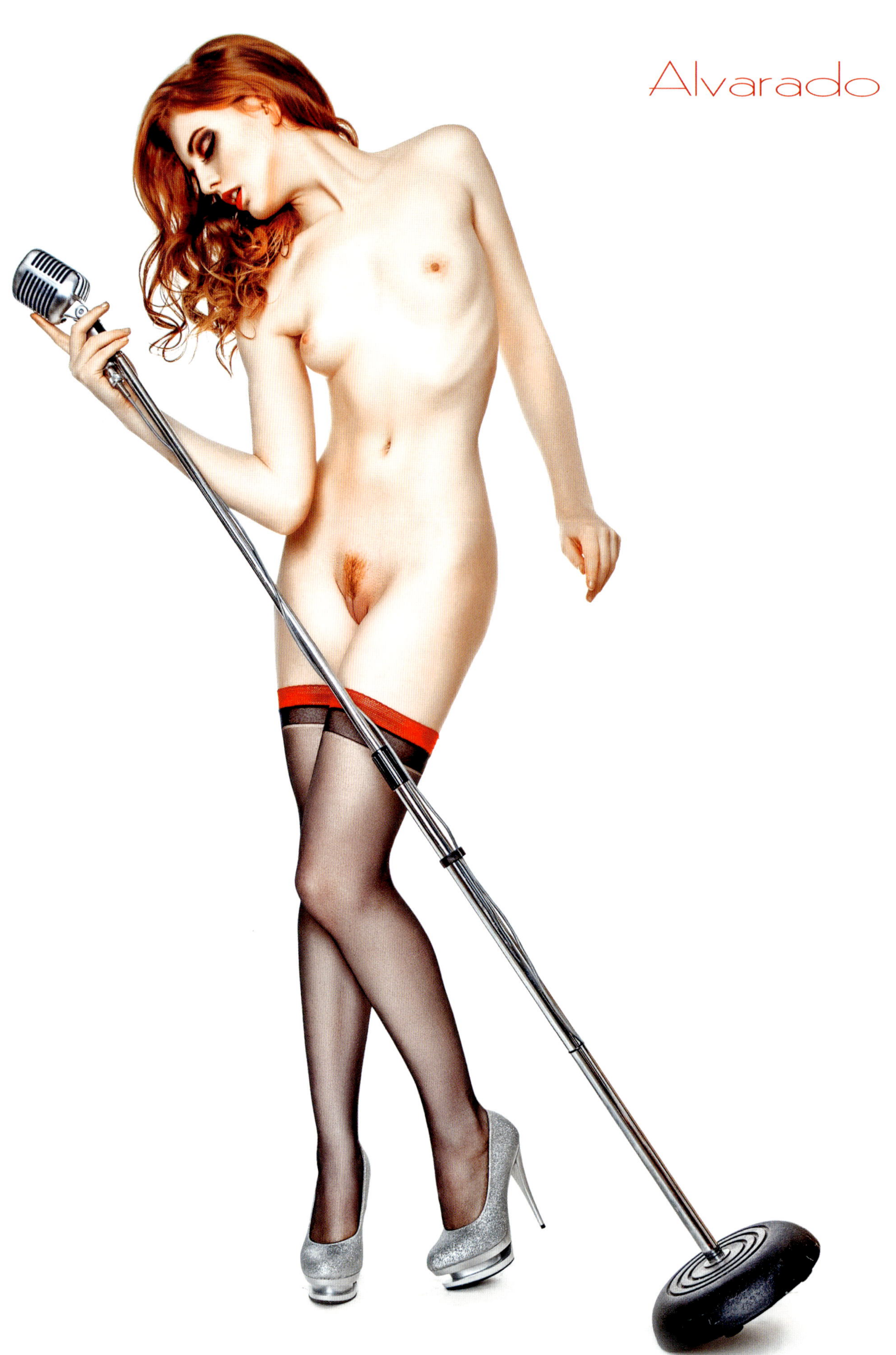

Alvarado

Alvarado

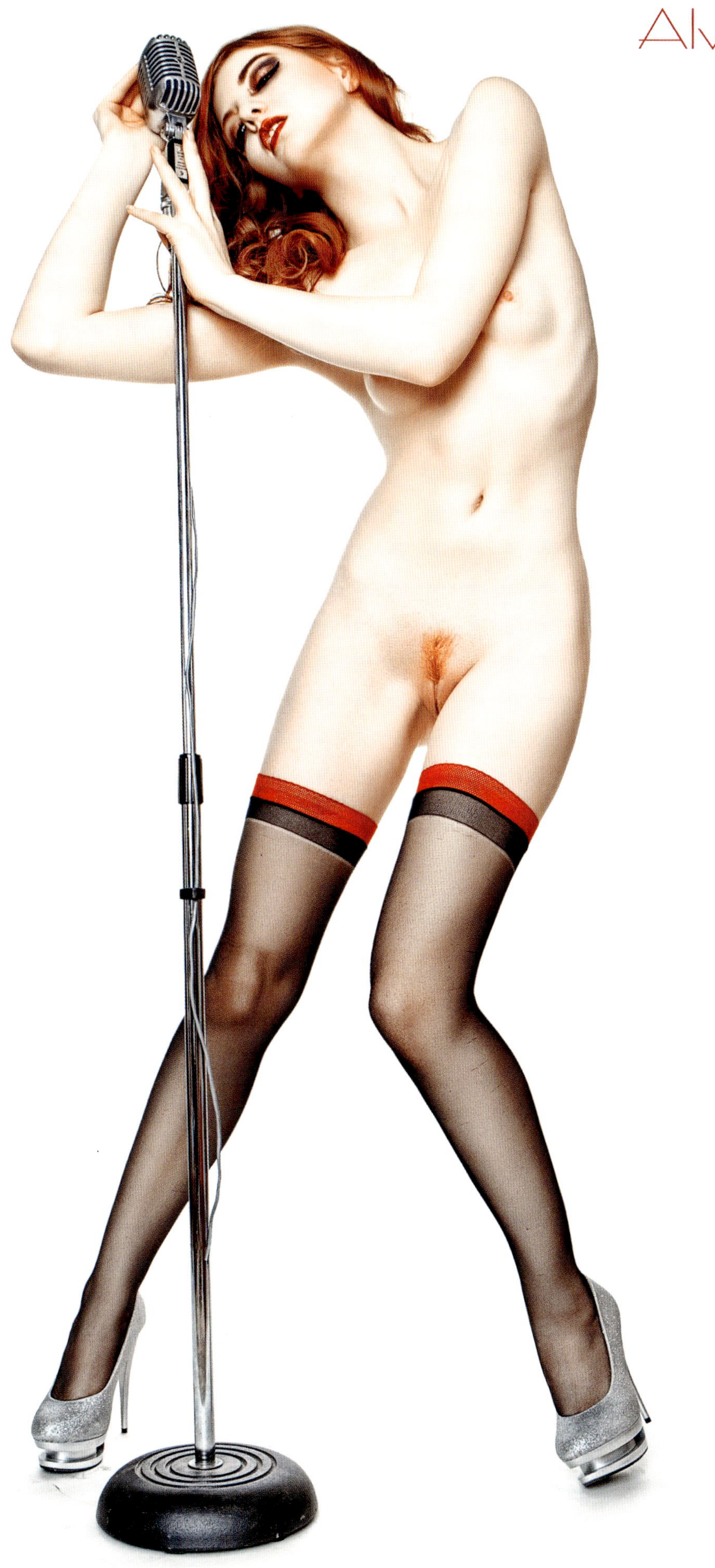

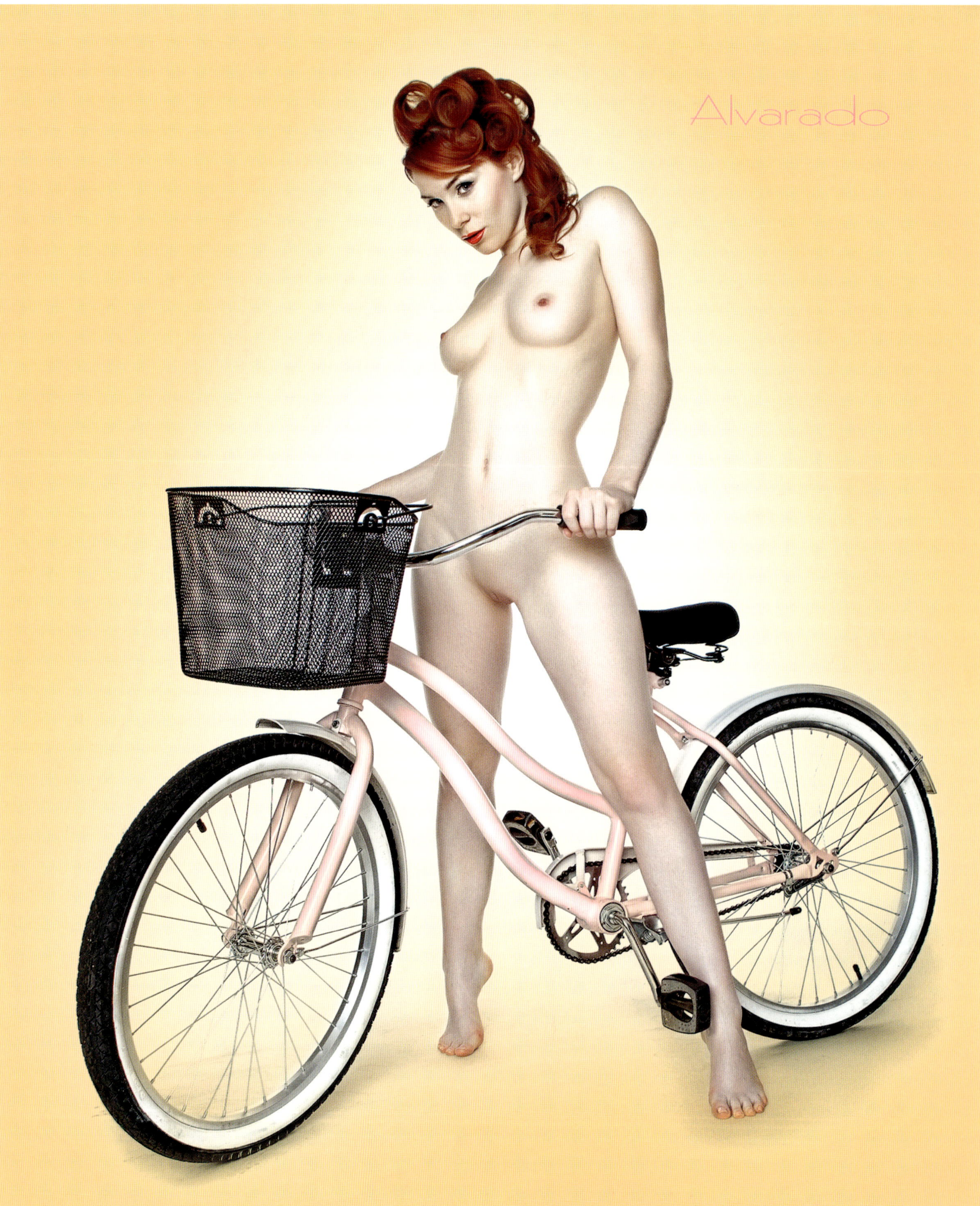
Alvarado

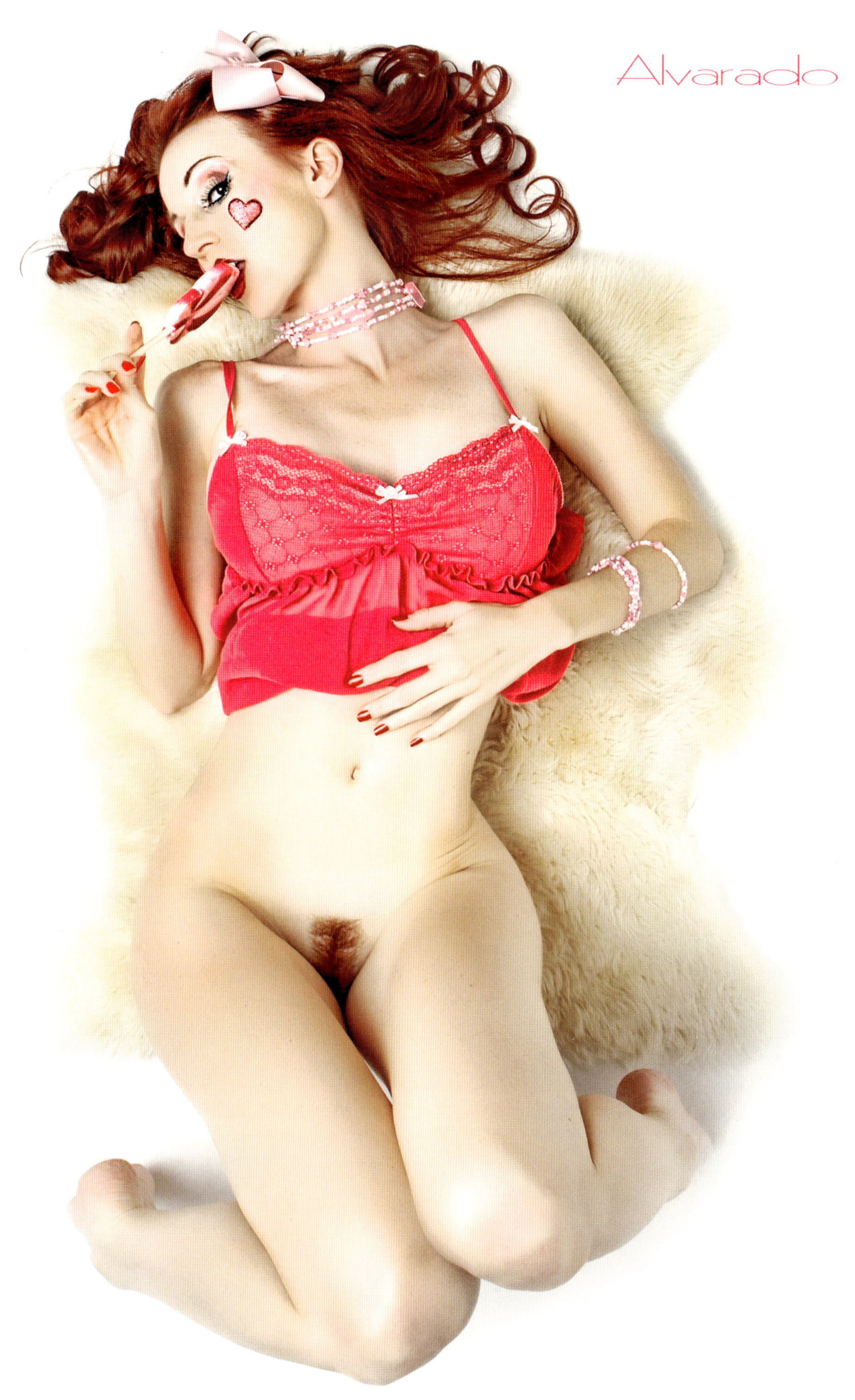

Alvarado

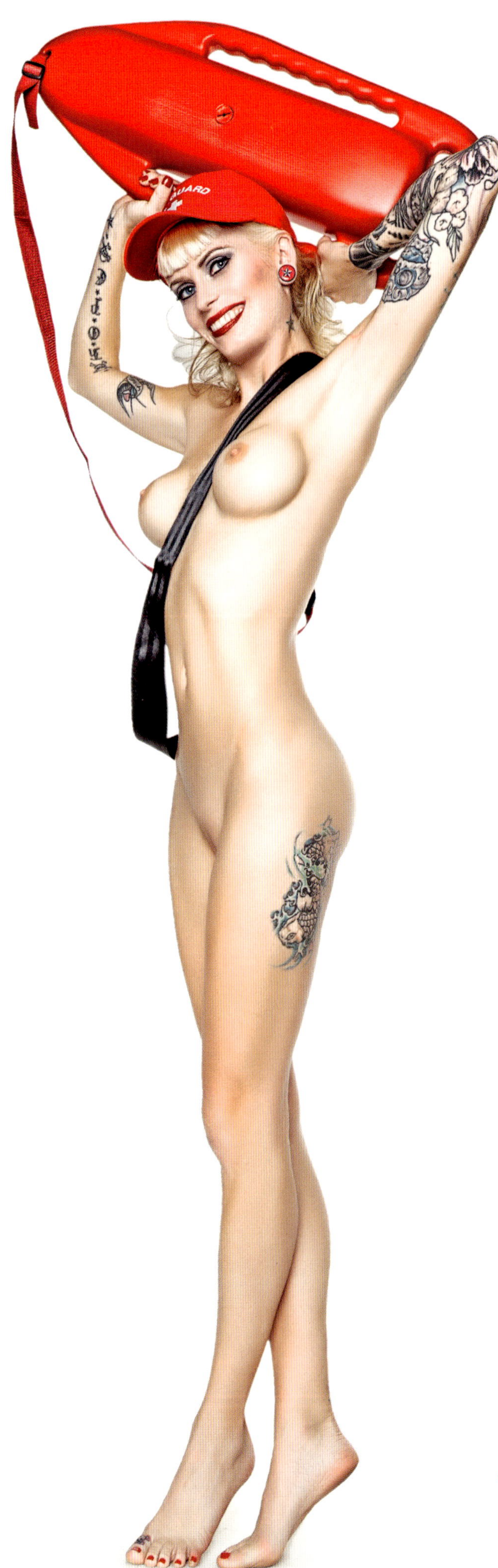

Alvarado

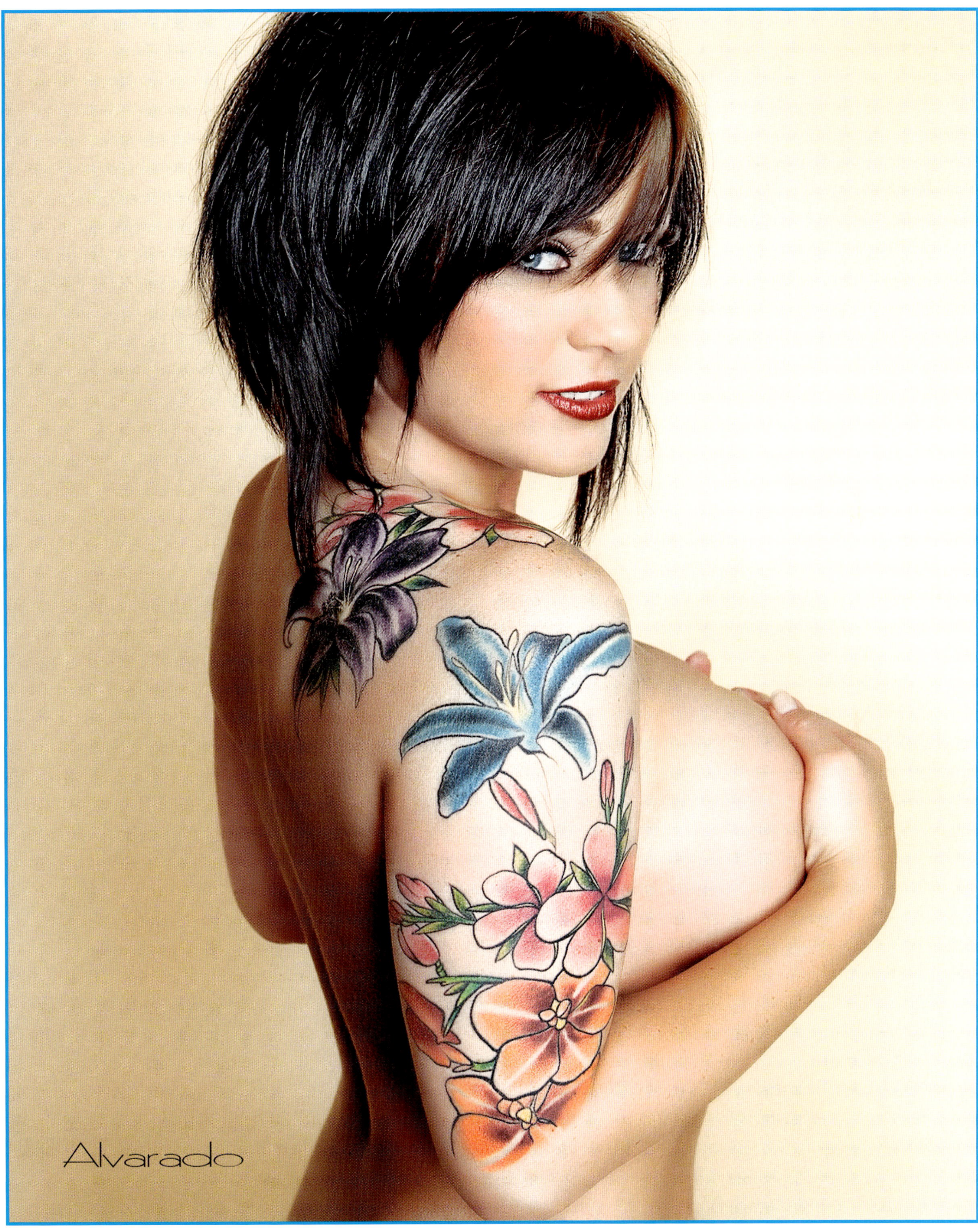
Alvarado

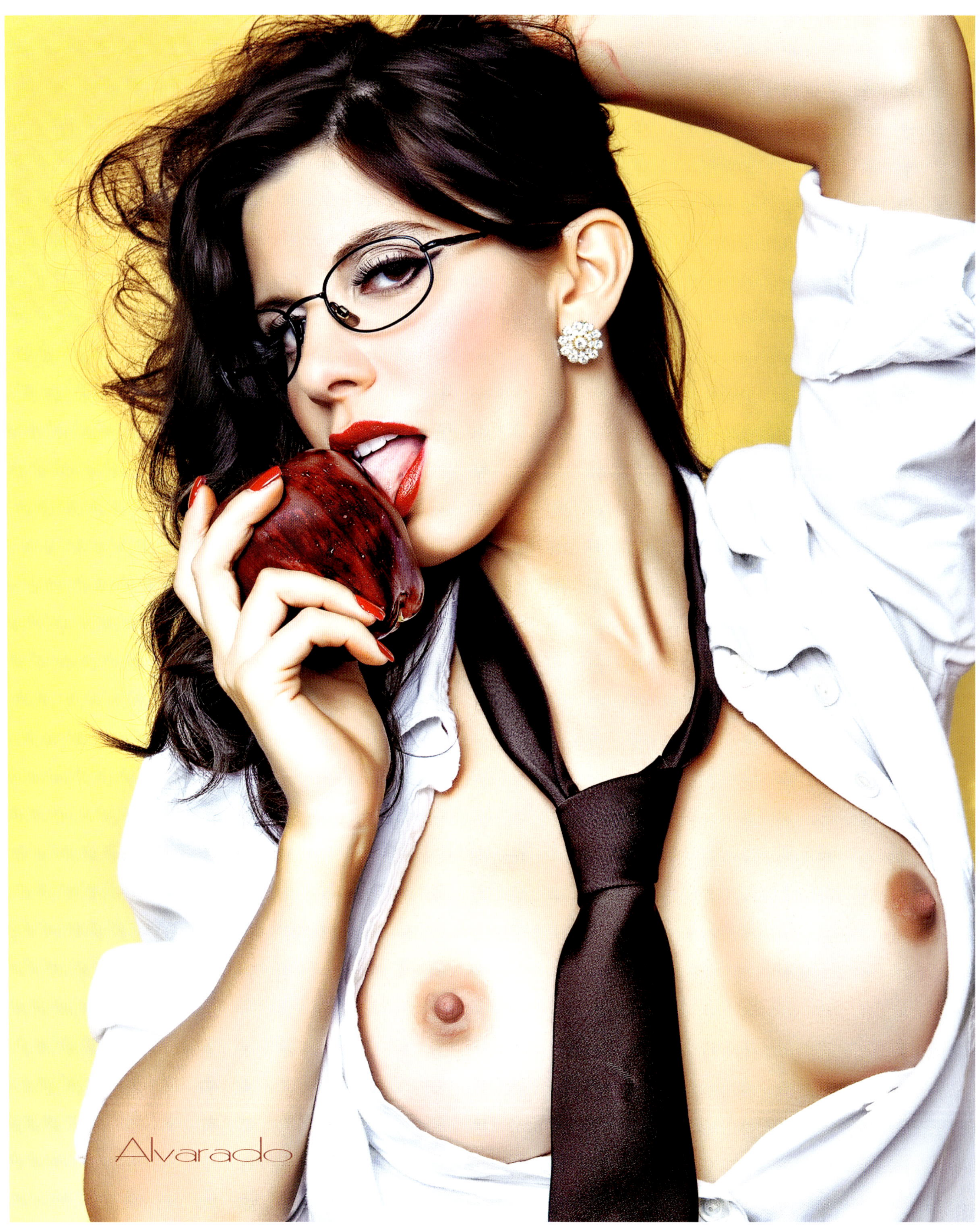
Alvarado

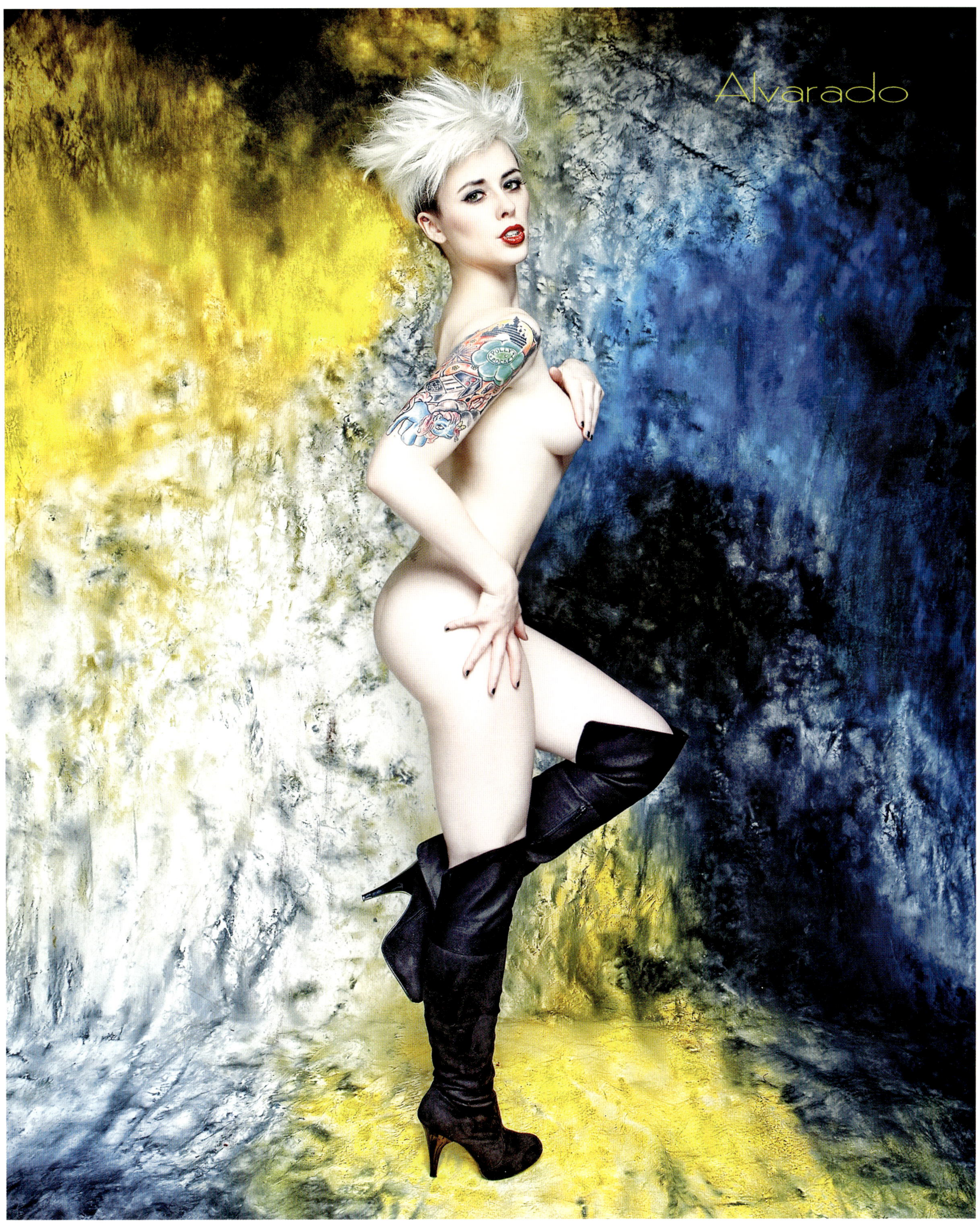
Alvarado

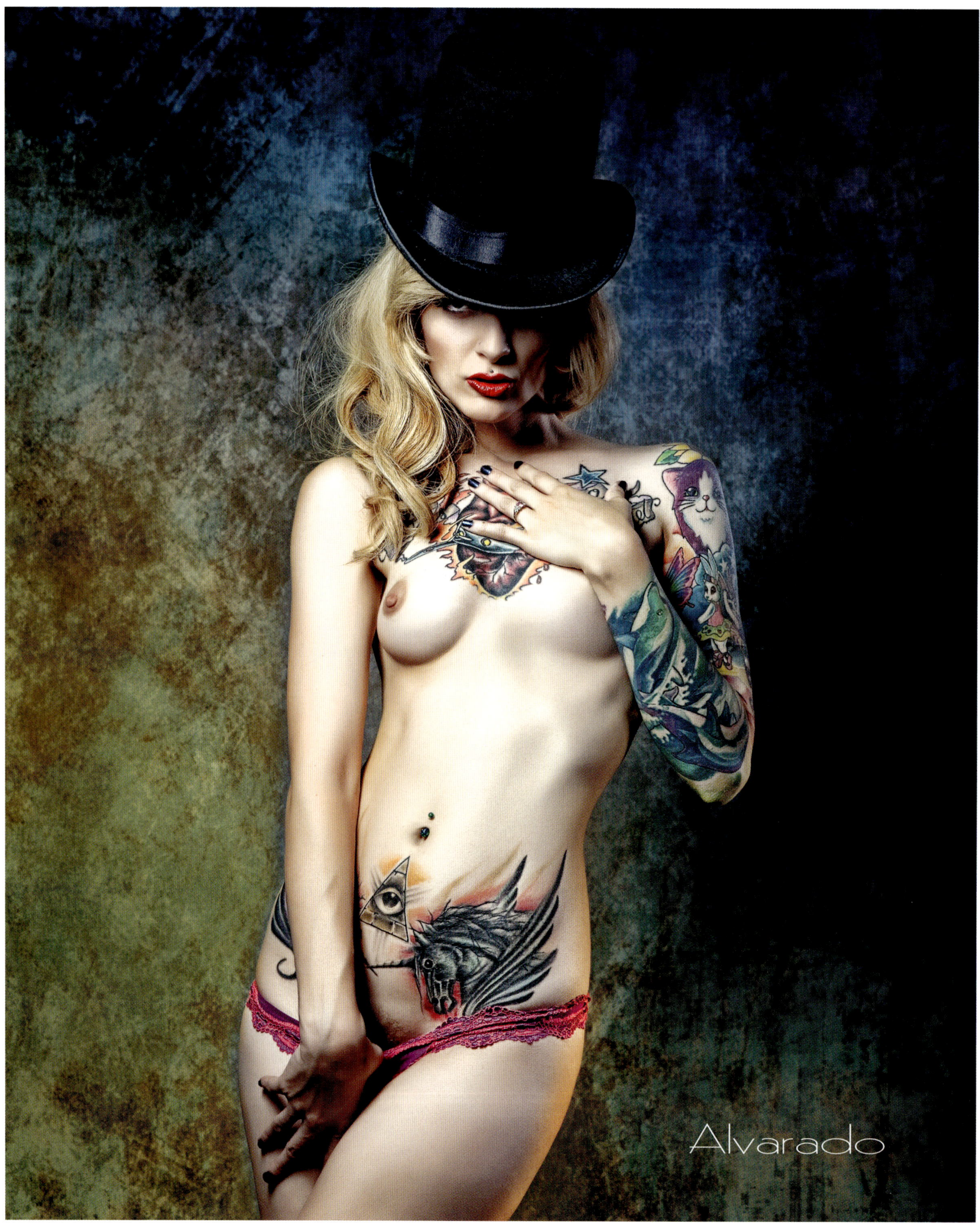
Alvarado

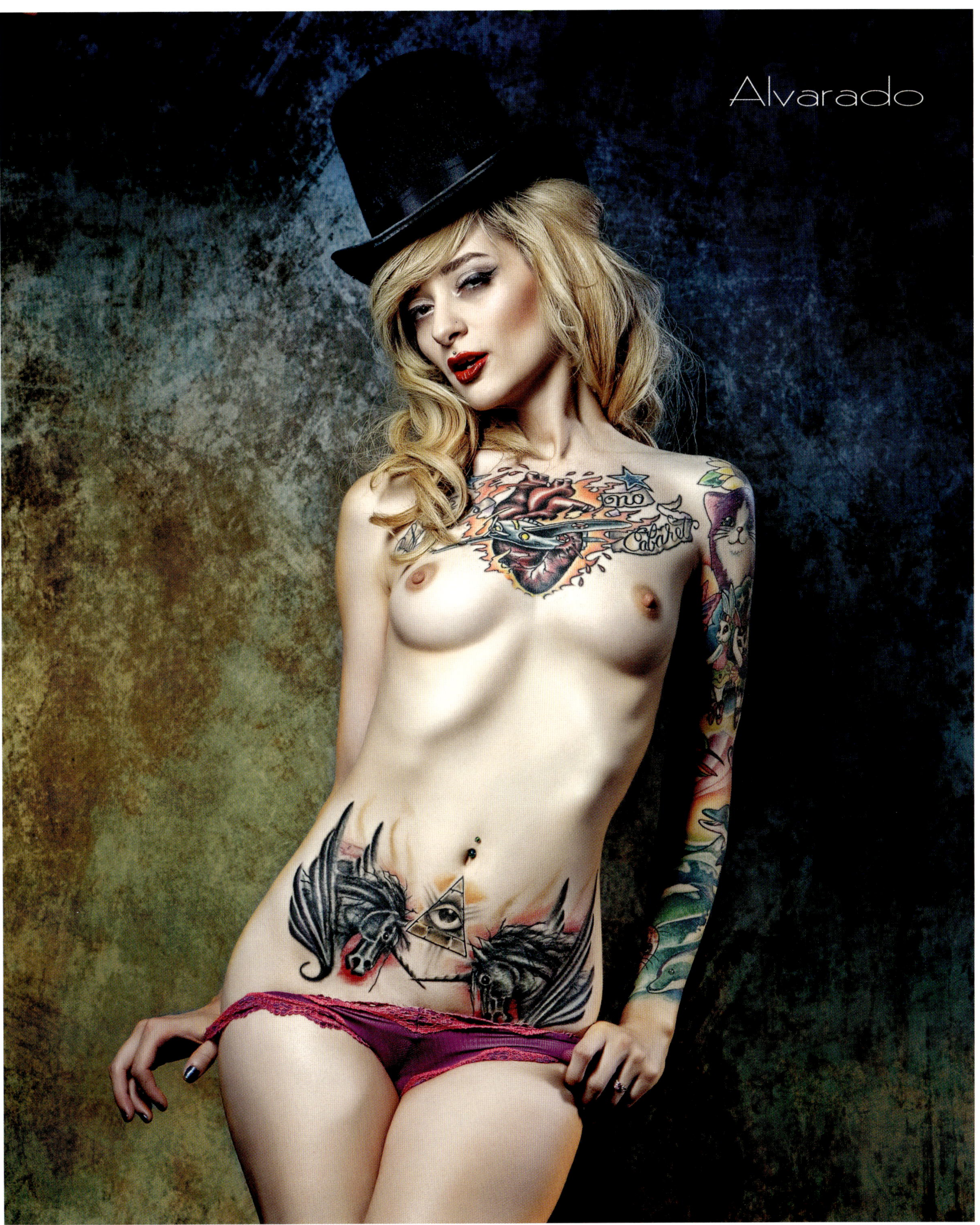
Alvarado

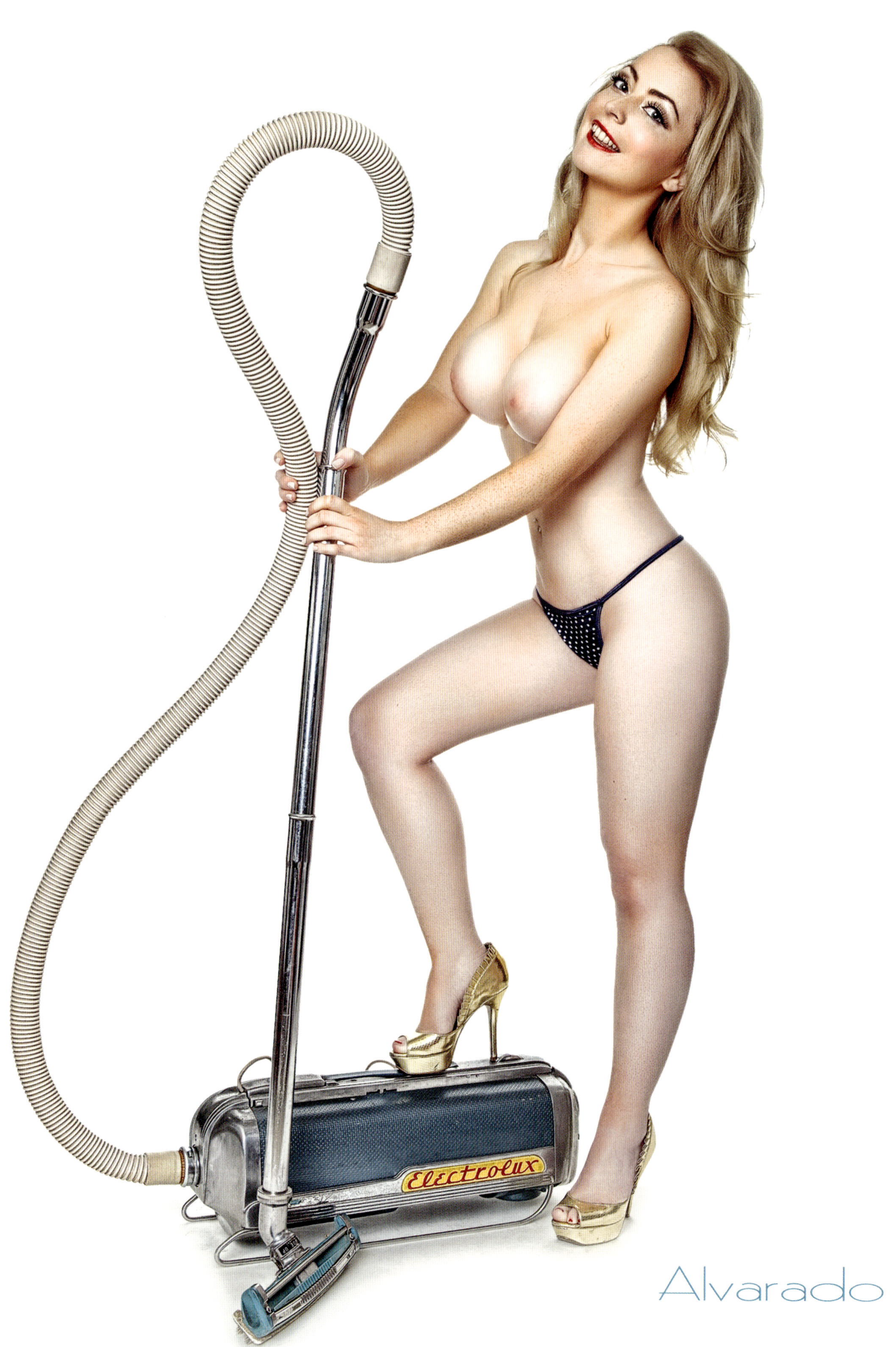
Electrolux
Alvarado

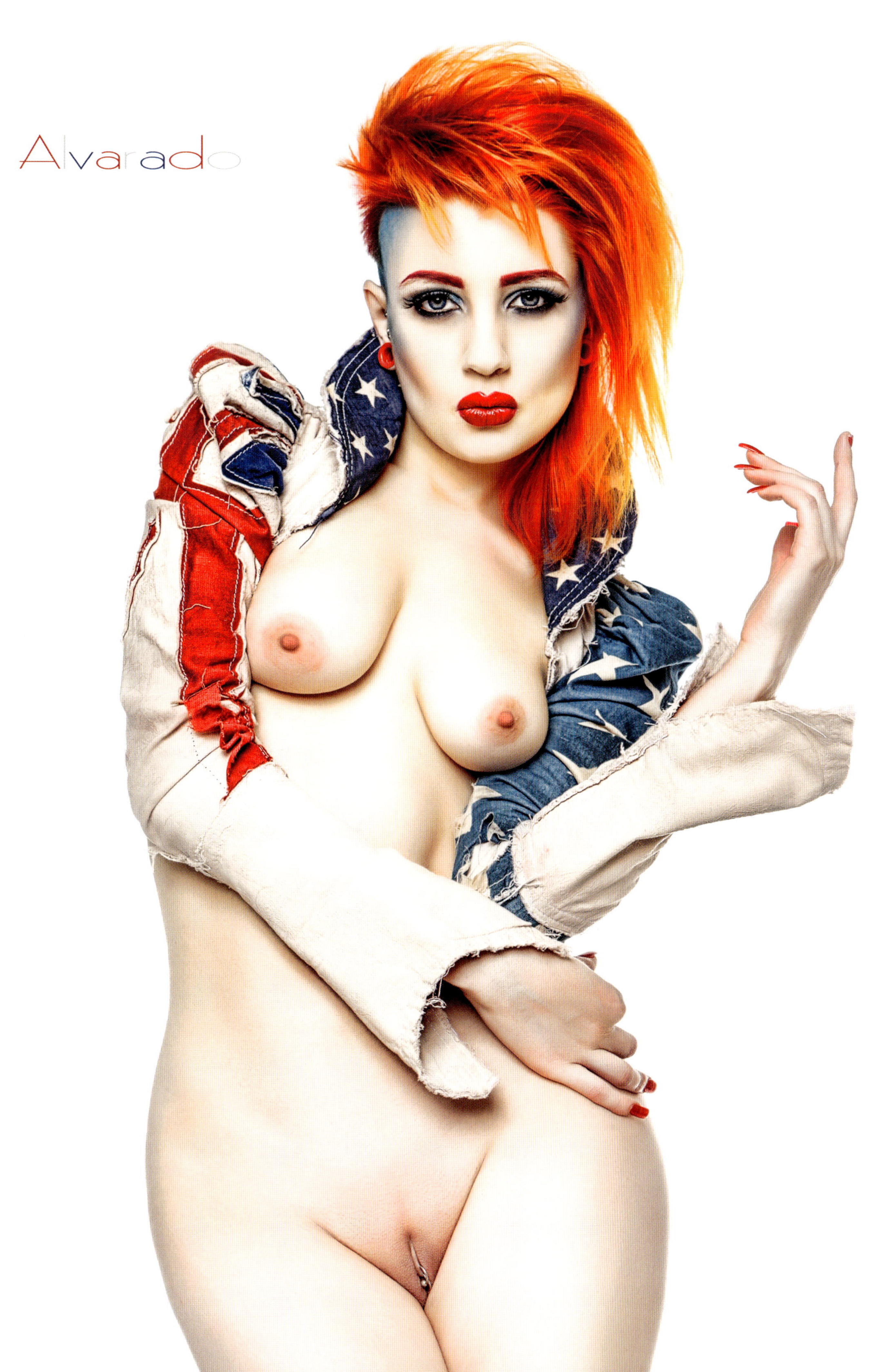
Alvarado

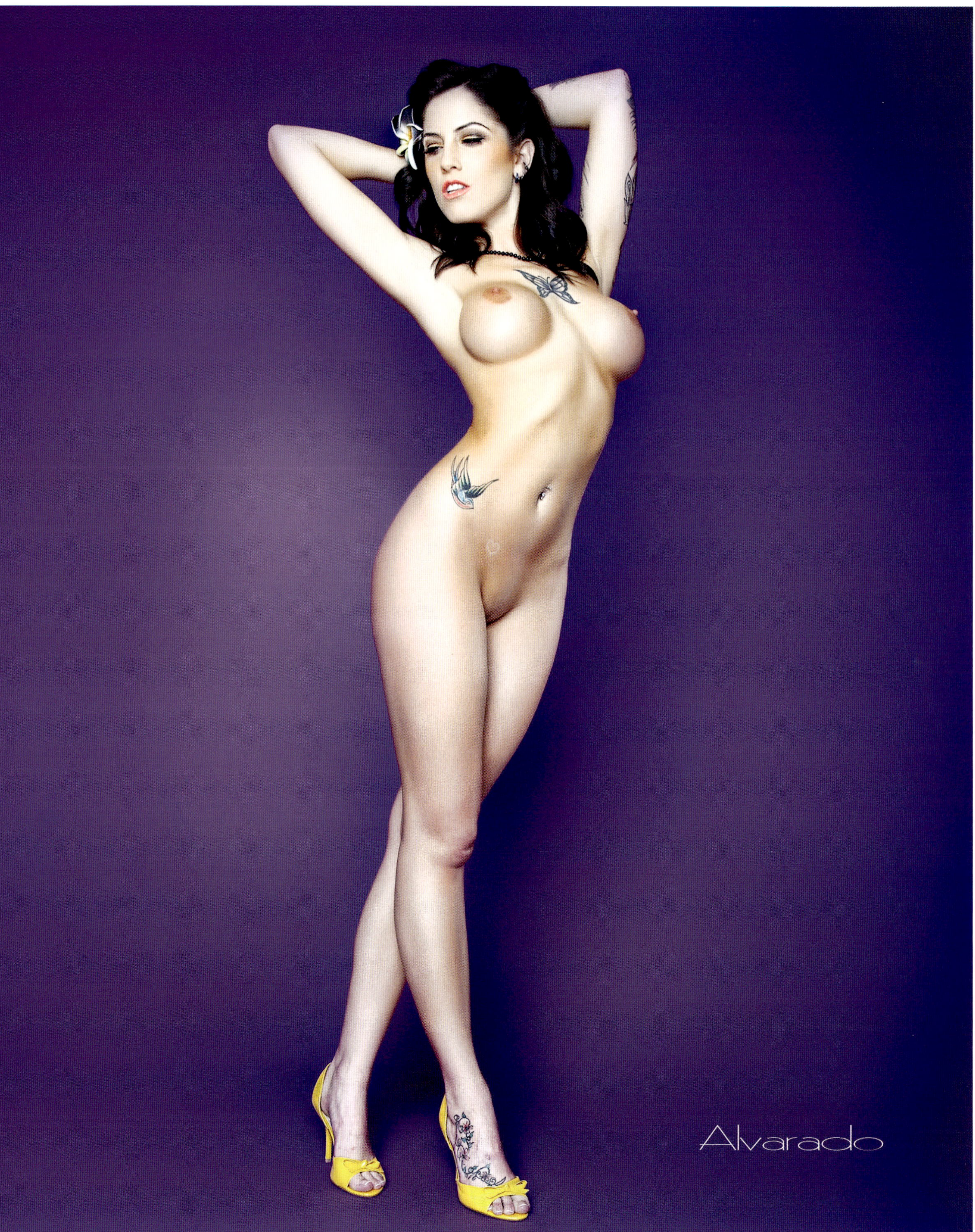
Alvarado

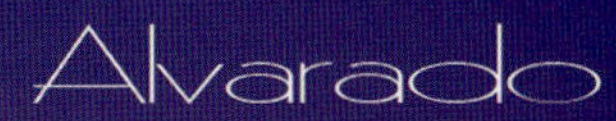
Alvarado

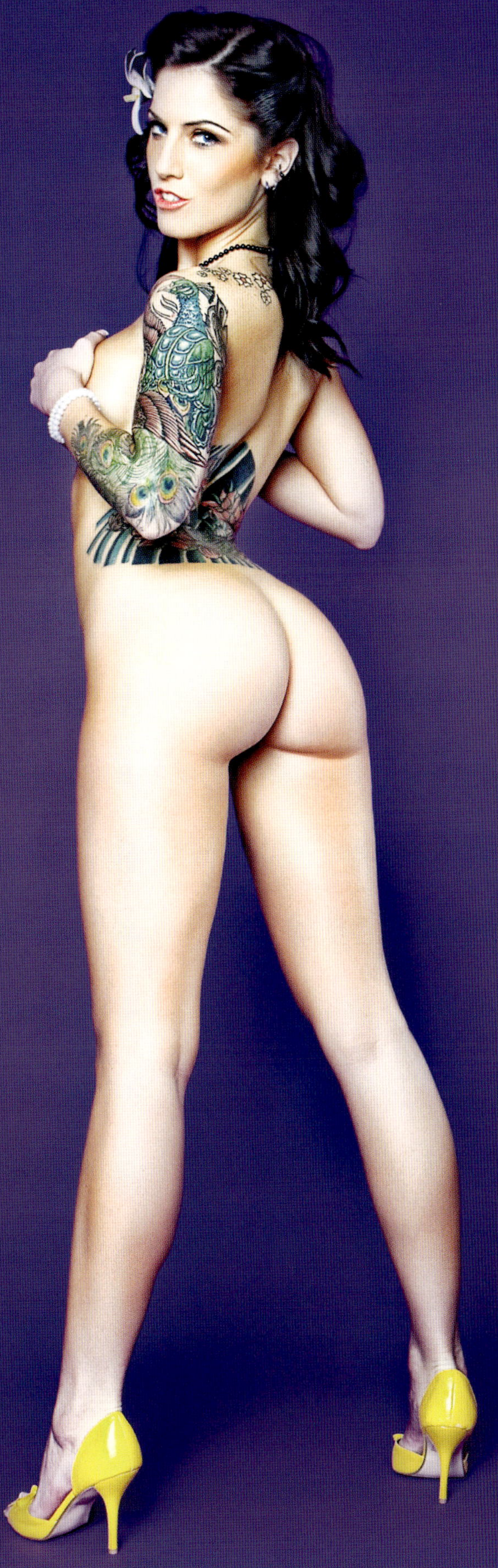

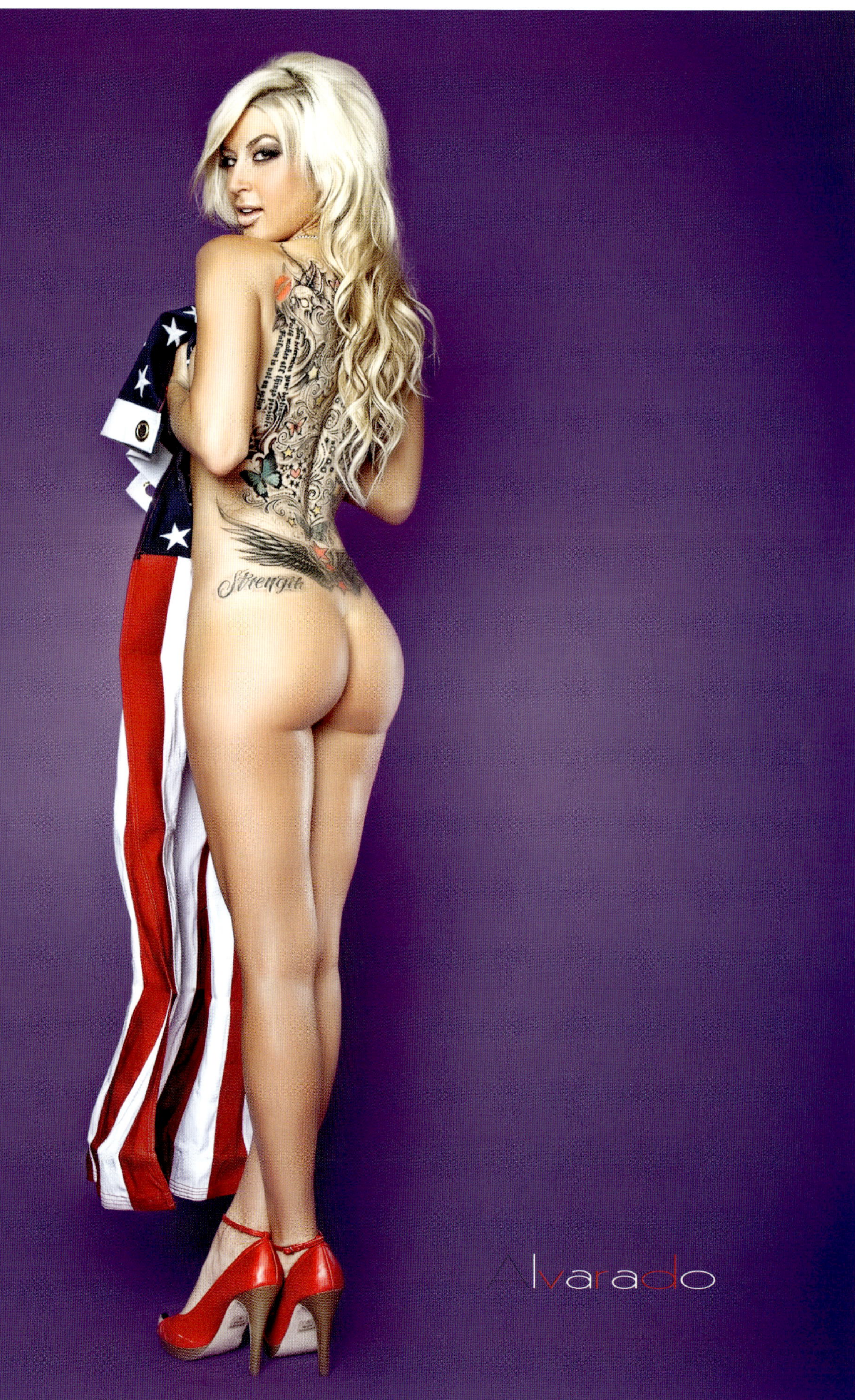
Alvarado

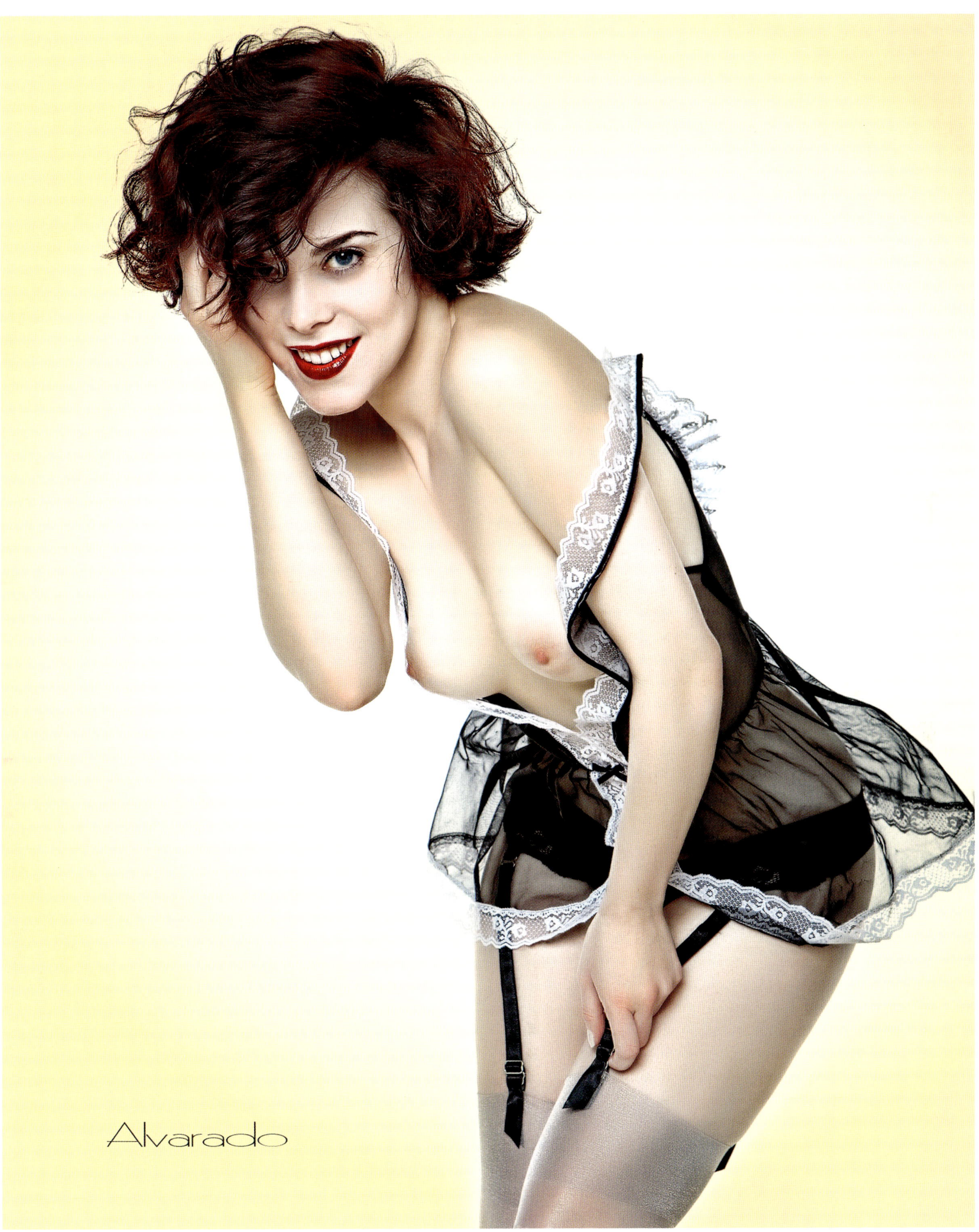
Alvarado

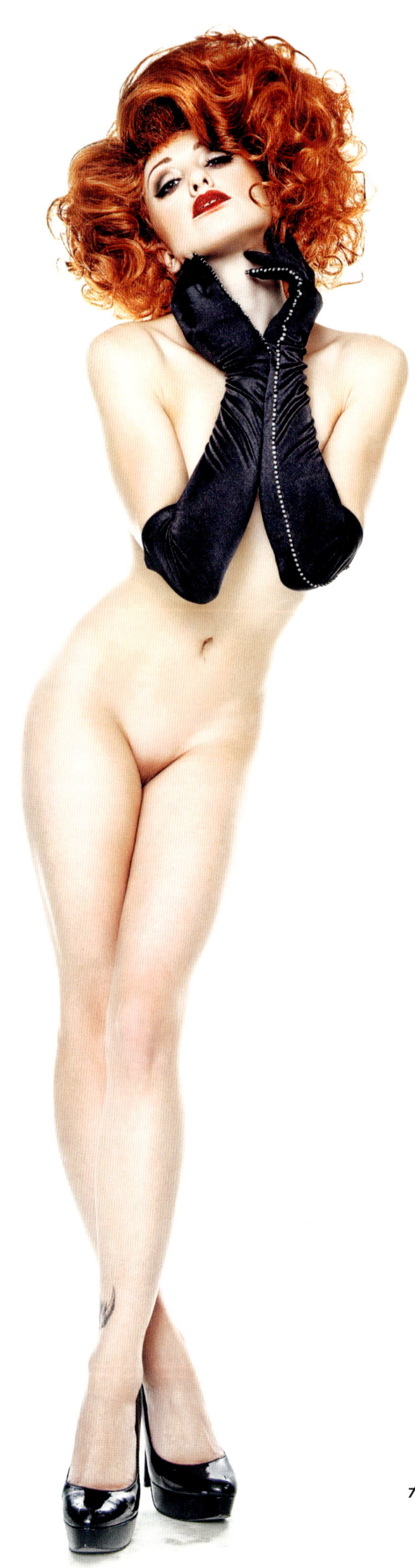

Alvarado

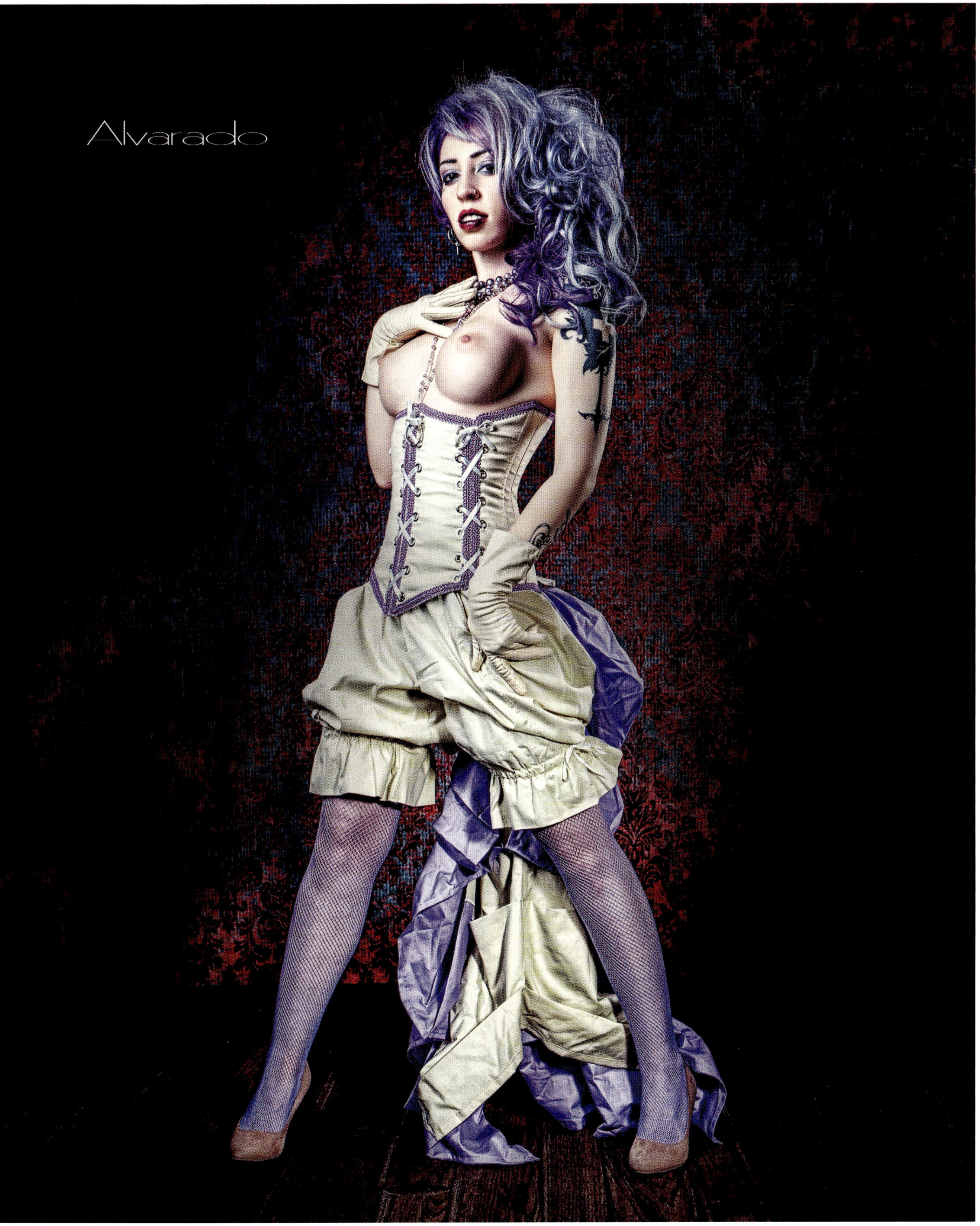
Alvarado

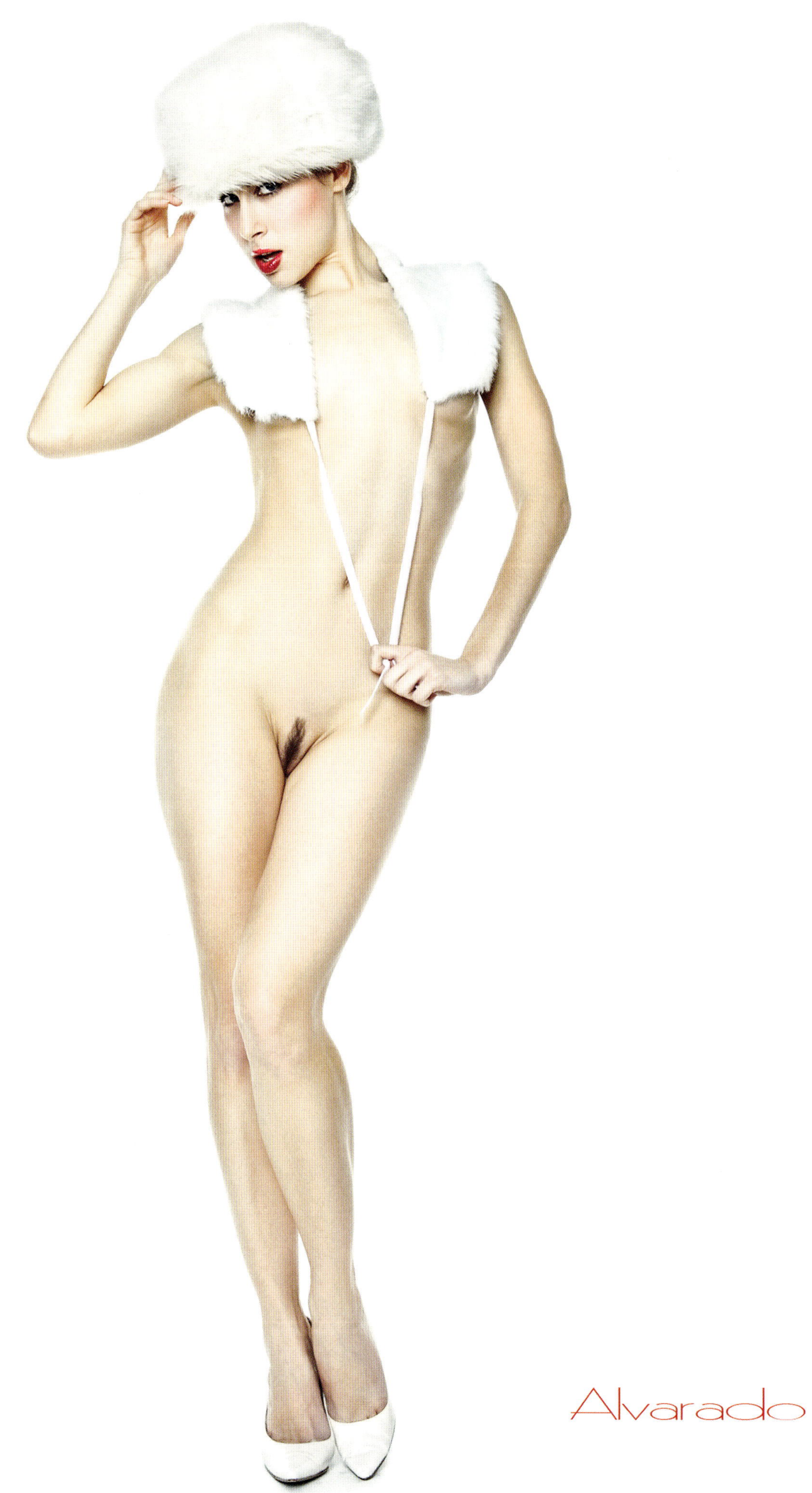

Alvarado

Alvarado

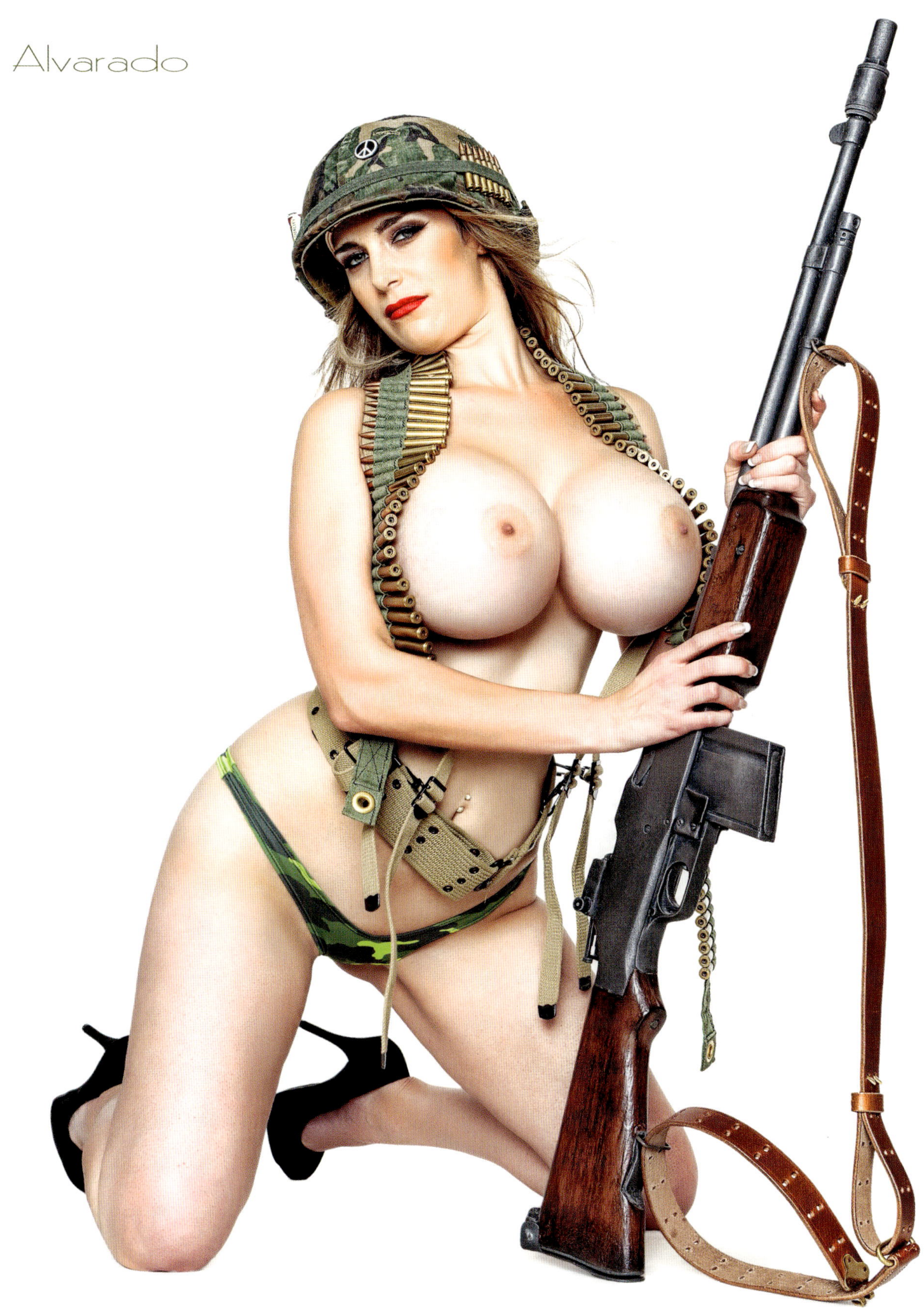

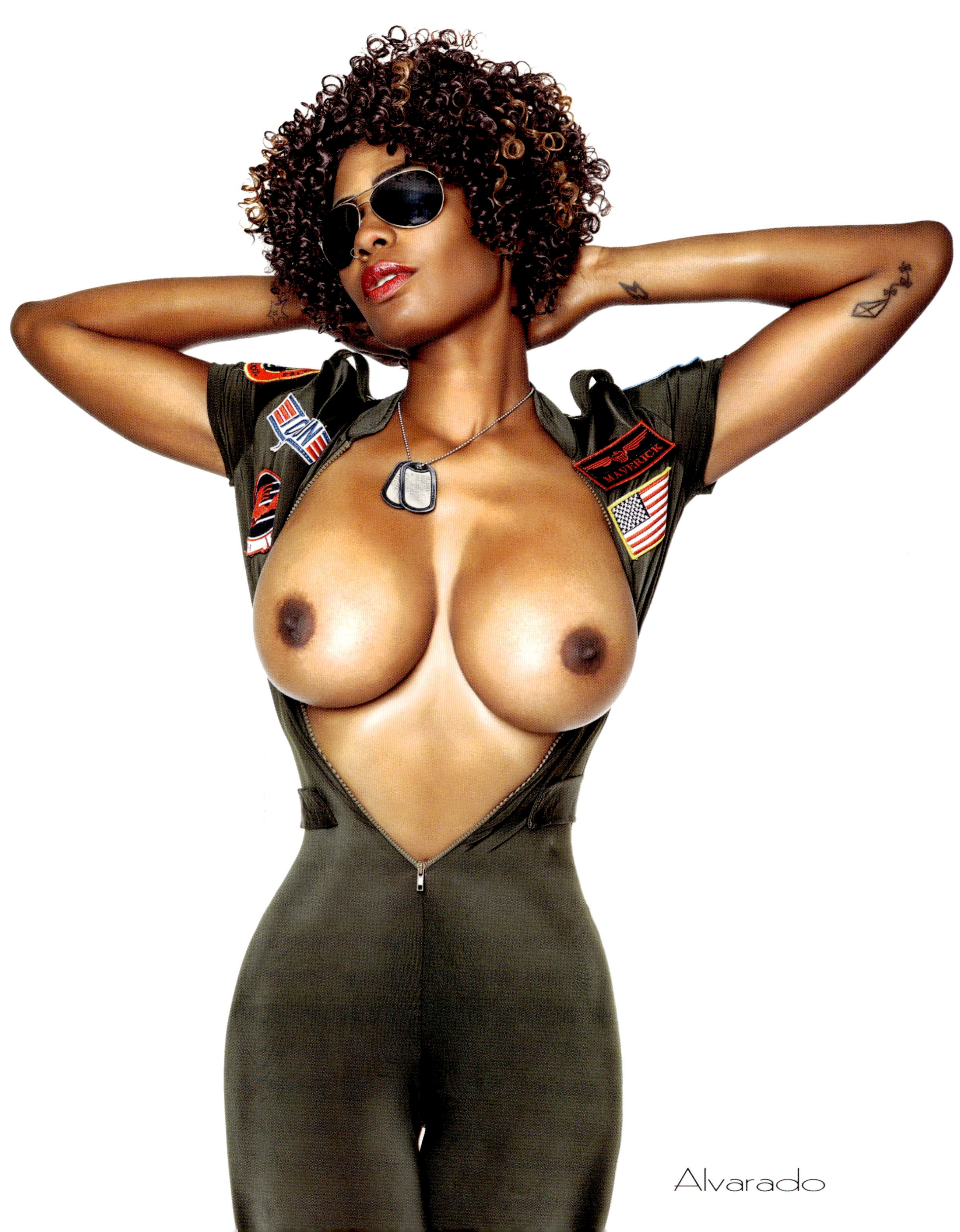
MAVERICK
Alvarado

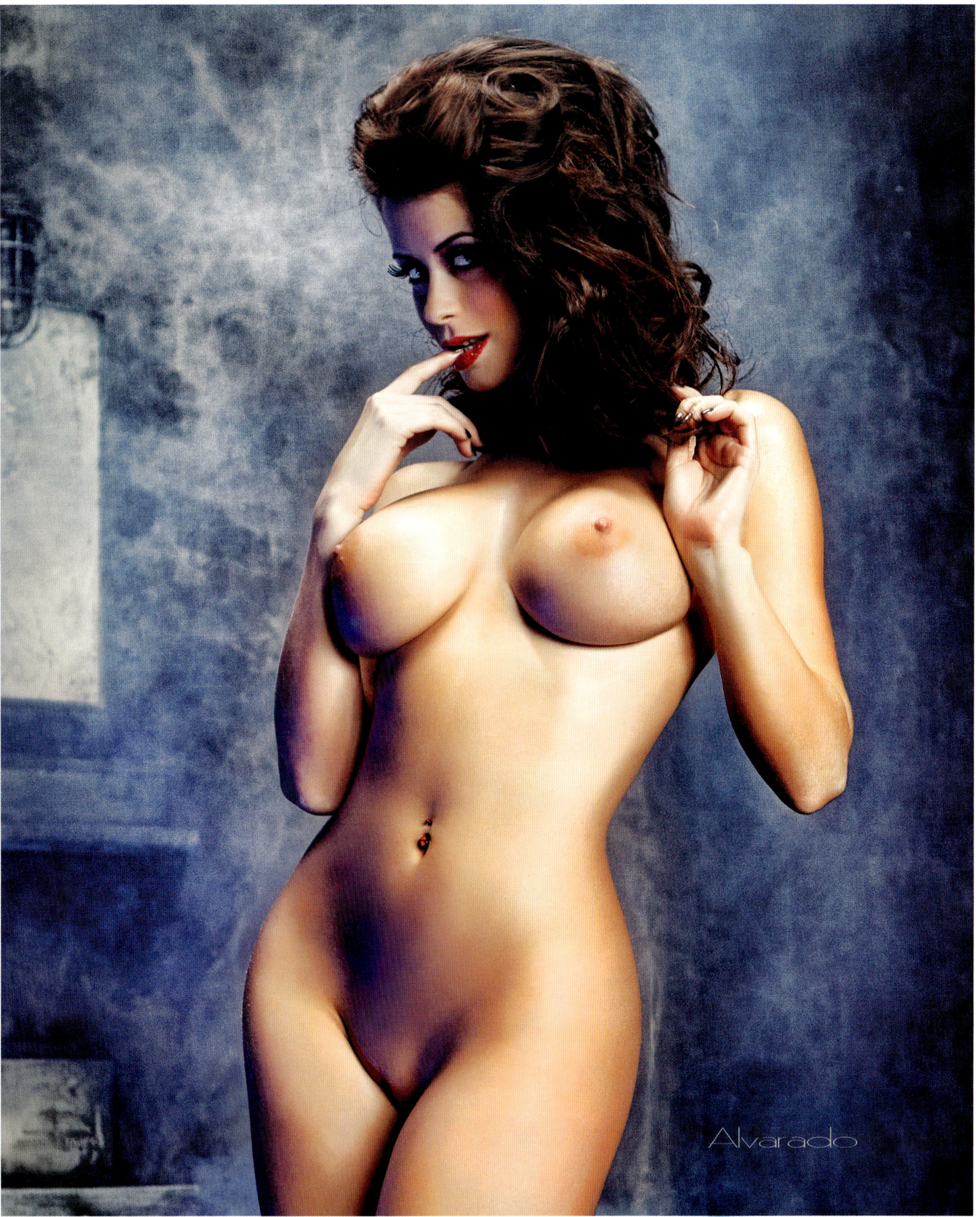
Alvarado

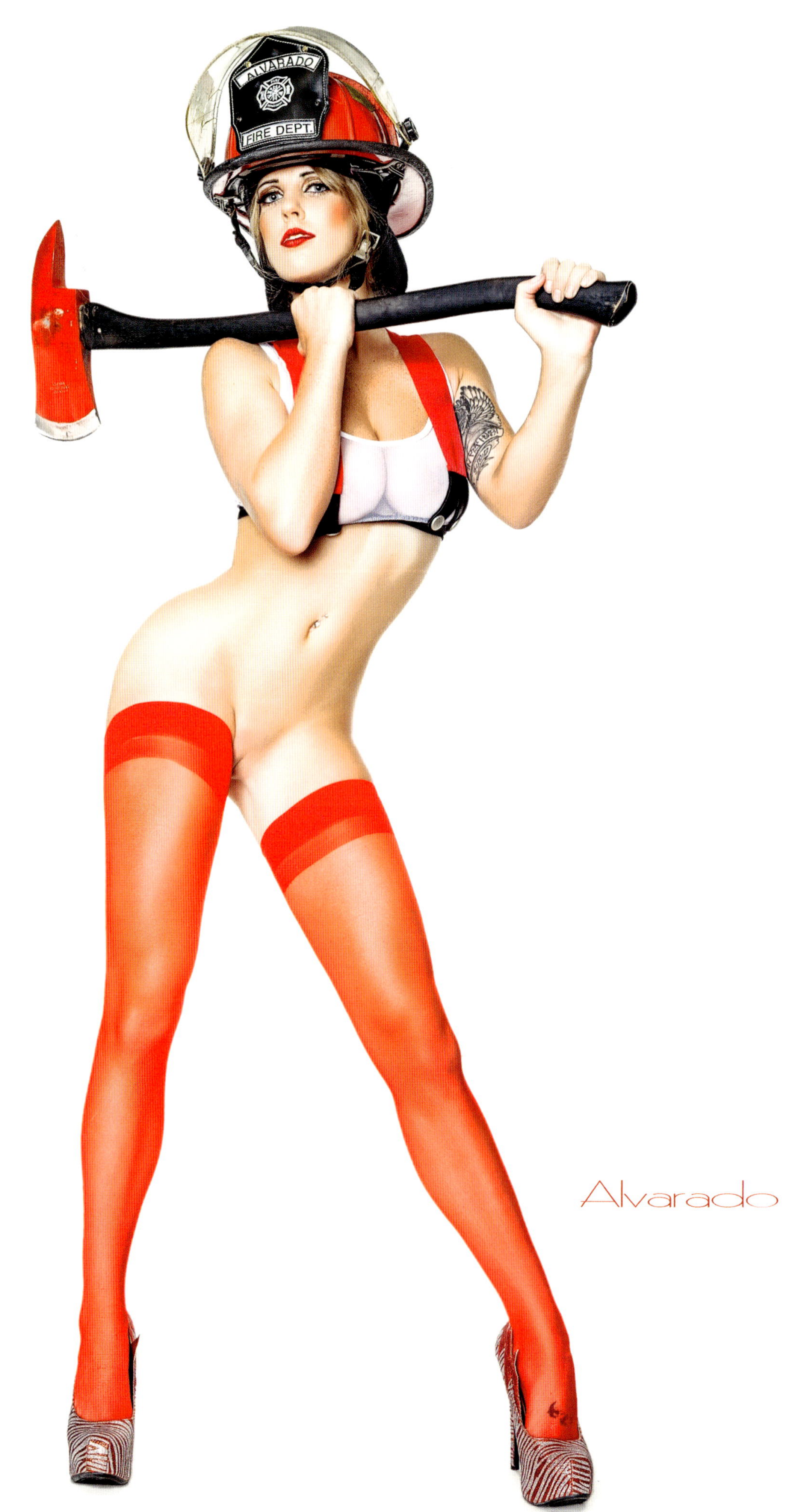
ALVARADO
FIRE DEPT.
Alvarado

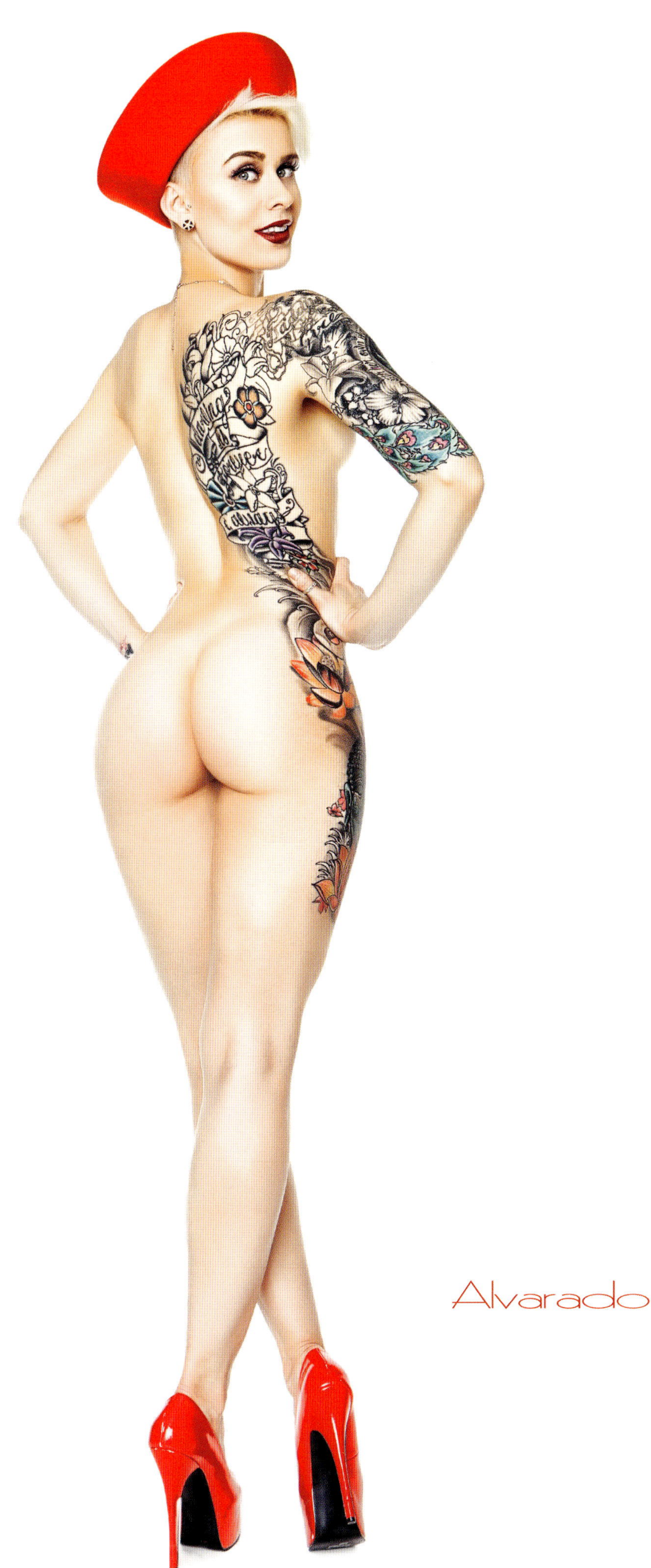
Alvarado

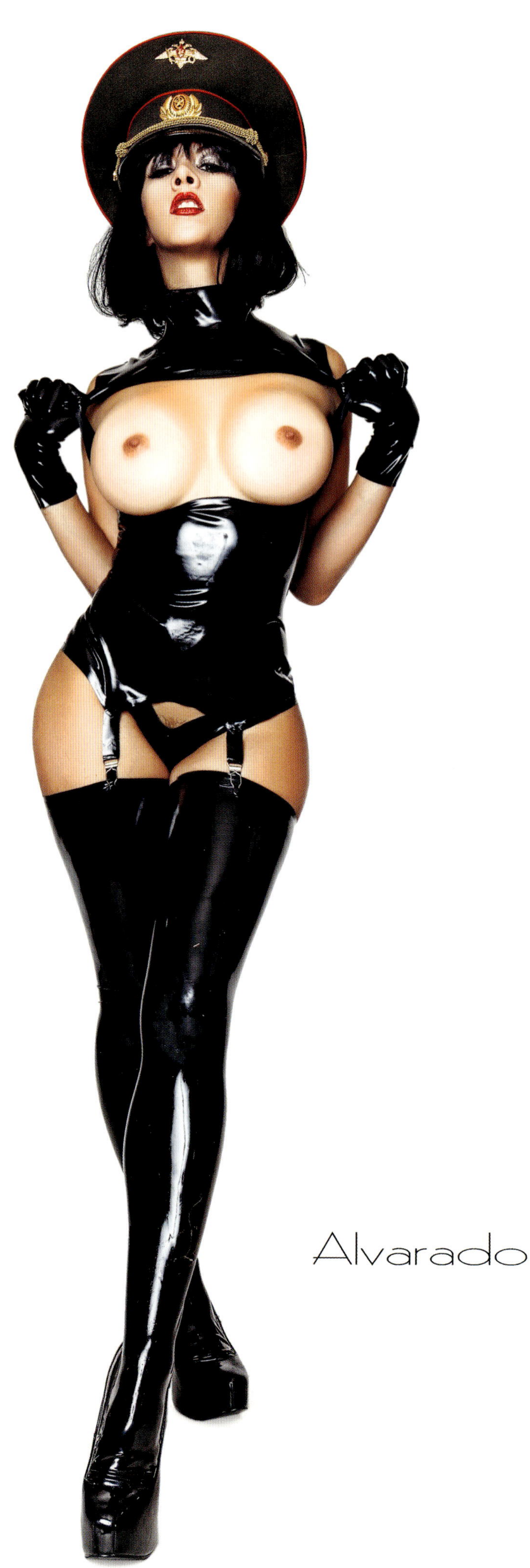

Alvarado

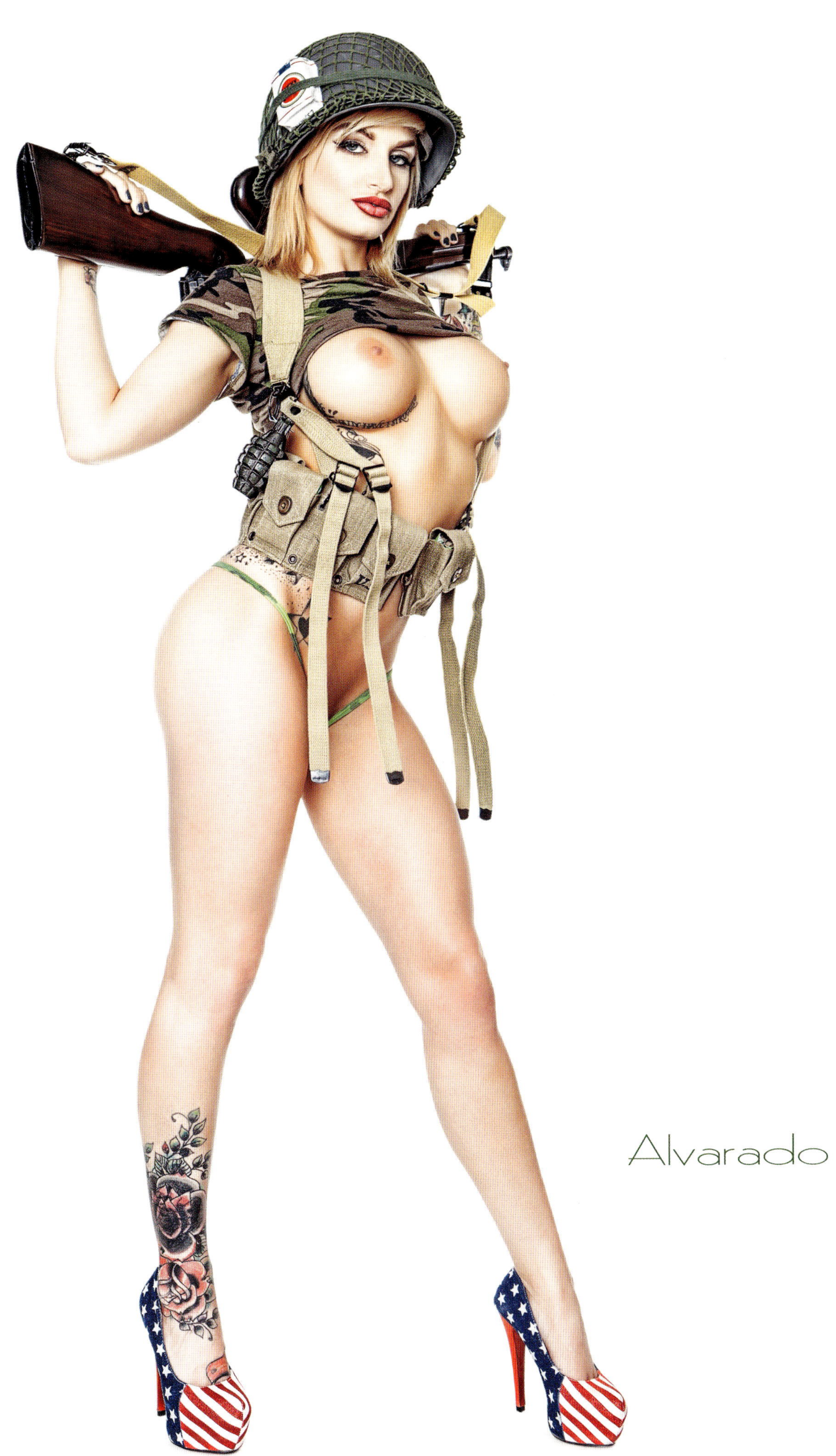
Alvarado

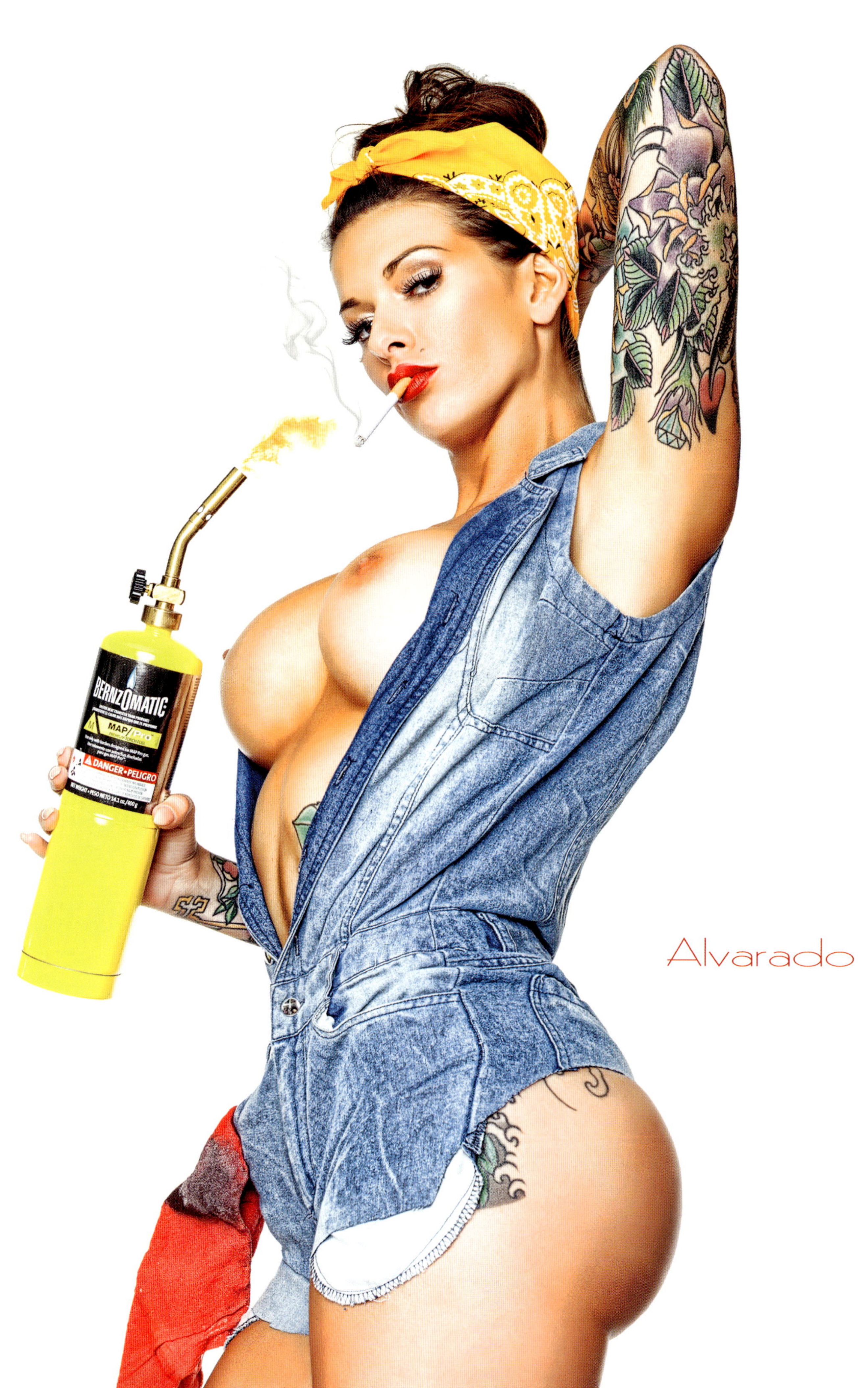

Alvarado

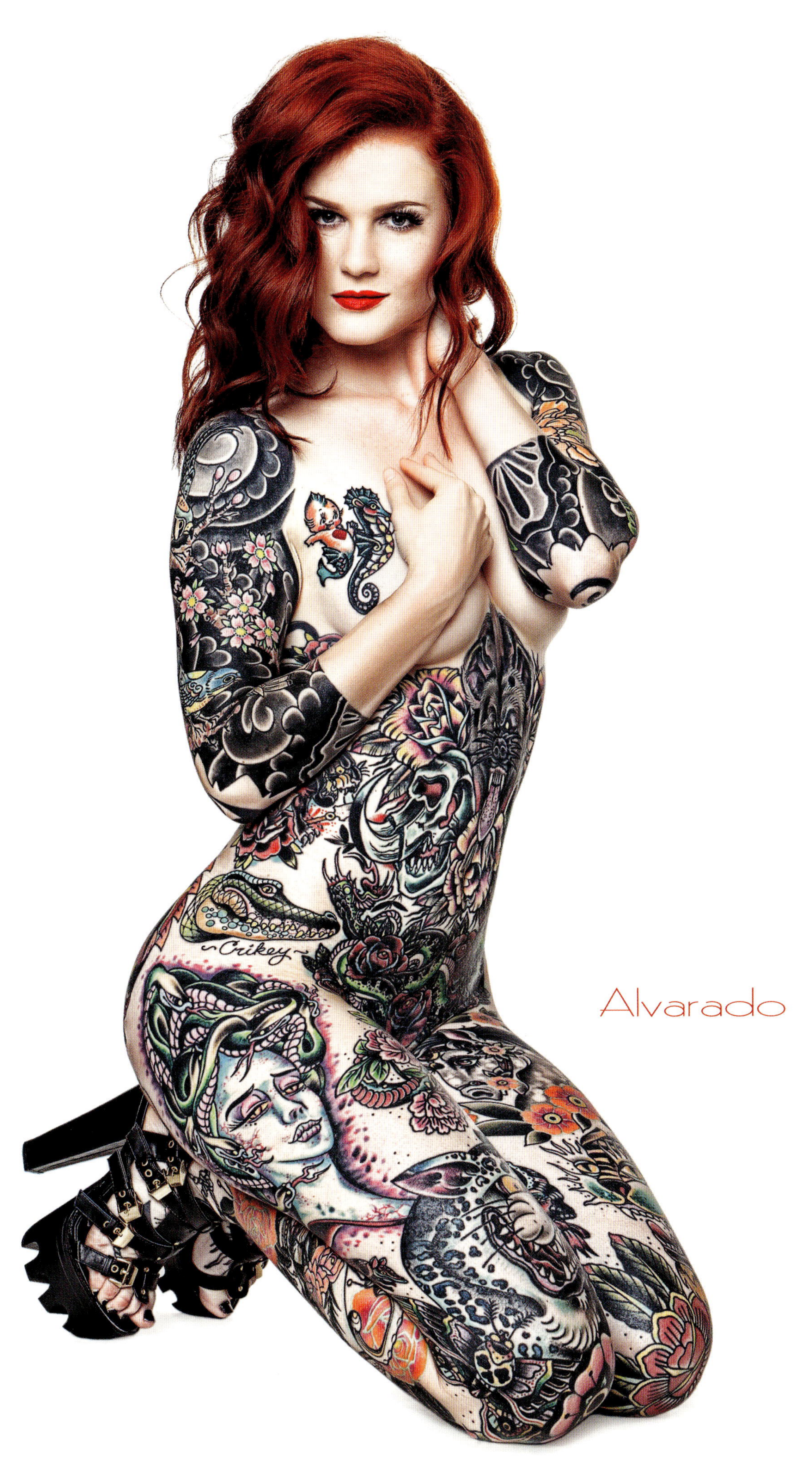

Alvarado

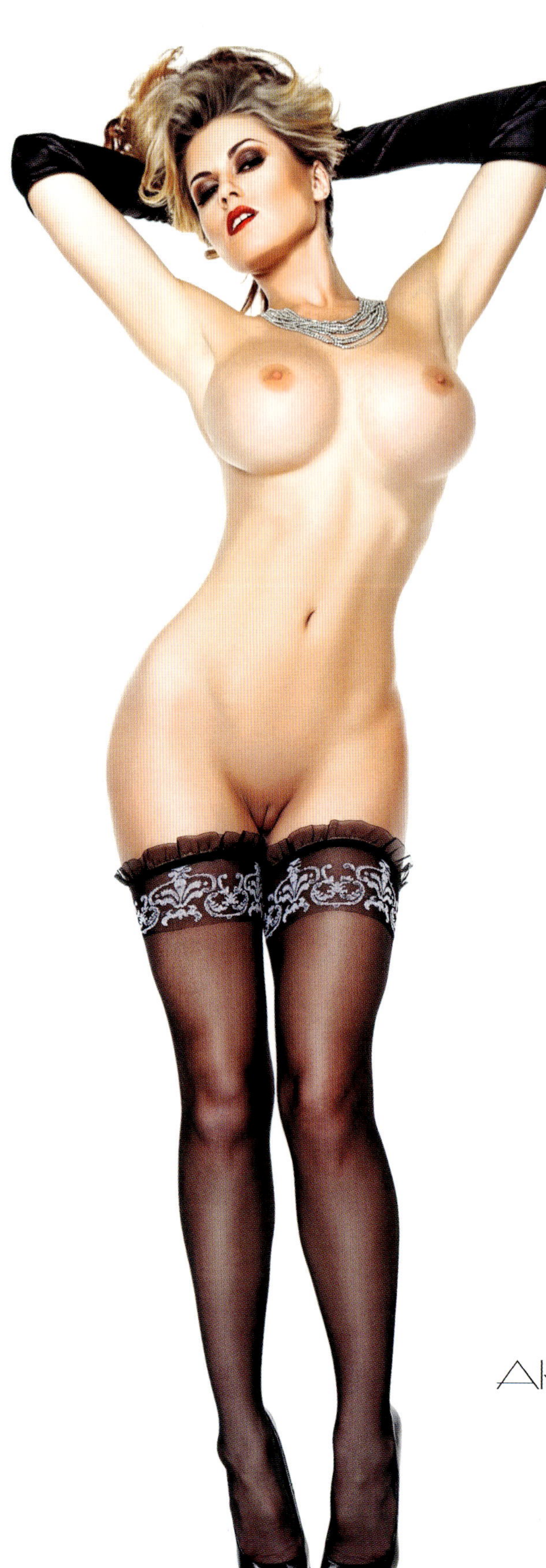

Alvarado

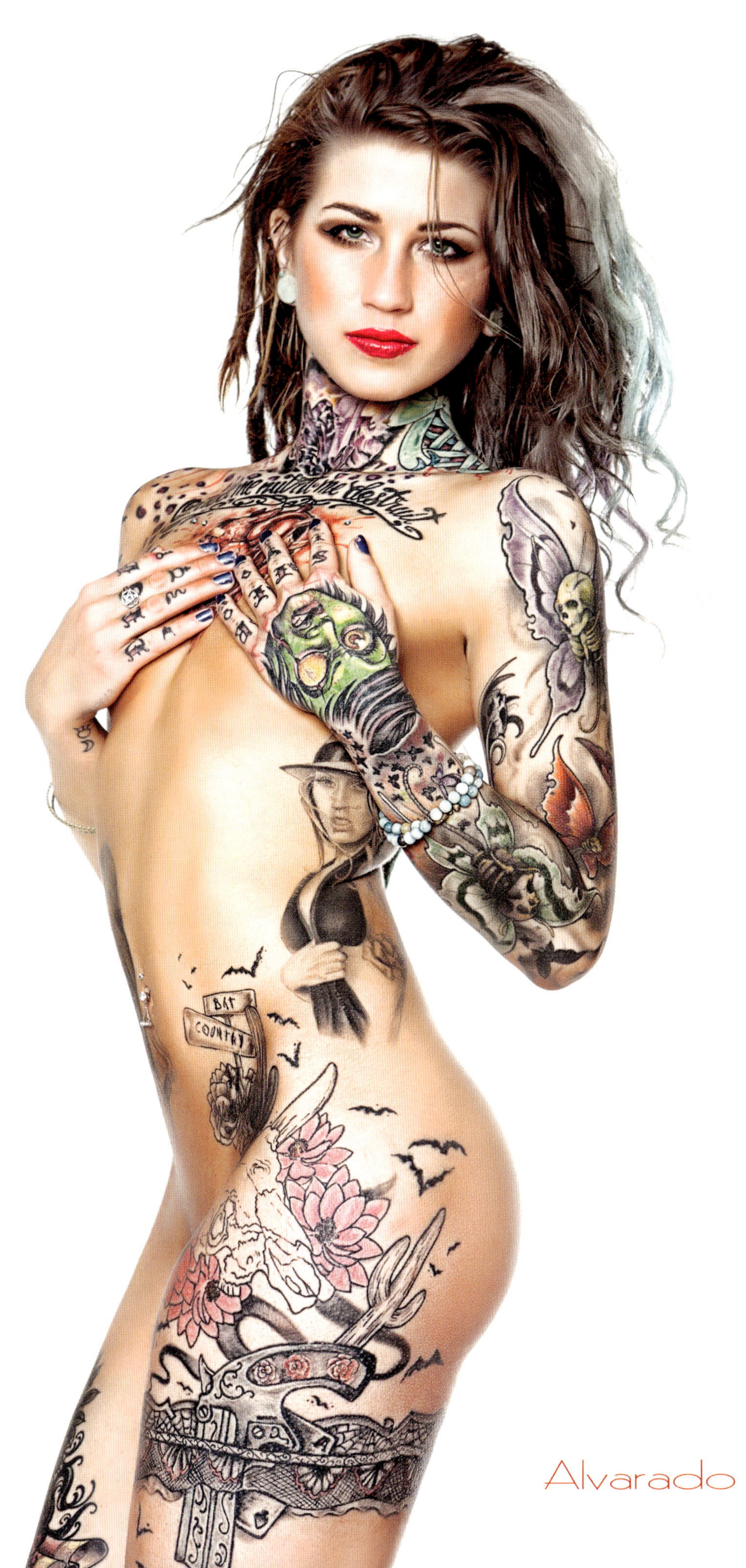

Alvarado

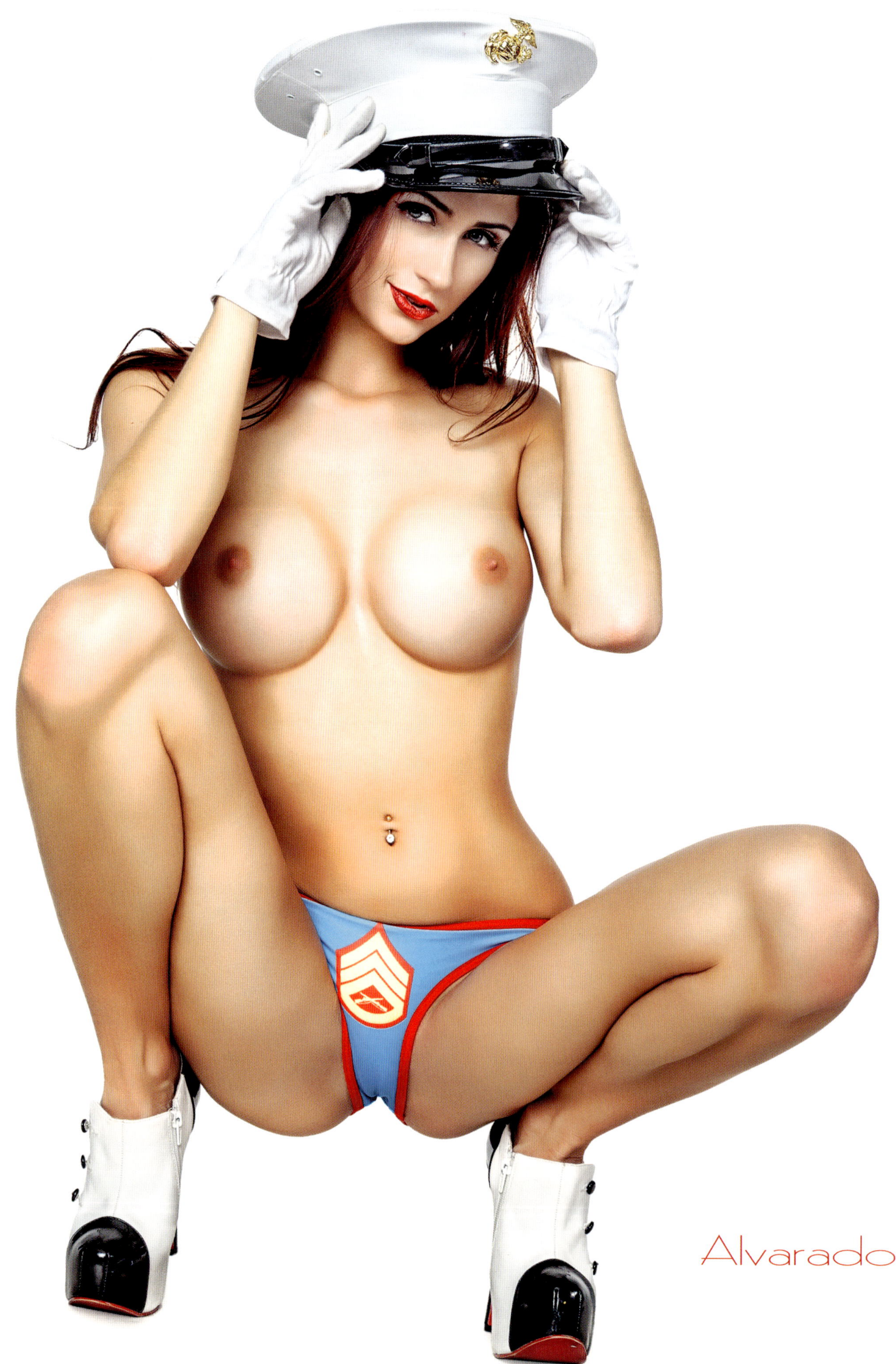
Alvarado

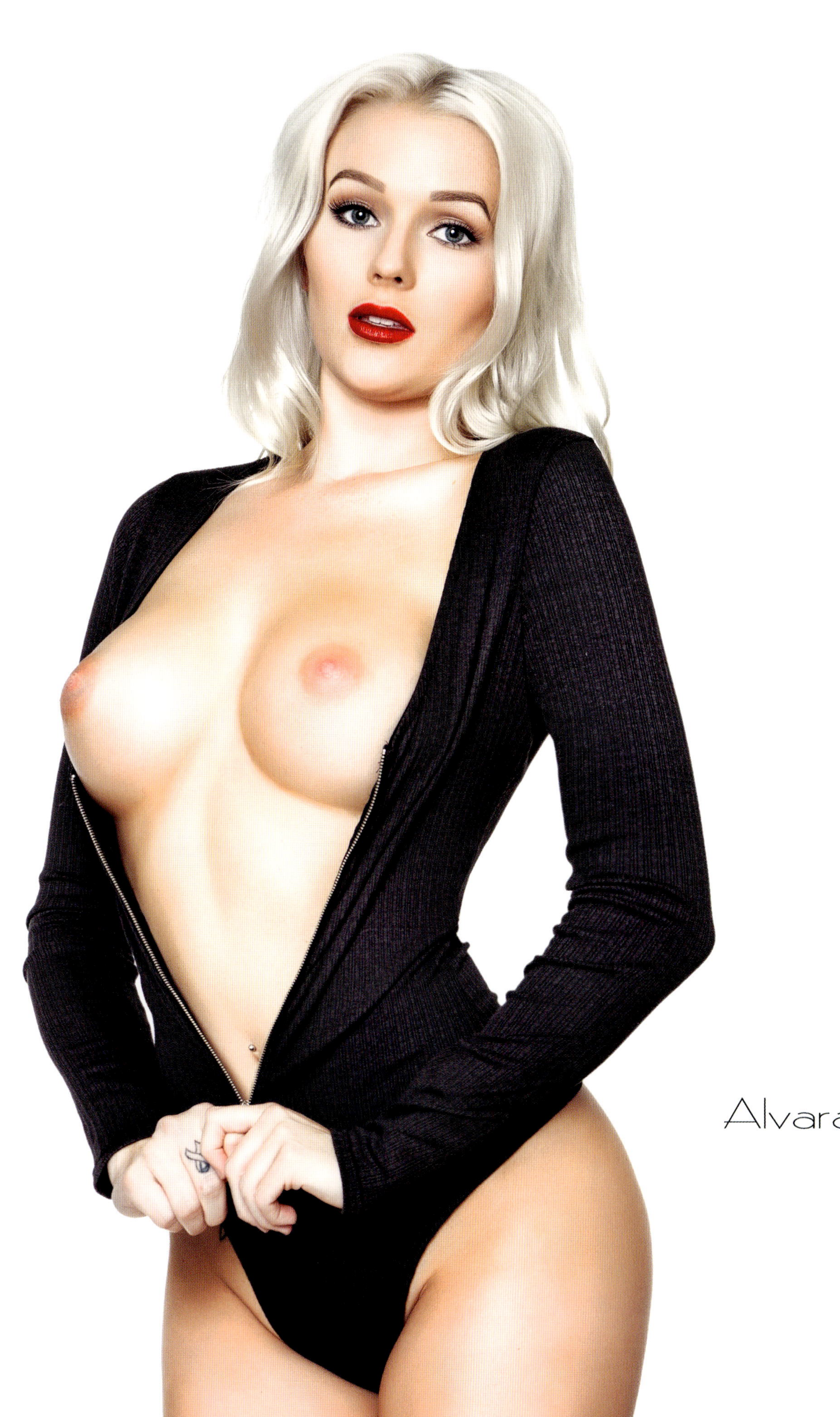

Alvarado

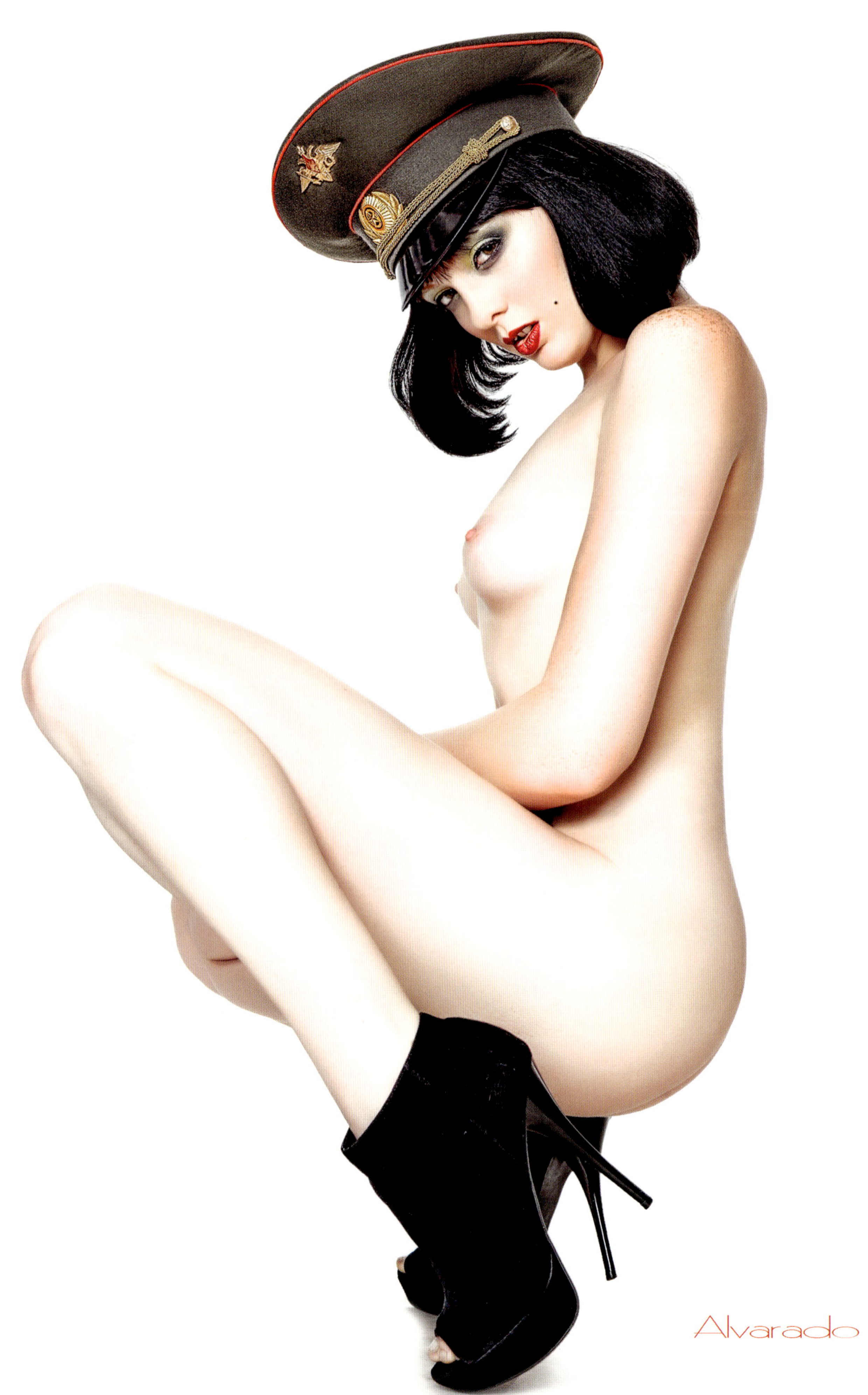
Alvarado

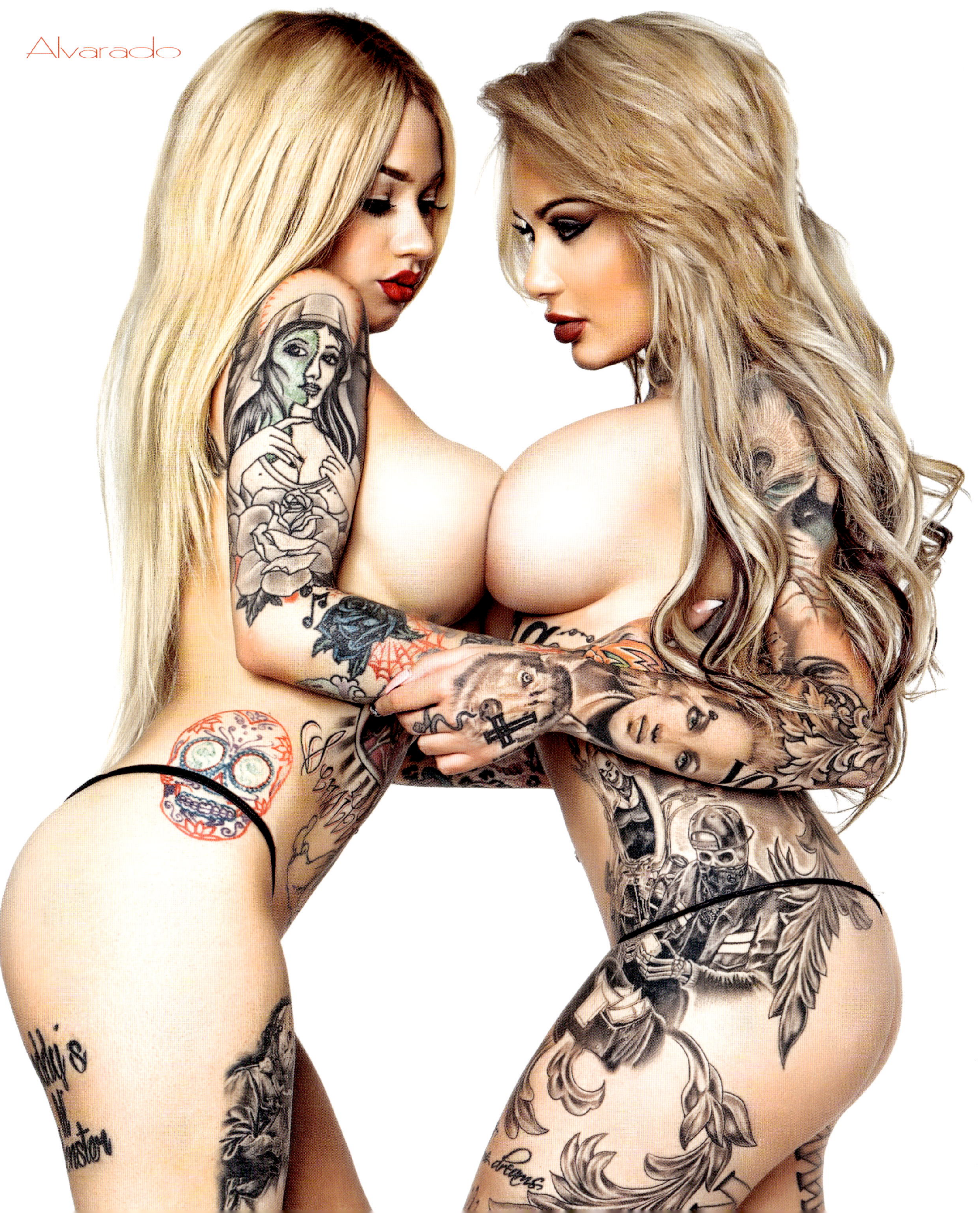
Alvarado

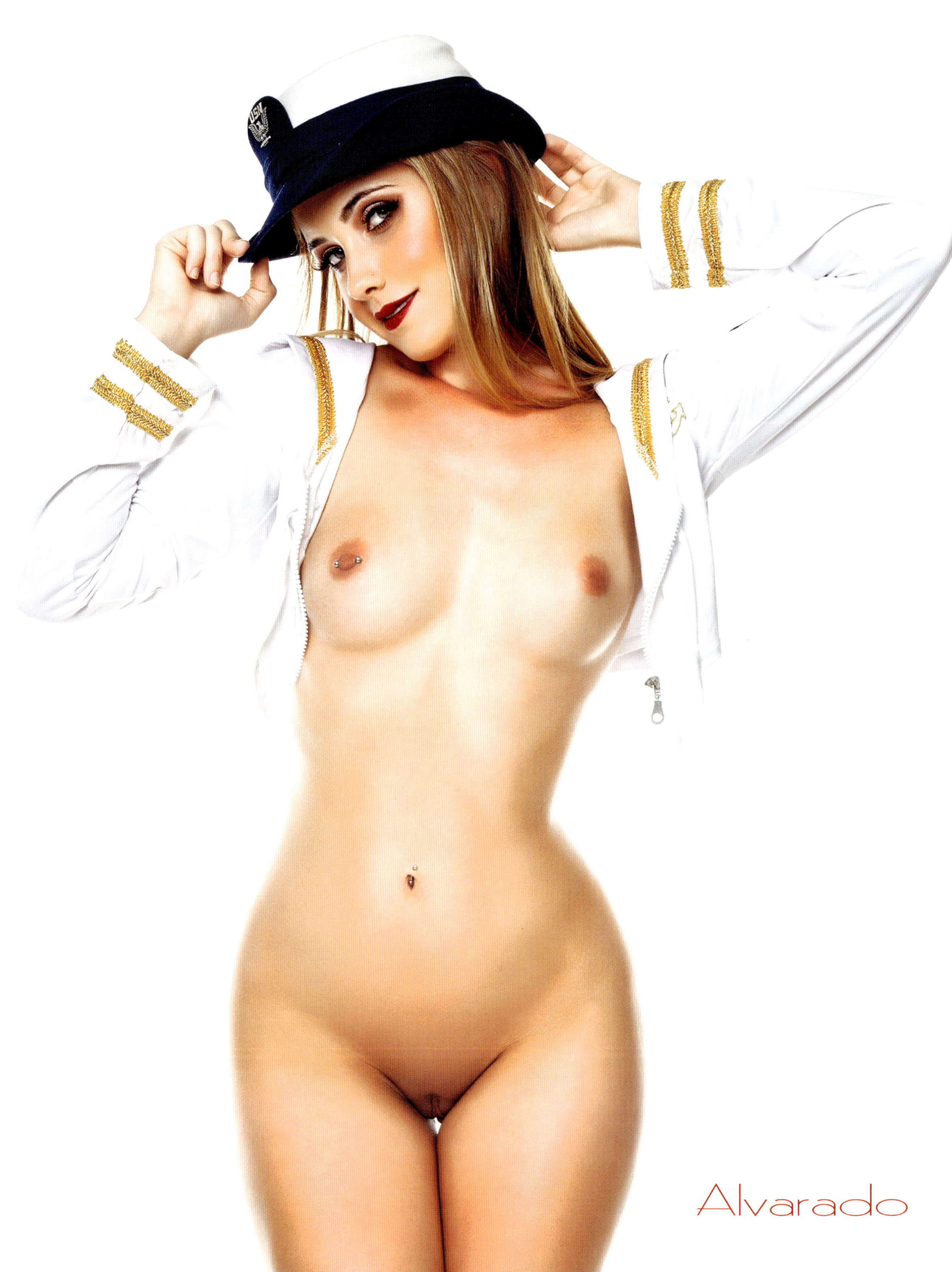
Alvarado